WHAT COLERIDGE

THOUGHT

ह‌‌‌ह‌‌‌ह‌

BY

Owen Barfield

WESLEYAN UNIVERSITY PRESS

Middletown, Connecticut

ISBN: 0–8195–4040–4
Library of Congress Catalog Card Number: 73–153100
Manufactured in the United States of America
FIRST EDITION

To
KATHLEEN COBURN
with admiration, gratitude
and affection

Here undoubtedly lies the chief poetic
energy:—in the force of imagination
that pierces or exalts the solid fact,
instead of floating among cloud-pictures.
            —GEORGE ELIOT (*Daniel Deronda*)

Contents

Acknowledgments

MY THANKS are due to Messrs. Routledge & Kegan Paul the publishers, and to Professor Kathleen Coburn the Editor, of *Inquiring Spirit* (1951) for allowing me a lengthy quotation from her Introduction to that valuable anthology of Coleridge's prose; also to the same publishers, and to the author Professor David Bohm, for permission to quote from *Causality and Chance in Modern Physics* (1957). It is with the permission of the Clarendon Press that I have included in one of my notes a passage from Professor Thomas McFarland's *Coleridge and the Pantheist Tradition* (1969). I am further indebted to A. H. B. Coleridge Esq. and to Victoria College, Toronto, for kindly allowing me to transcribe and reproduce two hitherto unpublished MS notes in the possession of the College. Dr. Frances Yates, of the Warburg Institute, London, not only found time to reply at some length to two enquiries I addressed to her concerning Giordano Bruno, but has also been kind enough to allow me to quote a passage from one of her letters in a note to the Appendix.

Courtesy and copyright apart, the debts of gratitude I owe are too plentiful for me to attempt their enumeration. There are for instance those labours of love, the careful editions we already possess of the greater part of Coleridge's letters and his notebooks, and now also (since this book was begun) of the *Friend* as the first fruits of the *Collected Coleridge*. Something of what I have gained from others who have written on Coleridge must appear, I think, from the text and notes which follow, where I have endeavoured to supply full details of any book or article referred to. But it would be a mistake to infer that those referred to are the only, or even necessarily the most valuable, of all those I have had the benefit of reading. Selection from such a point of view would be quite impossible, nor would it then be accurate or justifiable to limit myself to those who have actually written about

Coleridge. Indeed, if my own experience is any guide, the greatest helps of all towards divining what Coleridge thought are to be had from other thinkers, not a few of whom died before he was born.

Moreover, acknowledgments based on their value to myself or my book could not be limited even to writers, let alone to writers about Coleridge. Friends both old and new and the interest they have taken in my other books and in the progress of this one; acquaintances I have only conversed with; some of the students I have latterly had the privilege of teaching in the U.S.A.; I should soon be betrayed into a sincere, but perhaps rather priggish, acknowledgment to my fellow human beings in general for all, such as it is, that I am and know.

Agoraphobia must not however prevent me from expressly mentioning Professor Craig W. Miller of the University of British Columbia, whose hospitality I once enjoyed there, with whom I have had the benefit of correspondence extending at intervals over a number of years, and to whose own work on Coleridge up to date I have taken occasion to refer. Professor Gian N. G. Orsini of the University of Wisconsin was so generous as to send me a copy of his *Coleridge and German Idealism* (1969), which reached me, to my regret, only after this book was already completed. For help in the arduous business of proofreading and indexing respectively, I thank my two friends John Griffiths and Walter Hooper, who most willingly bestowed on it not only their time and trouble but also the benefit of much previous experience.

There is one still more personal acknowledgment, which I should dearly like to express if I can safely do so without appearing to claim for this interpretation of STC the cachet of the truly illustrious editor of his *Philosophical Lectures* and his *Notebooks* and general editor of the *Collected Coleridge*. Any such claim would be quite false, and it is with no such intention that I record the sense of inner support I have been deriving for some years now from a sort of warm west wind of benevolent interest blowing gently but steadily across the Atlantic and just occasionally freshening into an actual meeting in the neighbourhood of the British Museum; or that I identify the source from which it came as the lady to whom my book is dedicated.

WHAT COLERIDGE THOUGHT

Introduction

THERE was a period following his death in 1834, during which more attention was paid to Coleridge as a thinker than to Coleridge as a poet and critic. This was the time of which an observer who weighed his words as carefully as John Stuart Mill could write: "Bentham excepted, no Englishman of recent date has left his impress so deeply on the opinions and mental tendencies of those among us who attempt to enlighten their practice by philosophical meditation." It was followed by a much longer period of almost exclusive interest in the poet and critic. In the last few decades, beginning perhaps with the publication in 1930 of J. M. Muirhead's *Coleridge as Philosopher,* the pendulum has on the whole been swinging back again. Prose works long out of print are again becoming available; unpublished prose is being published. A full edition both of the *Letters* and the *Notebooks* is gradually coming from the press; the *Collected Coleridge,* under the general editorship of Kathleen Coburn, gave birth to the first two of its sixteen projected volumes while this book was being written; there has been a steadily increasing flow of books and articles on what Coleridge thought about other things as well as literature and the drama.

I do not know how many people will have read all these books and all these articles, which of course differ widely from each other. I certainly cannot claim to have done so. But I have read a good many, and if I were asked whether, in spite of their generous variety, and in addition to the high quality of the scholarship many of them display, there are any leading characteristics common to practically all of them, my answer would be: Yes, there are two—the predominance firstly of what I would call the biographical/comparative approach and secondly of the biographical/psychological approach; and I should hope that the terms I was using were reasonably self-explanatory. One good reason for this—though not, I think, the only one—is that the best known of

Coleridge's prose works is his *Biographia Literaria*. It is indeed the only one, apart from the *Lectures on Shakespeare,* that is at all widely known; and it is the only one that has even remained in print uninterruptedly since it first appeared. It has much to say about the various philosophies with which he came into intellectual contact during his life; so much so that *Biographia Philosophica* would have been an equally, if not more, accurate title. From Coleridge himself, then, we first *learn* of his philosophy through his biography, and we first learn of its relation to other philosophies to the accompaniment of an historical, and sometimes anecdotal, account of his personal encounters with them.

But whatever the reason, the comparative approach has its disadvantages. A student, for instance, who picks up a contemporary book on Coleridge, in order to find out what he thought about things, is likely to find himself involved in a complex and allusive web of comparative philosophy, which is certainly not, to begin with, what he needs. But that is not all. There are inherent disadvantages in the comparative approach not only for the readers of such a book, but for its writer also. It keeps him too much outside the intellectual content with which he is dealing. J. A. Appleyard, who has employed the biographical/comparative approach so instructively and so well in his *Coleridge's Philosophy of Literature,* came to feel, in doing so, that a different approach altogether was also needed. For he wrote in his Introduction:

> What is wanting in the sizable bibliography of literature on Coleridge is a full-scale study of the development of his philosophy which will consider him on his own terms and not as a representative of something else, whether it be German idealism, English Platonism, pantheistic mysticism, semantic analysis, or depth psychology. The idea or organizing insight ought to be internal to his thought, so as to see what that thought is and not merely what it is like or unlike.

When, in 1966, I first came upon these words, I had already begun assembling the material for the present volume. They at once struck me— indeed they rather leaped from the page—as a fair description of what I myself should actually be trying to do. And I venture to quote them as the best and shortest statement I can imagine of the general aim of the book, some such statement being perhaps required to justify its rather unusual form. It may serve for instance to explain why in Chapter 1 the reader is plunged so unceremoniously into philosophy, while the more familiar territory of Coleridge on imagination is not reached until Chapter 6.

Professor Appleyard, it is true, supposes a study of the "development" of Coleridge's philosophy and in that respect I cannot claim to be even trying to meet his requirements. That he did develop it during his life is of course not in doubt and he said so himself in his *Table Talk*. Moreover the nature of this development and the extent to which it involved substantial changes are disputed questions which have received a good deal of attention. I have not made it my concern, nor stressed (though I have occasionally indicated) the dates of the quotations I have used. My own opinion is that the development was so consistent or, if it is preferred, "organic," that later views are for the most part implicit in the earlier. They are at all events not contrary, so that what is explicitly stated in, say, 1830, may (to borrow a neat phrase from Professor J. R. de J. Jackson) be "relevant as a foreseen conclusion" to a passage from 1816 or earlier. This is in fact my opinion, but I do not assume that the reader will necessarily agree with it. If not, perhaps instead of laying down the book in disgust at this point, he will mentally substitute for the title it bears some such alternative title as: "What Coleridge Thought towards the End of his Life."

That there was a unity in this; that in his own mind his "system" was indeed a coherent system and not a hodge podge of "inspired fragments"; that he had a muddled life, but not a muddled mind—all this is by now widely, though not universally, accepted: ". . . fragmentary, 'atomic' as Thelwall calls it, is just what Coleridge's thought is not," wrote Kathleen Coburn in her Introduction to the *Philosophical Lectures,* and other contemporaries could be quoted to the same effect. The fact remains of course that, although the reverse of fragmentary in his own mind, its elaboration *is* fragmentary on paper. The *Letters,* the *Notebooks* and the *Marginalia* are of inestimable value. But, if my own experience is any guide, they are not indispensable for an understanding of the system or philosophy itself. For it happens that my own study of Coleridge's prose, conducted unsystematically and at intervals over a long period of years, was limited to the five published works, *Biographia Literaria,* the *Friend,* the *Statesman's Manual* (with the *Theory of Life* scheduled to it), *Aids to Reflection* and *Church and State,* together with some part of the *Treatise on Logic,* which, though hitherto unpublished, is far from being a fragment. It was only much later that I began on the 'fragments'; and it will be seen that I have made a fairly extensive use of them for the purpose of exposition. Here, if not indispensable, they are to say the least of it welcome. The condensed argument of, for instance, much of Chapter XII of the *Biographia Literaria* is made easiest to understand by seeing it expanded, exemplified, applied in one direction and another and, where Coleridge himself has done this, it is his voice we want to hear and not his exponent's. For one thing he is likely to have done it better.

Another issue that has been frequently, and sometimes hotly, debated in connection with Coleridge's thought is the old charge of plagiarism, which began during his lifetime and was answered by Coleridge himself on more than one occasion. Here too, although it still forms the staple of many specialised articles, the general opinion has been moving against it. Since I have largely ignored the issue in what follows, I venture a few observations here. Verbal plagiarism, as a labour-saving breach of the law of copyright, is a matter of determinable fact, and there is not much doubt that, as the law now stands, Schelling could have sued Coleridge in respect of one or two pages in the *Biographia Literaria*. Psychological plagiarism, or "borrowing," on the other hand, depends on a number of imponderables such as the way a man reads, the way he thinks and, in the last resort, on your view of the nature of mind. Coleridge himself in a letter of 1811 divided human heads into two types, the *tanks* and the *springs*. It is only the tanks who may be accurately said to *borrow* the thoughts, together or not with the words, of others. The spring adopts them. To quote Miss Coburn's admirable Introduction once more, Coleridge "borrows only when his own thinking has reached almost the same point as his creditor's." He remarks in another letter that he "read for truth, and not to make a book," and it is really obvious that in saying so he was *speaking* the truth. He was not interested in "originality," if the word is taken to mean novelty. For the principles advanced in his Essays on Method he claimed "no other merit, than that of having drawn them from the purest sources of Philosophy, ancient and modern." He would whole-heartedly have accepted James Russell Lowell's definition in his essay on *Thoreau*: "Originality consists in the power of digesting and assimilating thoughts, so that they become part of our life and substance."

If, as I hope, the thought here attributed to Coleridge is in the main that which had become part of his life and substance, the issue of borrowing is irrelevant. And in this connection it is significant that, in order to preserve it as a reproach, he has to be accused, as he not infrequently is, of confused and inconsistent borrowings. Such accusations assume in advance that he was a tank and not a spring; for a spring must continue to give in the act of receiving. "Rarely," and I again venture to quote Appleyard, "was he much concerned with the precise and actual meaning an idea had for another writer; almost always it was its interaction with his own thinking that mattered most to him." The word *interaction* is important. The ground is cut from beneath a good deal of what has been written about Coleridge and Kant for instance by a simple observation of Professor McFarland's in his *Coleridge and the Pantheist Tradition*: "Kant provided Coleridge with instruments, not with a philosophical orientation." That did not prevent him from revering Kant as "a very *very* great man."

There is a right as well as a wrong use of the comparative approach or method. The tragedy of the wrong one—which Carlyle once disparaged as "view-hunting"—and of its wide prevalence is that, without more, it actually hinders people from reading Coleridge in the only way he wanted to be read; which is a way more in accord with his own habit of reading—and "borrowing." "What are my metaphysics?" he asks in the *Friend*—"merely the referring the mind to its own consciousness for truths indispensable to its own happiness." He desired, as he says Plato desired, "to excite the germinal power that craves no knowledge but what it can take up into itself." His object was not to indoctrinate; but neither was it to become one more appetising quarry for the view-hunter. It was to goad his readers into thinking for themselves. In the *Friend* and the *Aids to Reflection* "the aim of every sentence is to solicit, nay tease the reader to ask himself whether he actually does, or does not, understand distinctly."

Now this is exactly what a predominantly comparative, or biological/comparative, approach prevents a reader from doing. Its learned debates have something in common with the waters of Lethe. To become immersed in them is to risk forgetting that one at least of the interesting questions about almost any thought is the question whether it is sound or unsound, valid or invalid, true or untrue. If I find it depressing when a distinguished literary critic complains that "Coleridge has little insight into the incompatibility of different trends of thought," it is because this seems to me to betray a deplorable inability to distinguish between philosophy and talking about philosophy. Philosophy is, to my mind, not much concerned with "trends" of thought. It is concerned with thought. Is it seriously suggested that Coleridge was incapable of detecting the incompatibility of one *thought* with another? Or with proven fact? If so, let us first be shown the point or points at which this occurred. Time enough then to start investigating the confused borrowings, or the unconscious motivation, that seduced him to it.

A fairly extended perusal of comment on Coleridge's prose works reveals the existence of what I have come to call the "somehow" convention. According to the somehow convention, instead of burrowing into Coleridge's thought to see what it looks like from inside, you stand *be*side it, equipped with three or four prefabricated frames or grids (for instance, subjective idealism, Neoplatonism, Christian Theology) and proceed to superimpose them one after another. You then read off from each grid in succession what it allows to appear and finally remark with surprise, or perhaps with a twinkle of amusement *de haut en bas,* that Coleridge "somehow" managed to keep them all going at the same time.

This is apt to lead fairly quickly into the still more limiting superficialities of the biological/psychological approach, when "somehow" turns out to have meant his emotional needs or unconscious motivation or something of the sort. As an example of this, it is frequently affirmed in parenthesis, that Coleridge's philosophy was really determined by his emotional need for the Christian faith. I say in parenthesis because, although it has for many years been constantly repeated, I have never seen it satisfactorily demonstrated. I myself have found virtually no evidence for it and I am now convinced that, from actual *study* of Coleridge's philosophy, it is a conclusion impossible to reach without the help of a prescinding aversion from Christianity, or at the least from the Christian Church. Without that overriding persuasion it is not, even on its own personalist grounds, convincing. For after all what kind of a man was Coleridge? He was almost the discoverer of the unconscious mind and one who was constantly and penetratingly pondering his own. Moreover his cardinal sin was indolence, and his besetting weakness a pitiful dependence on the approbation of others and the affection of those around him. He was constitutionally *dependent* and he abhorred having to exert his will. But what kind of Christianity was it that he argued? Read the *Theory of Life* and, along with it, the *Essay on Faith.* It was a Christianity of *energy,* or, if it is preferred, of the *energeia* of the Pauline Epistles; a doctrine of the sovereign independence and initiative of the human spirit. *Porphyrogeniti sumus,* he proclaims: we are born in the purple; and his evolutionary theory of life culminates in the claim on behalf of man: "Henceforward, he is referred to himself, delivered up to his own charge; and he who stands the most on himself, and stands the firmest, is the truest, because the most individual, Man." It is true that humility is also demanded of him. "The intensities must be at once opposite and equal. As the liberty, so must be the reverence for law. As the independence, so must be the service and submission to the Supreme Will." He is never to forget his coronation oath, but neither dare he abdicate and relax before Omnipotence operating *ab extra*. Life itself, when it has reached its apex in Man, is to say, with Racine's Emperor Titus:

> Mais il ne s'agit plus de vivre, il faut regner.

Now Coleridge had, if anything, *less* inclination for reigning in sovereign independence over either himself or others than Racine's Titus. In the depths of his soul, if not in those ultimate depths of his spirit, which he conceived himself to share with mankind as a whole, he was all for life with Berenice. He knew it, as he knew most things about himself. When he said in a letter that he had a "passion for Christianity," he at once went on to admit, or bemoan, that it was "an intellectual passion"; and there is a more poignant admission to the same effect in the *Notes on Leighton*. A man who loathes getting up early and frequently fails to do so, may nevertheless be convinced that early-rising is the one indispensable virtue; and, if he is a writer, he may proclaim his conviction far and wide, meekly enduring the inevitable reproach of hypocrisy. But he is hardly likely to rig the evidence in order to become convinced in the first place. Would not the wishful-thinking recipe be not less, but a good deal more, available to us, if, instead of an intellectual passion for Christian *energeia*, Coleridge had succeeded in developing quite a different metaphysic—a "black" one for instance, to assure himself that because life has no meaning, it calls for no moral exertion?

That, for what it may be worth, is my contribution to the corpus of personalist interpretation. It is not important. Because, as far as Coleridge's *thought* is concerned, the real objection to personalist exegesis is, not that it is liable to stop short at hasty conclusions and get stuck in them, but that it would be irrelevant even if it were profound. If a train of thought has been biassed and thus flawed by unconscious drives, it is the flaws that need pointing to first, not the drives. Are you telling me that the steering-column was out of order? I will join you in taking it to pieces after you have shown me the marks on the road, where the car swerved because of it. Without some such *prima facie* evidence of aberration we should be wasting our time. And you have produced none.

What is the relevance of Coleridge to our own time, and what chance has the *Collected Coleridge,* as it progressively sees the light, of being read at all widely? The answer to the second question seems to me to depend on the ability and the willingness of the rising generation to distinguish between what is significant and what is merely trivial in their own immediate reaction to what is put before them. His style in general, the sometimes inordinate length of his sentences, for example, and his addiction to parenthesis, are decidedly repugnant to contemporary taste. Much will depend on whether the worship of contemporary taste simply because it is contemporary continues to prevail so strongly that it prevents people from accepting even the *necessary* discrepancies between his characteristic utterance and our own. Partly his style is expendable; he himself for instance commented on the way it had been influenced by his extensive reading in leisurely and prolix seventeenth century writers. Partly on the other hand, it is inextricable from the radical difference between the *quality* of his thought and that of nearly all his own contemporaries, let alone ours. Long sentences may sometimes be required to penetrate to the sap of a topic and flow with that into its exterior and delicate ramifications. Again it is arguable, and Coleridge himself argued, that only shallow thinking can dispense with parentheses in writing.

But literary style is of course not the only impediment. There is an area that lies somewhere between style and personality, for which "attitude" is perhaps the only word. Here again there are elements in Coleridge's that are distasteful to a good many of us. I will confine myself to the single example of his highly developed bump of reverence. It is difficult not to feel that he protests too much. With the assistance of his penchant for slipping easily into apostrophe, he too often *obtrudes* his reverence on us. He seems at such times to have forgotten that the twin-brother of reverence is reticence; and that is something we are not likely to forget today, as we watch them both disappearing hand in hand. Here again it is a question of ability to distinguish the expendable from the essential. The obtrusion is expendable, but the reverence itself is not; since reverence is not simply a virtue for which we may expect full marks in heaven, or a device for bolstering up the social establishment. It is an organ of perception for a whole range of qualities that are as imperceptible without it as another whole range is imperceptible without an ear for music. And Coleridge's aim, it must be remembered, was precisely to supplement the current metaphysic, and the current science, of quantities with a metaphysic and a science of qualities.

This brings me to the other question: that of his actual relevance to our time, whether it should be recognised or not. It is one on which it is better to leave the reader to make up his own mind than for me to argue it. Indeed the principal object of the book is to assist him in doing so. I have however occasionally commented in detail from that point of view, mainly in the Notes. And Chapter 11 considers at some length the relevance of Coleridge's thought to one particular aspect of modern life, a very important one, namely natural science and physics in particular. Beyond that—he was so seminal a thinker that his insights and *aperçus* tend to "sprout in the brains" with a fertility that is positively dangerous. I have generally resisted the temptation to detect exciting links with up-to-date, and perhaps ephemeral, developments such as generative grammar, structuralism and so forth. At one point even Gödel's theorem (which I understand to be an undermining critique of all "closed systems" of thought) beckoned to me for mention in connection with Coleridge on the understanding, but I resolutely looked the other way. So too with another exciting link. I mean that vast and unwieldy body of speculation concerning the unconscious mind, betokening (as I feel) the shadowy appearance there during the last few decades—at the opposite pole from the physical world, where their appearance has been far from shadowy—of those "lost Dynameis," those conflicting but productively conflicting forces, on which Coleridge's entire system was based. I feel the Jungians, the Yin and Yang votaries and others will easily perceive the link for themselves. And I believe this will also be the case, only more so, with the small but growing number who have come to acknowledge the pre-eminence of Rudolf Steiner, to whom however I have expressly referred in a note to Chapter 11 and again in Chapter 13.

It will become apparent to anyone who has the patience to reach the end of this book that I find the relevance of Coleridge's thought to our time where he himself located its relevance to his own. It resides, above all else, in his radical critique of one or two major presuppositions, upon which the immediate thinking, and as a result the whole cultural and social structure of this "epoch of the understanding and the senses" (including supposedly radical revolts against it) is so firmly—or is it now infirmly?—established. As long as this is ignored,

I doubt if he has much to say to us, whether as a philosopher or as a sociologist. It is partly for that reason, but partly also because my book is already, if anything, too long for its main purpose, that I have touched on his political theory only very briefly in the latter part of the last chapter. I notice that David Calleo found it necessary to include an early chapter on "The Philosophical Underpinnings" in his excellent book on *Coleridge and the Idea of the Modern State;* and I feel sure that that chapter is the golden bridge on the crossing whereof by his readers the persuasiveness of the rest depends. If then I should have made it a little easier for any puzzled mind to cross that bridge, I may perhaps claim to have done something at least for Coleridge's contribution to sociology.

A final word is needed concerning the Appendix on "polar logic." I have been suggesting that there is something to be said for the practice of ascertaining what Coleridge thought before beginning to discuss when, or why, or in what company he thought it. This means that, while we are still examining the what, it is better to withdraw our attention from the why and the when and the with whom; and that is the general principle I have sought to follow.

In the book itself references to other philosophers are made either because Coleridge himself expressly referred to them, or because they seemed to help in elucidating Coleridge's own meaning, or occasionally in order to remove a current misconception. But this restraint was not occasioned by lack of interest. On the contrary the relation of his philosophy to others like and unlike it, and to historical trends of thought—in short, the comparative approach—is a matter that I have found of absorbing interest. Very much here, as I have already said, has been done by others; and I am deeply indebted to more than one of them: but a remark of Coleridge's in the *Biographia Literaria* concerning his indebtedness to "the polar logic of Giordano Bruno" does not seem to have attracted the attention it deserved. I have therefore attempted to investigate its significance, confining my view-hunting and source-hunting to an Appendix, which I offer as my own small and very imperfect contribution to the study of Coleridge's philosophy by the comparative method.

Thoughts and Thinking

On the 17th of March 1801 Coleridge's eldest son, Hartley, then between four and five years old, was looking out of the study window at some mountains. Coleridge picked up a mirror. "I showed him," he records in a notebook,

> the whole magnificent Prospect in a Looking Glass, and held it up, so that the whole was like a Canopy or Ceiling over his head, and he struggled to express himself concerning the Difference between the Thing and the Image almost with convulsive Effort.—I never before saw such an Abstract of *Thinking* as a pure act and energy, of *Thinking* as distinguished from *Thoughts*.[1]

It is a good point at which to make our entry into Coleridge's own thoughts, that is to say into the whole coherently conceived, though fragmentarily expounded, structure which he sometimes referred to as his "system," at other times as the Dynamic Philosophy, and occasionally as the Constructive Philosophy.

Coleridge himself was twenty-eight at this time. Decades later Thomas Carlyle was to despise and describe the old man at Highgate still expatiating on the relation between "subject" and "object" (which, owing to a catarrhal affliction, he pronounced "sum-m-mject" and "om-m-mject"); and those few who have really endeavoured to master his philosophy are likely to have concluded that a grasp of this relation, as Coleridge saw it, is the *pons asinorum* of the whole endeavour. In fact, however, if the definitions of *subject* and *object,* and the true nature of the relation between them, are the *pons asinorum,* the concept, and perhaps the *experience,* of thinking as an *act,* or as an 'act and energy,' are the toll-gate in the middle of the bridge, the barrier that has to be opened before we can get across.

Most of my readers will have observed a small-water-insect on the surface of rivulets, which throws a cinque-spotted shadow fringed with prismatic colours on the sunny bottom of the brook; and will have noticed, how the little animal *wins* its way up against the stream . . . This is no un-apt emblem of the mind's self-experience in the act of thinking.[2]

We must however distinguish between energy and effort. Both Hartley Coleridge and the water-insect give evidence of something like a struggle. But this is not *necessarily* the case. In a notebook entry of 1803 Coleridge observes: "In all inevitable Truths, e.g. that the two sides of a triangle are greater than the third, I feel my will active: I seem to *will* the Truth, as well as to perceive it. Think of this."[3]

Coleridge did not always obey the commands he laid on himself in his notebooks, but in this instance he clearly did so. One could almost say that he hardly ever ceased thinking of it; or certainly that it was always at the back of his mind and of almost any doctrine he was pro-pounding at the moment. There is evidence enough in his prose-writings throughout his life;* and, towards the end of it, in a work which was to have formed part of the "Magnum Opus" that he frequently re-ferred to but never achieved, he advises the reader that the only way of overcoming a certain difficulty (to which we shall refer again shortly) is:

> . . . by placing yourself in such situations or as it were positions of mind as would be likely to call up that act in our intellectual being and then to attend to it so far as its necessary transient and subtle nature will permit . . . When connecting 2 bright stars, the one directly above the other as the extremities of the same line I seemed to have a something between a sense and a sensation of length more perfect than any actual filling up of the interval by a succession of points in contact would have given me. I seemed to find myself acting as it were in the construction of that length undisturbed by any accompanying perception of breadth or inequality which must needs accompany all pictures of a line . . . in other words it was a self-conscious act snatched away as it were from the product of that act.[4]

We have here an act which is normally performed unconsciously, though the *result* or *product* of the act is part of "the spontaneous con-sciousness natural to all reflecting beings."[5]

---

* See for instance *Philosophical Lectures*, p. 115 ("To comprehend the philos-ophy of Pythagoras, the mind itself must be conceived of as an act"); p. 333; and elsewhere.

This is perhaps easiest to grasp in the case of geometry: "I need not I am sure tell you that a line upon a slate is but a picture of that act of the imagination which the mathematician alone consults." [6]

Mathematical lines, points and surfaces are "acts of the imagination that are one with the product of those acts." [7] And this remains true of the figures constructed with them. A geometrician draws three meeting lines on a slate; but the 'triangle' which he then sees merely represents to him (and imperfectly) an ideal figure he has first had to produce by an act of thought or (it is practically the same thing) an act of imagination.

[the] spirit in man (that is, the will) shows its own state in and by its acts alone: even as in geometrical reasoning the mind knows its constructive faculty in the act of constructing, and contemplates the act in the product (that is, the mental figure or diagram) which is inseparable from the act and co-instantaneous.[8]

Both the act and the product of the act ("the mental figure or diagram") are already there before the pencil has touched the slate. They are inseparable from one another or normally so, but that does not entail that they are indistinguishable. Indeed it is precisely as we do begin to distinguish them that we come at "the mind's self-experience in the act of thinking."

Coleridge was perfectly clear about this distinction in his own mind. But he had the utmost difficulty in getting it across to his contemporaries—a generation, we should recall, which had not been familiarized by Freud and his followers with at least the *notion* of at least the possibility of there being such a thing as unconscious mental activity. In the following quotation we ought not to let ourselves be put off by Coleridge's use of the word *transcendental*. What he designated as *transcendental philosophy* is what we should be more likely today to call epistemology. It was no wise mystical. It was reasoning about thinking.[9]

There is a *philosophic* (and inasmuch as it is actualized by an effort of freedom, an *artificial*) consciousness, which lies beneath or (as it were) *behind* the spontaneous consciousness natural to all reflecting beings. As the elder Romans distinguished their northern provinces into Cis-Alpine and Trans-Alpine, so may we divide all the objects of human knowledge into those on this side, and those on the other side of the spontaneous consciousness; *citra et trans conscientiam communem.* The latter is exclusively the domain of pure philosophy, which is therefore properly entitled *transcendental,* in order to discriminate it at once, both from mere reflection and *re*-presentation, on the one hand, and on the other from those flights of lawless speculation which, abandoned by *all* distinct consciousness, because transgressing the bounds and purposes of our intellectual faculties, are justly condemned as *transcendent.*[10]

But, though it is not mysticism, to reason about thinking does entail our being led inward from the product of thinking to the act itself. And this does require a certain discipline. Here is the root-cause of the charge of 'obscurity,' which was levelled during his life, and has so often been levelled since his death, against both Coleridge himself and his philosophy.

A system, the first principle of which it is to render the mind intuitive of the spiritual in man (i.e. of that which lies *on the other side* of our natural consciousness) must needs have a great obscurity for those, who have never disciplined and strengthened this ulterior consciousness.[11]

It will have been noticed that, in the passages cited, the expressions "act of thinking" and "act of imagination" are treated as equivalent. This will call for further consideration later; but meanwhile it may help to prevent the mistake we might otherwise make of assuming that by the act of thinking all he means is 'attending.'

The difference between these two goes very deep and cannot really be grasped, as Coleridge apprehended it, without reference to his fundamental and well-known (though not often well-understood) distinction between Reason and Understanding. This, too, must await a later chapter. Meanwhile it may be observed that the difference between attending and thinking is perhaps most readily *experienced* in situations where the object of attention is itself a train of thought, and one which is being presented by another mind. We listen, let us say, to a lecture which is full of thought and deeply interesting, and which holds our attention from start to finish. A day or two later someone who was not there asks us: "What was the lecture like?" "Very good indeed!" "What did he say?" Whereupon we find ourselves completely at a loss; we just cannot answer, though we can recall plenty of disconnected observations. So it is not our memory which is at fault.

On another occasion, after the lecture is concluded, we summon up the energy to 'go through' it in our own minds, reproducing for ourselves the main and subsidiary threads of the discourse. And this time, if we are asked the same question, we can answer it pretty satisfactorily. Or it may be a chapter from a book.

> By thought I here mean the voluntary production in our own minds of those states of consciousness, to which, as to his fundamental facts, the Writer has referred us: while attention has for its object the order and connection of thoughts and images, each of which is in itself already and familiarly known.[12]

Elsewhere he speaks of the *effort* of attention and the *energy* of thought.[13] Attention, in spite of the effort it requires, is *intellectually passive*. "On whatever subject the mind feels a lively interest, attention, though always an effort, becomes a delightful effort." [14] But though the two motions of the mind must be carefully distinguished, they are also closely related—as is the case with understanding and reason. The lower is the only way to the higher and attention is "a habit or discipline without which the very word, thinking, must remain a thoughtless substitute for dreaming with our eyes open . . ." [15]

Coleridge once wrote in his notebook: "*A Thought* and Thoughts are quite different words from *Thought*—as a Fancy from Fancy, a Work from Work, a Life from Life, a Force and Forces from Force, a Feeling, a Writing, etc." [16] What he is pointing out is that, just as "a" work, which is a *thing,* is the finished product of 'work,' which is an *act,* so is "a" thought the product of the act of thought. When they are used in the singular and without the article before them, all these words are in effect participial, so that to use the term *thinking* (instead of *thought*) for the *act* makes the distinction clearer. Hitherto we have been concerned mainly with the act of thinking as he experienced and reflected on it. It remains to consider (observing his own verbal distinction) what Coleridge understood by 'a thought' or 'thoughts.'

It will be recalled that the *act* of thinking is normally performed unconsciously. By contrast, *thoughts* can be defined as all the content of consciousness in so far as that is not sense or feeling. It covers memories, speculations, fancies, theories, reverie and all else that goes on while we remain conscious. But not those alone. It is a truism today, though it was not in Coleridge's, that a great part, if not the whole, of what for practical purposes we classify as 'perception' includes a thought-component. The 'koenaesthesis,' as it is sometimes called, which constitutes

our experience of a common world external to and independent of ourselves, is derived from that component. Nature itself, so far as it has
form and quality, is a compound of thoughts and perceptions.[17]

The difficulty here, as in the case of the act of thinking and its product, is that in ordinary life we never consciously experience the one
separately from the other. We 'perceive,' as we say, an 'object,' but the
object is already 'nature' in the above mentioned sense, that is to say, a
construct owing, not to our senses but to our minds its total form, and
thus its unity, and thus its presence *as* an object. A single percept, uncombined, unmodified and unadopted by any element of mental construction, is as much outside our normal experience as is pure thinking,
uncombined with *any* element of representation borrowed from the
senses.

Yet this does not alter the fact that thinking and perceiving are two
clearly distinguishable functions, the one active and the other passive.
Indeed that is part of what the words *mean*. Whatever his views on the
subject of free will and determinism, it remains true for everyman that
thinking is self-originated in a way that perceiving is not. Thinking is,
by contrast, something which (however unconsciously) he *does;* perceiving is, by contrast, something which he suffers.

Put that way, the point may perhaps seem so obvious as to be scarcely
worth making. But there was in Coleridge's day a strong current of
philosophical and scientific thought which was founded on the denial of
precisely this distinction. There was for example the philosophy of
Hume and there was the associationist psychology of David Hartley,
which had played so great a part in Coleridge's own intellectual development.[18] In our own day we are familiar enough with the behaviourist
upholders of the same tradition. This refusal to *distinguish* between
thinking and perceiving, and thus between the mind and the senses,
was (so Coleridge divined) based on the fact, to which attention has
just been drawn, that the two are in practice found to be inseparable.
And it is for this reason that we so frequently find him turning aside
from a particular topic he is pursuing to expose on general grounds the
fallacy implicit in the assumption that we cannot 'really' distinguish
components we cannot divide.

The assumption is as strange as it is persistent. Water can be really
separated into drops—but each drop is no less really composed of hydrogen and oxygen, in spite of the fact that we cannot, as long as it remains
water, separate the one from the other. Coleridge attributed the pre-

valence of this mental blind spot to what he sometimes referred to as "the despotism of the eye." But we will pursue our present policy of letting him speak for himself:

> In order to obtain adequate notions of any truth, we must intellectually separate its distinguishable parts; and this is the technical process of philosophy. But having done so, we must then restore them in our conceptions to the unity in which they actually co-exist; and this is the result of philosophy.[19]

Again:

> It is a dull and obtuse mind, that must divide in order to distinguish; but it is a still worse, that distinguishes in order to divide.[20]

The second ("still worse") type of mind is evidently not worse by being still *more* dull and obtuse, but rather the opposite; for it is the type of mind which possesses 'keenness' without subtlety:

> Few men of genius are keen; but almost every man of genius is subtle. If you ask me the difference between keenness and subtlety, I answer that it is the difference between a point and an edge. To split a hair is no proof of subtlety; for subtlety acts in distinguishing differences—in showing that two things apparently one are in fact two; whereas to split a hair is to cause division, and not to ascertain a difference.[21]

> Distinct *notions* do not suppose different things. When I make a threefold distinction in human nature, I am fully aware that it is a distinction, not a division, and that in every act of mind the *man* unites the properties of sense, understanding and reason. Nevertheless it is of great practical importance, that these distinctions should be made and understood, the ignorance or perversion of them being alike injurious . . .[22]

Now let us hear him on the psychological source of this still very prevalent assumption that we cannot distinguish except where we can divide; or that, if we do so, the distinction is 'unreal.'

> Under that despotism of the eye (the emancipation from which Pythagoras by his *numeral,* and Plato by his *musical* symbols, and both by geometric discipline, aimed at, as the first *propaideutikon* of the mind) —under this strong sensuous influence, we are restless because invisible

things are not the objects of vision; and metaphysical systems, for the most part, become popular, not for their truth, but in proportion as they attribute to causes a susceptibility of being *seen,* if only our visual organs were sufficiently powerful.[23]

. . . Locke told us, in defining words, we ought to have distinct images or conceptions . . .[24]

Now it is clear that the materialist excludes all facts that are not immediately the objects of his senses. By his very hypothesis he cannot have a theory, for he determines first of all rather to place effect for cause than to concede any one thing which his reason dictates if his senses do not at the same time give him a picture of it.[25]

Thus, as materialism has generally been taught, it is utterly unintelligible, and owes all its proselytes to the propensity so common among men, to mistake distinct images for clear conceptions; and vice versa, to reject as inconceivable whatever from its own nature is unimaginable. But as soon as it becomes intelligible, it ceases to be materialism.[26]

. . . this difficulty* . . . arises wholly out of That Slavery of the Mind to the Eye and the visual Imagination or Fancy under the influence of which the Reasoner must have a *picture* and mistakes surface for substance.[27]

There is an interesting corollary to the above quotations, and particularly perhaps to the first two of them. Coleridge rarely let slip an opportunity of emphasising "the great advantages to be obtained from the habit of tracing the proper meaning and history of words"; and we find him towards the end of his life vigorously recommending this discipline as a means towards liberating mind from sense. Perhaps, in a history-conscious age it is a likelier one than those formerly adopted by Pythagoras and Plato.

In disciplining the mind one of the first rules should be, to lose no opportunity of tracing words to their origin; one good consequence of which will be, that he will be able to use the *language* of sight without being enslaved by its affections. He will at least save himself from the delusive notion, that what is not *imageable* is likewise not *conceivable.*

---

* The reference is to Milton's over the notion of creation out of 'nothing,' which led him to "assert the eternity of Matter to escape from it."

To emancipate the mind from the despotism of the eye is the first step towards its emancipation from the influences and intrusions of the senses, sensations and passions generally. Thus most effectively is the power of abstraction to be called forth, strengthened and familiarized, and it is this power of abstraction that chiefly distinguishes the human understanding from that of the higher animals—and in the different degrees in which this power is developed, the superiority of man over man largely consists.

Hence we are to account for the preference which the divine Plato gives to expressions taken from objects of the ear, as terms of Music and Harmony, and in part at least for the numerical symbols, in which Pythagoras clothed his philosophy.[28]

Tinted glasses make the clearest blue sky look leaden and overcast. Coleridge will continue to be called 'cloudy' even by his admirers, because he will continue to be misinterpreted by readers who are not willing to grasp, and to remember once they *have* grasped, the elementary principles which consciously permeate almost every other sentence he constructs, and which it is hoped the foregoing quotations sufficiently illustrate. These are: first, that thinking is an act. Secondly, that it is normally, though not necessarily and always, an unconscious act. Thirdly, that though we are not normally conscious of the act, we *are* normally conscious of the product of the act (which we call 'thoughts'), and indeed it is this, which actually constitutes our self-consciousness as human beings.

It must not be thought, because a number of the quotations selected instance occasions when the act itself did become conscious—"snatched away as it were from the product" *—that Coleridge rested the validity of his system on abnormal experience. He held that the peculiar relation between act and product is implicit in the very concept of thought or mind;[29] and that this can be demonstrated by analysis. Indeed he spent a large part of his energies in seeking to demonstrate precisely this, by every means in his power and at every opportunity that offered itself.

---

* See p. 14, above.

∂ 2 ↣

Naturata and Naturans

In nature nothing remains constant. Everything is in a perpetual state of transformation, motion and change. However, we discover that nothing simply surges up out of nothing without having antecedents that existed before. I believe nothing ever disappears without a trace, in the sense that it gives rise to absolutely nothing existing at later times. This general characteristic of the world can be expressed in terms of a principle which summarises an enormous domain of different kinds of experience and which has never yet been contradicted in any observation or experiment, scientific or otherwise; namely, everything comes from other things and gives rise to other things.

This principle is not yet a statement of the existence of causality in nature. Indeed, it is even more fundamental than is causality, for it is at the foundation of the possibility of our understanding nature in a rational way.

David Bohm: *Causality and Chance in Modern Physics;*
Chapter 1, Introduction.[1]

THIS is a concept of nature which Coleridge would have approved and accepted. Nature was, for him "the term in which we comprehend all things that are representable in the forms of time and space, and subjected to the relations of cause and effect: and the cause of the existence of which, therefore, is to be sought for perpetually in something antecedent." [2] Characteristically, he adds that the word itself expresses this in the strongest manner possible: "*Natura,* that which is about to be born, that which is always *becoming*." [3] *Natura* is of course the Latin rendering of Greek *physis* and, as Bohm begins by pointing out, it is this fundamental principle—the nature of Nature as a whole—with which the science of Physics is concerned.

But at this point the Coleridgean analysis takes a further step which differentiates his concept of nature sharply from that of most, if not all, modern physicists. To investigate scientifically the nature of Nature is to investigate the nature of phenomena as such. It is to ask the question: What is a phenomenon? True, "everything comes from other things and gives rise to other things." Of any particular phenomenon we can say, tracing the chain of cause and effect: "this comes from such and such another phenomenon or group of phenomena." But if it is really the origin of phenomena *as such* that we are seeking to investigate, there must come a point where this answer will no longer serve: "the solution of phenomena can never be derived from phenomena." [4]

Thus, the question: What is a particle? can never be answered in terms of "the relation of unproductive particles to each other." [5] Yet this is precisely the solution which the physical science of Coleridge's day was looking for. We are not at the moment concerned with the question whether the same is true of the physics of our own day, but it may be remarked that the concept of the 'field,' supplementing that of the particle if not replacing it altogether, has no doubt done something towards emancipating modern physics from "the despotism of the eye." [6]

The essence of the natural process is that it is 'productive,' in the wide sense of evolving phenomena from other phenomena,[7] and Coleridge held it to be a logical absurdity to suppose that this productive *power* is the same kind of thing as the phenomena themselves.

What then can be said, what can be ascertained about productive nature, as distinguished in thought from already produced (that is, phenomenal) nature? The proper answer to this question was one of the main concerns of Coleridge's life, and we may begin by quoting his opinion of what it is *not:*

—Aristotle's definitions of nature are all grounded on the petty and rather rhetorical than philosophical *antithesis* of nature to art—a conception inadequate to the demands even of his philosophy. Hence in the progress of his reasoning, he confounds the *natura naturata* (that is, the sum total of the facts and phenomena of the senses) with an hypothetical *natura naturans,* a Goddess Nature, that has no better claim to a place in any sober system of natural philosophy than the Goddess *Multitudo;*[8]

It is not of course the mere concept of a *natura naturans*—a nature linguistically denotable only by adding a verb to the noun, a nature 'naturing'—that Coleridge is objecting to here. On the contrary, it is one that he frequently uses himself:

> —in speaking of the world without us as distinguished from ourselves, the aggregate of phenomena ponderable and imponderable, is called nature in the passive sense,—in the language of the old schools, *natura naturata*—while the sum or aggregate of the powers inferred as the sufficient causes of the forms (which by Aristotle and his followers were called the substantial forms) is nature in the active sense, or *natura naturans*.[9]

What he criticises is, firstly, Aristotle's failure to *distinguish* clearly between *natura naturans* and *natura naturata* and, secondly, his attempt to remedy the defect by the hypothesis of a Goddess.

We may speak of *natura naturans* and *natura naturata;* or we may say that, in addition to the phenomena, there are the so-called 'laws' of nature, without which it is impossible to understand the phenomena. The laws themselves are not phenomenal and we only become aware of them in their effects. But we have, all the same, to distinguish them from the phenomena themselves. They are not the less real because they are not things.

Thus, the distinction between *natura naturans* and *natura naturata* reveals itself as resembling in quality that distinction between the act of thought and its product, which was discussed in the previous chapter— *natura naturata* being "the productive power suspended and, as it were, quenched in the product." [10]

It was the refusal of science to realise, or even consider, this principle that provoked Coleridge into such extreme pronouncements as we find, for instance, in the *Statesman's Manual,* where he casually remarks that "we have not yet attained to a science of nature." [11] He held that a true system must be grounded neither in a *thing* nor an *abstraction*.[12] And it is the inexorable presupposition in the minds of his readers, that whatever is not a thing *must* be an abstraction, which, more than perhaps anything else, has prevented his own system from being understood. In particular it has prevented them from even grasping, at the outset, what such a term as *natura naturans* signifies. For, once the author has made it clear that what he is talking about is not a thing, it is mentally docketed by 99.9 per cent of them as an abstraction. In fact, however, Coleridge's *natura naturans* is no more of an abstraction than, for instance, gravitation.

Natura naturans is supersensuous, but not supernatural. It has nothing to do with those 'occult qualities,' whose final expulsion (or intended expulsion) from the domain of science was one of the major achievements of the scientific revolution. Coleridge emphasised this on more than one occasion.[13] We shall see that, so far from reintroducing occult qualities, he considered his concept of spirit, as the antithesis or correlative to 'nature,' to be the only possible means of *eliminating* those occult qualities which in fact remain surreptitiously present in the vocabulary of science. There were not a few of them still left in Coleridge's time, and there are still some today. Comte complained long ago that the admission of so-called 'forces' into that vocabulary (the "force of gravity" for instance) was a relic of primitive animism. An 'occult quality' is anything that is deemed to possess an exclusively objective existence, in spite of being imperceptible.

This was the case with the hypothetical 'ether' to which so much speculative attention was directed during the earlier part of the time between Newton's day and our own. But it is equally true of any other 'plenum,' or hypothetical space-filler, conceived in the phenomenal mode, in order to solve the old problem of action at a distance—a problem indeed (he held), if not an absurdity, to all men who presuppose 'nature' to mean the *naturata* alone, in artificial abstraction from the totality which must include also the *naturans*.

We will conclude this chapter with an extract from Coleridge's notes written on his copy of the *De Divisione Naturae* of John Scotus Erigena:

> Such men, and their name is *legion*—consequently *demand* a *Matter* as a *Datum*. As soon as this gross prejudice is cured by the appropriate discipline and the Mind is familiarised to the contemplation of Matter as a product in time, the resulting Phenomenon of the equilibrium of the two antagonist Forces, Attraction and Repulsion, *that* the Negative and *this* the Positive Pole . . . the idea of *Creation* alone remains.[14]

In the chapter that follows we shall find that we cannot direct our attention on these "two antagonist Forces" and enquire what Coleridge meant by them, without finding ourselves in territory with which the average student of Coleridge's prose is already familiar.

Two Forces of One Power

APART from his poetry, the best-known work of Coleridge is the 'Literary Life,' or *Biographia Literaria*. It is really the only prose writing that is at all widely read today. Moreover, within the *Biographia Literaria* itself it is to one particular chapter that attention is mainly given. The critique of Wordsworth's poetry which fills four chapters in the second part of the book is, it is true, highly valued by all who are at all deeply concerned with English literature and its history; but it is the famous, truncated Chapter XIII, at the end of Part I, which comes to mind first and foremost, when the *Biographia Literaria* is mentioned. This chapter has been praised, criticised, confuted, confirmed, argued from, argued against, expounded, blessed and cursed over and over again and almost without intermission since the day it was published . . . or rather part of this chapter.

Chapter XIII consists of three parts. First there are three pages of philosophical exposition following, without any appreciable break, on the long philosophical disquisition which constitutes Chapter XII. Then there is a row of asterisks, followed by a letter, printed in italics, which the author says he had just received from a friend, whose practical judgment he has "ample reason to estimate and revere" and who had seen the part of the book already written. The letter begins: "You ask my opinion concerning your Chapter on The Imagination, both as to the impression it made on myself, and as to those which I think it will make on the Public . . ." It goes on to advise that the chapter, "which cannot, when it is printed, amount to so little as an hundred pages," would be quite out of place in a literary biography, and recommends the author to reserve it for "your great book on the Constructive Philosophy, which you have promised and announced." Even then it will be too revolutionary to be readily received. For both its opinions and its method of argument are "directly the reverse of all I had ever been accustomed to consider as truth . . ."

The chapter then concludes with three short paragraphs stating, says Coleridge, "the main result of the Chapter which I have reserved for that future publication."

This 'letter' we now know[1] to have been composed by Coleridge himself. It is on the third part of the chapter, the three final paragraphs already referred to, that attention has been mainly concentrated. They contain (1) Coleridge's distinction between the 'primary' and the 'secondary' Imagination, (2) his frequently quoted definition of the primary Imagination "as the living power and prime agent of all human perception, and as a repetition in the finite mind of the eternal act of creation in the infinite I AM," (3) his dictum that the secondary Imagination "is essentially *vital,* even as all objects (*as* objects) are essentially fixed and dead," and (4) though this had already been adumbrated in Chapter IV, the famous distinction between Imagination and Fancy.

So much for the content of the three paragraphs. Let us now tabulate what else we know about them. We know, firstly, that they form part of a chapter entitled "On the Imagination, or Esemplastic Power"; secondly, that Coleridge began writing this chapter with the thought that it might run to as many as a hundred pages; thirdly, that the three paragraphs* were substituted for what would have been at most a brief terminal summary of the conclusions ("the main result") to be drawn from the contents of those hundred or so pages; fourthly, that Coleridge had in contemplation a great book on the Constructive Philosophy, which was likely to contain opinions and a method of argument not merely different from, but "directly the reverse" of all that his contemporaries were accustomed to think.

The great book on the Constructive Philosophy never appeared, though it was often mentioned.[2] It was certainly never finished; but equally certainly it was more than merely begun, and there are two substantial MS volumes in the British Museum, which were undoubtedly intended to be the first part of it.† Moreover it is apparent from other published works such as the *Aids to Reflection,* the *Friend,* the *Philosophical Lectures,* and the *Theory of Life,* and it has been becom-

---

* In effect there are only two, since the first merely describes the other two.

† The *Treatise on Logic.*

ing more and more apparent during the last few decades from MSS, letters, marginalia, notebook entries etc., that the substance of his projected Magnum Opus was fully available to Coleridge's *mind* before he died, in the shape of a coherent and closely knit psychology, philosophy and cosmology.

How far it was already so available at the time when Chapter XIII was written and how far he continued to develop it afterwards is a matter which need not concern us.

Apart from all this, there is Chapter XII of the *Biographia Literaria* itself, which, though it is difficult reading, is perfectly intelligible, and from which, even if taken by itself, the skeleton of the constructive, or dynamic, philosophy, and in particular the precise significance of the term *primary imagination,* can be constructed by a little serious application.

Discouraging perhaps; but one would have thought that anyone who felt at all deeply concerned with Coleridge's views on imagination and who felt entitled to spread himself on the topic (Walter Pater for instance) would, if he could not bring himself to study Chapter XII, at least have taken the trouble to ponder the opening paragraphs of Chapter XIII *as well as* the three aphoristic paragraphs with which it closes. Yet, with a few honourable exceptions, these opening paragraphs have been completely ignored.

Let us then see how Chapter XIII does begin—omitting the quotations from Milton, Leibnitz and Synesius which are placed at the head of it:

Descartes, speaking as a naturalist, and in imitation of Archimedes, said, give me matter and motion and I will construct you the universe. We must of course understand him to have meant: I will render the construction of the universe intelligible. In the same sense the transcendental philosopher* says: grant me a nature having two contrary forces, the one of which tends to expand infinitely, while the other strives to apprehend or *find* itself in this infinity, and I will cause the world of intelligences with the whole system of their representations to rise up before you. Every other science presupposes intelligence as already existing and complete: the philosopher contemplates it in its growth, and as it were represents its history to the mind from its birth to its maturity.[3]

---

* See Chapter I, p. 15, above.

A cosmology, a philosophy, a psychology, which allows to imagination a 'primary' as well as a secondary role, must begin by recognizing two forces. These two forces will be its ultimate, unquestioned grounds in precisely the same way as matter and motion were the unquestioned grounds of most of the philosophy and all the science of Coleridge's contemporaries. They would appear therefore to be of some slight importance. Nevertheless the majority of those who up to now have sympathetically interpreted Coleridge to us, including some who have honestly sought to interpret him in depth—and have read very widely in him for that purpose[4]—have simply ignored them. To us, on the contrary, it has long been evident that neither his 'system' as a whole, nor his theory of imagination, which is an integral part of it, can be authentically apprehended without first coming to terms with those two forces; and it is with the idea of coming to terms with them at the outset that we have taken the unusual course of dealing, as far as in us lies, with Coleridge's concept of nature *before* coming on to his concept of mind (understanding and reason), of man, of imagination and other things.

To proceed in this order may have some disadvantages, but it will have two important merits. Firstly, everyman's personal experience of nature does precede in time his experience of the working of his own mind, and we have all learned much about the former before we begin to reflect on the latter. Secondly the positivist or materialist (many would say simply 'the scientific') world-view itself adopts this order. It begins by postulating a physical process (whether in terms of "matter and motion" or of energy or of some other physical substratum makes no difference here), it shows how this process produced the human brain (of which the mind is a function) and then proceeds, on the basis of a brain so conceived, to propound whatever it has to propound about the mind. All this, though rarely stated and perhaps not often consciously formulated, is operative as presupposition today whenever the mind, whether conscious or unconscious, whether in its creative or its analytical aspect, is debated or reflected on.[5] It is the tacit assumption of every received system of psychology, whether neural, Freudian, philosophical, theological or aesthetic. A certain concept of nature is in fact implicit in every concept of mind; and Coleridge's own concept of nature—"directly the reverse" of all that most of us "have ever been accustomed to consider as truth"—is implicit in all his reflections and all his utterances on the subject of the mind and its operations. Most of the criticisms to which these have been subjected, whether fretfully or thoughtfully, are found on analysis to be based on the substitution of the wrong set of presuppositions for the right ones. His conclusions are rejected for failing to accord with premises on which they are not based. In particular they have suffered from the circumstance that a non-Cartesian psychology will not fit into a Cartesian cosmos. Critics who prefer to bestow their attention on more immediate matters, while they take for granted as revealed truth the prevailing metaphysical climate of their age, are sometimes heard to grumble because Coleridge's theory of imagination is for some reason "still around." They are to be commended for their sincerity. There really is no room for Coleridge in their world. Something at least, then, will have been achieved by the method adopted here if it should be appreciated in future that Coleridge's doctrine of, for instance, imagination cannot be refuted, or even intelligently attacked, without first meeting and disposing of Coleridge's premises.

As before, we shall proceed by selecting and commenting on a few quotations, drawn from his published and unpublished writings, on the subject of these two 'forces' which, for Coleridge, took the place of the exclusively physical base presumed by the educated opinion of his day, and of our own, to lie at the foundation of the world. And we will look first of all at those early paragraphs of Chapter XIII of the *Biographia Literaria* from which we quoted above. They are, then, "contrary" forces (p. 28); but on the other hand they are "real" and not mere logical opposites. It is not Hegel but Kant, whom he cites to the effect that:

> Opposites . . . are of two kinds, either logical, that is such as are absolutely incompatible; or real, without being contradictory . . . a body, at one and the same time in motion and not in motion, is nothing, or, at most, air articulated into nonsense. But a motory force of a body in one direction, and an equal force of the same body in an opposite direction is not incompatible, and the result, namely, rest, is real and representable.[6]

Are they physical forces, then? Certainly not, though they do (as will be seen later) give rise to physical forces. The instance of a body at rest, because two physical forces are acting on it from opposite directions, was an illustration only, offered as some help to the imagination. But our two forces are "prior to all direction"; they "counteract each other by their essential nature"; they are "the primary forces from which the conditions of all possible directions are derivative"; they are "both alike infinite, both alike indestructible." To which we may add (from the Essay on the *Principles of Genial Criticism*): they are "two conflicting principles of the FREE LIFE and the CONFINING FORM." [7]

They thus fulfil his own stipulation that a true system must be grounded neither in a *thing* nor an *abstraction;** and, because they are not abstractions but realities, it is possible for us to "contemplate" them intuitively.

> Every power[8] in nature and in spirit must evolve an opposite as the sole means and condition of its manifestation: and all opposition is a tendency to re-union. This is the universal law of polarity or essential dualism, first promulgated by Heraclitus, 2000 years afterwards re-published and made the foundation both of logic, of physics, and of meta-physics by Giordano Bruno.[9]

Now follows one of the passages in which Coleridge attempts to express the relation between the two forces in abstract philosophical language, and where his adoption of 'Hegelian' (more properly Fichtean) terminology has perhaps hindered rather than helped effective grasp of his meaning by most of his readers:

> The principle may be thus expressed. The identity of *thesis* and *antithesis* is the substance of all being; their opposition the condition of all existence or being manifested; and every thing or *phaenomenon* is the exponent of a *synthesis* as long as the opposite energies are retained in that *synthesis*.[9]

After which he continues with another attempt, this time taken from chemistry, to illustrate concretely and pictorially, the *nature* of "polar opposition":

> Thus water is neither oxygen nor hydrogen, nor yet is it a commixture of both; but the *synthesis* or indifference of the two: and as long as the *copula* endures, by which it becomes, or rather which alone is water, it is not less a simple body than either of the imaginary elements, improperly called its ingredients or components. It is the object of the mechanical atomistic philosophy[10] to confound *synthesis* with *synartesis,* or rather with mere juxta-position of corpuscles separated by invisible interspaces.

---

* Chapter 2, p. 24, above.

I find it difficult to determine, whether this theory contradicts the reason or the senses most: for it is alike inconceivable and unimaginable.[11]

"Every power in nature and in spirit . . ." As has already been emphasised, we are beginning with Coleridge's concept of nature; moreover in this chapter we confine ourselves largely to his concept of *inorganic* nature, the bearing of the two forces on biological evolution being left for subsequent treatment. This again has some disadvantages, since their interpenetration within the processes, alike of organic growth and of phylogenetic evolution makes a readier appeal to the imagination, which is helped there by the rich variety of familiar and picturable forms wherethrough they manifest themselves. Nevertheless it is believed that on the whole the disadvantages are outweighed by other considerations. In any case the question would quickly be raised, which is now raised at the very outset, by the words "in nature and in spirit"; and that is of course the question of the 'ontological status' of the two forces.

To ask some such question as: are they real or are they purely conceptual? would be to accept in advance a categorical disjunction which Coleridge spent much of his life in denying and (as he believed) disproving. A less loaded question would be to enquire if they are of such a nature that any use can be made of them by experimental science. But that is a question to which no answer can be attempted until we have heard a great deal more than we have yet done of what Coleridge had to say about them.

We will begin by hearing what they are *not*. They are not phenomenal; another way of putting it would be to say that, unless we are prepared to accept, at least for the sake of argument, the distinction, already discussed, between *natura naturata* and *natura naturans,* and to accept it as a distinction between two forms of reality, we had better not trouble ourselves further with them. For it is only in *natura naturans* that we shall ever find them. But let us hear Coleridge himself on the subject:

All our inquiries respecting Nature (that is, the objects of the senses, or whatever is seen, heard, smelt, touched, tasted or weighed) may be generalized into two questions:

First, what are the *Powers* that must be assumed in order for the Thing to *be* that which it is: or what are the primary constituent *Powers* of Nature, into some modification or combination of which all other Natural *Powers* are to be resolved?

Second Question. What are the Forms in which these Powers *appear* or manifest themselves to our senses—or What are The primary *Things,* into some combination of which all other *things* are to be resolved, as into their first Elements?

Answer to the First Question. In answer to the First Question I say, that all the primary Powers of Nature may be reduced to Two, each of which produces two others, and a third as the union of both.[12]

In the second place they are not hypotheses invented to "account for" phenomena. Coleridge himself carefully distinguished between accounting for a thing and "explaining" it in his *Theory of Life,* but it will be better to deal with this when we come on to the relation, in his system, between a 'law of nature' and an 'idea.' Meanwhile any sceptic may quite properly *treat* them as hypotheses and therefore decline considering them further if he finds the notion of them incompatible with fact observed or verified.

But that is of course quite different from rejecting them simply because they are not to be found among the phenomena observed, or the hypotheses invented, in trim with post-Cartesian scientific method. When for instance Sir Herbert Read remarks that: "The *Natur-geist* [*natura naturans*] is not a phenomenon recognized by natural science," one can only reply, patiently and with all due courtesy: "But *of course* it isn't!" How could that which is by definition not a phenomenon be recognized as a phenomenon by anyone? And how could it be recognized *even as a hypothesis* by a natural science, which up to the present has proceeded on the assumption that "the final solution of phenomena" *can* "itself be a phenomenon"; for which "nature" is, not only theoretically but also methodically, presumed to be exclusively *natura naturata?* [13]

The two forces, then, are not parts of phenomenal nature; they are not body, nor in any conventional sense the "causes" of what is bodily. They are not material in the sense that, for instance, the forces of electricity and magnetism are material. These 'constituent powers,' as Coleridge calls them in the passage previously quoted, are acts or energies that are "suspended and, as it were, quenched in the product." * They are the 'inside' of anything to which we can apply the noun *matter* or the adjective *material.*[14]

---

* Chapter 2, p. 24, above.

It is peculiar to the Philosophy, of which I have given this slight sketch as far as its introductory Science is concerned, to consider matter as a Product—coagulum spiritus—the pause, by interpenetration, of opposite energies . . .[15]

And here the word *pause* is important. It will be recalled that in Chapter XIII of the *Biographia Literaria* the two forces are characterised as "both alike infinite and indestructible." It follows that, when they are "quenched" in their product, they do not simply cease to exist. They are merely "suspended." (In the illustration, hydrogen and oxygen *are* water "so long as the copula endures"—but they are also still potentially hydrogen and oxygen.) Consequently the 'constituent powers,' which have given rise to a body, may then 'reappear' in it as its function:

a Power, acting in and by its Product or Representative to a predetermined purpose is a Function . . .[16]

The first product of its energy is the thing itself: *ipsa se posuit et iam facta est ens positum*. Still, however, its productive energy is not exhausted in this product, but overflows, or is effluent, as the specific forces, properties, faculties, of the product. It reappears, in short, as the function of the body.[17]

And this will be particularly important for biology, where

The vital functions are consequents of the Vis Vitae, Principium Vitale, and presuppose the Organs, as the Functionaries.[18]

Before however we can proceed to the organic level, there is still some more to be said on the general subject of the two forces and the relation between them at the inorganic level.

One way of putting it, as has perhaps appeared, would be to say that, in order to think with Coleridge, we have to supplement the familiar contrast between 'potential' and 'kinetic' energy with some such contrast as that between 'energy as free power' and 'energy as structure.' [19] It is however a peculiarity of the two forces that we cannot even imagine them without at the same time imagining the special *relation between* them. This is the relation for which Coleridge normally used the word *polarity,* and which was for him such a common and indispensable tool of thought that in his notebooks, marginal annotations and some of his letters to friends he habitually employed the symbol)(, to avoid the tedium of writing out in full some such phrase as "is polarically related to" or "is the polar opposite of"; as others, writing in a hurry, will often put "=" for "is equivalent to" or "is the same as."

We come, then, to the question: what *is* this "polarity"? And perhaps, to begin with, a few observations on the word itself may be of some assistance. Originally it derived its meaning from terrestrial magnetism, being found in the seventeenth century (according to the Oxford Dictionary) both in the particular sense of "the quality or property possessed by a lodestone or magnetised bar of iron turning so as to point with their two extremities to the two (magnetic) poles of the earth" and then in the general sense of a quality or property *analogous* to that of magnetism. The dictionary subdivides the general sense into two branches (*a*) and (*b*), of which (*a*) is defined as "the having of an axis with reference to which certain physical properties are determined; the disposition of a body or an elementary molecule to place its mathematical axis in a particular direction." It is in this sense that the word is used in, for instance, crystallography. Subdivision (*b*) is still more generalized: "The quality of exhibiting contrasted properties or powers in opposite or contrasted directions; the possession of two points called poles having contrary qualities or tendencies"; and here the earliest supporting quotation is dated 1818 and taken from Coleridge himself: "Contemplating in all Electrical phenomena the operation of a Law which reigns through all Nature, viz. the law of *polarity,* or the manifestation of one power by opposite forces." [20]

We shall return in a moment to the reference to "Electrical phenomena." Meanwhile the precise wording should be carefully noted. Polarity is, according to Coleridge, a "law"; it is a law which reigns through all Nature; the duality of the "opposite forces" is the *manifestation* of a prior unity; and that unity is a "power." It is not, that is to say, any abstract "principle of unity" or of identity—a point which it is hardly possible to over-emphasise, since that is precisely what it is commonly presumed to be by the few who go so far as to interest themselves at all in these fundamentals of Coleridge's thought. Moreover, most of the much that has been written, in the last few decades, concerning the "reconciliation of opposites" in literature, and often with express reference to Coleridge as its putative father, betrays a lamentable failure to understand what "opposites" and their "reconciliation" actually signified in Coleridge's vocabulary. There is a world of difference between

Coleridge's polarity and those "gorgeous ballets of dialectical opposition," [21] to which we have been treated not only by literary critics theorising about poetry, but also by psychologists, and more lately by theologians seeking to 'reconcile' the sacred and the profane.*

Polarity is dynamic, not abstract. It is not "a mere balance or compromise," but "a living and generative interpenetration." [22] Where logical opposites are contradictory, polar opposites are generative of each other—and together generative of new product. Polar opposites exist by virtue of each other *as well as* at the expense of each other; "each is that which it is called, relatively, by predominance of the one character or quality, not by the absolute exclusion of the other." [23] Moreover each quality or character is present *in* the other. We can and must distinguish, but there is no possibility of *dividing* them.[24]

But when one has said all this, how much has one succeeded in conveying? How much use are definitions of the undefinable? The point is, has the imagination grasped it? For nothing else can do so.[25] At this point the reader must be called on, not to think about imagination, but to use it. Indeed we shall see that the apprehension of polarity is itself *the basic act of imagination*.

For that reason a single vivid picture of the law of polarity at work in nature may well prove more effective than a dozen definitions or statements of principle; and it happens that the 1933 Supplement to the Oxford Dictionary gives us just such a picture, when it hazards as an additional definition of *polarity:* "The tendency observed in some animals of a severed head-piece to develop a tail or of a severed tail-piece to develop a head; a similar tendency in parts of plants."

To think of directionally opposed mechanical forces, giving rise by their equilibrium to a state of rest, is very well; and at least it shakes us out of any obsession with merely logical contradictories. But to think *only* of that will in the end prove more of a hindrance than a help. We do better to envisage something like two nations at total war, each with a network of spies and a resistance movement, distributed throughout the whole of the other's territory—and each with a secret underground passage opening into the citadel in the heart of the enemy's metropolis.

---

* Though I am not aware that he ever did, STC might very well have invented the words *contrafaction* and *contrafactories,* to set against *contradiction* and *contradictories.*

Coleridge remained all his life deeply interested in the progress and the problems of natural science.[26] His Notebooks, in particular, are replete with observations on chemistry, biology, metallurgy and other sciences. He was an intimate friend of Sir Humphry Davy. His foremost concern was with electricity and magnetism, then still in their infancy, and particularly the no-mans-land between electricity and chemistry—so much so that, among the many misunderstandings which he suffered from his friends as well as from his enemies, was the belief that he held electricity to be "the foundation of life." [27]

This is of course a complete misconception. Coleridge's two indestructible "forces" are located in *natura naturans,* and are pre-phenomenal. The positive and negative forces or energies of electricity, though they are not directly perceptible (as neither, for that matter, are mechanical forces), are nevertheless present in the phenomenal world. The way he himself put it was to say that, though they are not embodied, they *are* "material." [28]

But though the material, and precisely quantifiable, positive and negative energies which we meet with in electricity are not the two forces spoken of at the beginning of Chapter XIII of the *Biographia Literaria,* they are, like the rest of the material world, effects, or products, of those forces and they happen, in their relation to each other, to provide a particularly telling illustration both of the two forces themselves and of the peculiar relation (polarity) which subsists between them. To this they come, so to speak, so near that one could almost say: Here we have *natura naturata* masquerading as *natura naturans.*

It is to this circumstance that we must look for an explanation of Coleridge's abiding interest in all he could learn about electricity and magnetism. The poles of the magnet, positive and negative electricity—these were not in themselves the "two antagonist Forces" that all creation entails. But they were forcing men's attention to themselves; and in so doing they were compelling them to begin thinking about nature in a different way, a way which might end in their again finding the forces themselves—in the only realm where they can be found—a realm to which the understanding alone has no access, but which is communicable, between one mind and another, only by an understanding laced with imagination.[29] The very histories of the two sciences and the contrast between them seemed to him to rub this in. Thus, we find him writing in the *Friend:*

But in experimental philosophy, it may be said how much do we not owe to accident? Doubtless: but let it not be forgotten, that if the discoveries so made stop there; if they do not excite some master IDEA; if they do not lead to some LAW (in whatever dress of theory or hypotheses the fashions and prejudices of the time may disguise or disfigure it):—the discoveries may remain for ages limited in their uses, insecure and unproductive. How many centuries, we might have said millennia, have passed, since the first accidental discovery of the attraction and repulsion of light bodies by rubbed amber etc. Compare the interval with the progress made within less than a century after the discovery of the phaenomena that led immediately to a THEORY of electricity. That here as in many other instances, the theory was supported by insecure hypotheses; that by one theorist two heterogeneous fluids are assumed, the vitreous and the resinous; by another, a plus and minus of the same fluid; that a third considers it a mere modification of light; while a fourth composes the electrical aura of oxygen, hydrogen, and caloric; this does but place the truth we have been evolving in a stronger and clearer light. For abstract from all these suppositions, or rather imaginations, that which is common to, and involved in them all; and we shall have neither notional fluid or fluids, nor chemical compounds, nor elementary matter,—but the idea of *two-opposite-forces,* tending to rest by equilibrium. These are the sole factors of the calculus, alike in all the theories. These give the *law,* and in it the *method,* both of arranging the phaenomena and of substantiating appearances into facts of science; with a success proportionate to the clearness or confusedness of the insight into the law. For this reason, we anticipate the greatest improvements in the *method,* the nearest approaches to a *system* of electricity, from these philosophers, who have presented the law most purely, and the correlative idea as an idea: those, namely, who, since the year 1798, in the true spirit of experimental dynamics, rejecting the imagination of any material substrate, simple or compound, contemplate in the phaenomena of electricity the operation of a law which reigns through all nature, the law of POLARITY, of the manifestation of one power by opposite forces; who trace in these appearances, as the most obvious and striking of its innumerable forms, the agency of the positive and negative poles of a power essential to all material construction; the second, namely, of the three primary principles, for which the beautiful and most appropriate symbols are given by the mind in the three ideal dimensions of space.

The time is, perhaps, nigh at hand, when the same comparison between the results of two unequal periods, the interval between the knowledge of a fact, and that from the discovery of the law,—will be applicable to the sister science of magnetism. But how great the contrast between magnetism and electricity at the present moment! From remotest antiquity, the attraction of iron by the magnet was known and noticed; but, century after century, it remained the undisturbed property of poets and orators. The fact of the magnet and the fable of the phoenix stood on the same scale of utility. In the thirteenth century, or perhaps earlier, the polarity of the magnet, and its communicability to iron, were discovered; and soon suggested a purpose so grand and important, that it may well be deemed the proudest trophy ever raised by accident in the service of mankind—the invention of the compass. But it led to no idea, to no law, and consequently to no Method: though a variety of phaenomena, as startling as they are mysterious, have forced on us a presentiment of its intimate connection with all the great agencies of nature; of a revelation, in ciphers, the key to which is still wanting. I can recall no event of human history that impresses the imagination more deeply than the moment when Columbus, on an unknown ocean, first perceived one of these startling facts, the change of the magnetic needle.

In what shall we seek the cause of this contrast between the rapid progress of electricity and the stationary condition of magnetism? As many theories, as many hypotheses, have been advanced in the latter science as in the former. But the theories and fictions of the electricians contained an *idea,* and all the same idea, which has necessarily led to METHOD; implicit indeed, and only regulative hitherto, but which requires little more than the dismission of the imagery[30] to become constitutive like the ideas of the geometrician. On the contrary, the assumptions of the magnetists (as for instance, the hypothesis that the planet itself is one vast magnet, or that an immense magnet is concealed within it, or that of a concentric globe within the earth, revolving on its own independent axis) are but repetitions of the same fact or phaenomenon looked at through a magnifying glass; the *reiteration* of the problem, not its solution. The naturalist, who cannot or will not see, that one fact is often worth a thousand, as including them all in itself, and that it first *makes* all the other facts, who has not the head to comprehend, the soul to reverence, a central experiment or observation (what the Greeks would perhaps have called a *protophaenomenon*),—will never receive an auspicious answer from the oracle of nature.[31]

We have already emphasised the fact that the difficulty in expounding Coleridge's concept of nature lies, not in its being incoherent or fragmented, but rather in its total integration; so that every part of it tends to involve every other. Thus, the foregoing quotation virtually plunges us into the issue of the relation between 'law' and 'idea,' and of both of these to 'method,' which it is our plan to reach only later. This much however should perhaps be said here: that the bearing, on precisely this issue,* of the discoveries that were being made in the domain of electricity was another (and yet, in a way, it is the *same*) reason for the special concern Coleridge felt with them. The understanding can apprehend only phenomena (that is, *natura naturata*) and the causal chain that links them together. If it 'goes behind' them, it can go only to other phenomena, hitherto unapprehended but forming part of the chain. Accordingly there must be ultimate phenomena, behind which the understanding cannot go. The understanding has played its part when it has delivered them to the imagination to contemplate (and here again we find ourselves pushed ahead into the issue of the relation between understanding, imagination and 'Reason'). These are the *protophaenomena*—"central phenomena," or Goethe's *Urphänomene*—and they are by no means confined to electricity and magnetism. They demand, though they rarely receive, our attention in every growing plant. But the positive and negative 'charges' with which electrical research in Coleridge's time, and now also atomic and nuclear research, are at last confronted, are conspicuous examples of them. To look beyond that stage for still other 'supporting' phenomena is (so Coleridge held) to wander off into the realm of fancy. At this point it is no longer for the understanding to continue exploring and analysing what the senses deliver to it, but for the mind to recognise the presence in itself of the naked 'idea' and, as it were, to exclaim: "Oh, it was *you*, was it!"

---

* See Chapter 10 (conclusion).

4

Life

In his *Studies in Words*[1] C. S. Lewis remarks that the modern usage of "one privileged abstract noun" reveals a state of mind that is startlingly close to the Platonic. Conformably with his method through the book he divides his treatment of the word *life* into a number of sections, each of which is devoted to one of its many senses as currently employed, and the above remark occurs in the section on *Life (Biological)*. He assembles a number of revealing quotations from modern writers, ranging from Nietzsche's "orgiastic, mystical sense of oneness, of life as indestructibly powerful and pleasurable," through Bernard Shaw's dramatic characterisation of evolutionary biology as "the science of the everlasting transformations of the Holy Ghost in the World" to D. H. Lawrence's "sense of richness and oneness with all life," and then reduces them analytically to what they mean if life is in fact only an abstract noun, a mere *ens rationis* or 'creature of discourse.' A man's inner conviction that life is a real thing would then amount to "a conviction that organisms exist," which, as Lewis observes, is a conviction hardly worth mentioning. He concludes that what people in fact have dimly in mind, when they use the word *life* in this sense, is, not a nominal abstraction from particular instances of the living, but a transcendent entity of the kind to which Plato gave the name *eidos,* or *idea.*

It is because the word so very often *is* used in that way that it is well worth while to ponder Lewis's conclusion: "If we want to know what it felt like to be Plato thinking about Beauty, we can get some inkling by noticing how people use *Life (Biological)*." But there is a further reason, too. When *life* appears in such contexts as are quoted above, the chances are that it has been introduced by way of contrasting, explicitly or implicitly, the speaker's own way of thinking about things in general with another way. And what is this other way? The other way is precisely the way which reduces *life* (and all other nouns that are not the names of things) to an abstraction. In other words, what is being positively affirmed is, not only the fact that life is valuable, or that it is one, or that it is pleasurable etc., but also that it is *not* an abstraction, but a factually antecedent unity. Lewis makes it clear that, whenever we speak or think in that sort of way about life, either we are referring to that antecedent unity, or else we mean nothing at all and merely show that we are happy to intoxicate ourselves with vocables.

At the conclusion of the last chapter we spoke of "the mind recognizing in itself the naked idea." And it has seemed worth while to point to an instance of the kind of reflection that can, or perhaps must, lead to some such recognition. Lewis's allusion to the Greek philosopher may perhaps, as he himself suggests, be of some importance for university students (and their name is probably legion) who are being authoritatively informed by their instructors in the history of philosophy that "Plato thought abstract nouns were proper names"; but that is not the main point. The main point at the moment is the recognition itself. What, more precisely, Coleridge meant by an *idea*—whether of life or of anything else—and how it differed from what Plato meant by it, are matters to come to later. But in the meantime it would be quite impossible to give an account of what he thought about "life," and about the way in which it should be defined, without some tolerably sympathetic understanding in the reader's mind—at least for what this word *idea* will *not* mean when it occurs in a quotation.

Coleridge realised that all disputes about the nature or origin of life that fail to take account of this antecedent unity are necessarily misconceived, because life is that very unity in operation. And, because most of the disputes that were going on in his time refused altogether to recognise this, he set himself to secure its recognition. This, he saw, was the main issue; not the secondary question, on which attention was being concentrated: What is the difference between organic and inorganic phenomena? Before we can profitably consider that, we must have some understanding of the principle of existence that is common to them both. And what is common to them both is that they appear and disappear. That is why they are called "phenomena"—the Greek word for "appearing," as Coleridge was wont to emphasise by spelling it "phaenomena." As was brought out by the quotation at the head of Chapter 2, it is not only living organisms that behave in this way. On the contrary, "Everything is in a perpetual state of transformation, motion and change." The true idea of life therefore involves the idea of change.

But in Coleridge's view the idea of change had been ousted from the phenomenal world by the Cartesian dichotomy. The change of an A into a B, as distinct from the mere substitution of B for A, involves the total disappearance of A and the appearance of B, but it also involves the persistence, through the change, of a somewhat which A and B have in common. To look for the "causes" of change in the macroscopic world, no further than to re-arrangements in its microscopic components, is to have abandoned the idea of change altogether. What persists through the event of change of one body into another cannot itself be a "body"; if it were, there would in fact be no such thing as change, but only a macroscopic illusion of it. "The solution of *phaenomena* can never be derived from *phaenomena*." [2] The idea of change entails total disappearances as well as appearances. It requires discontinuity as well as continuity.

We can never reach and recognise the idea of changes in nature, if our idea of nature itself is exclusively a picture of bodies already formed. This very picture however is the one which the Cartesian dichotomy between mind and matter had been busy riveting on the mind of the Western world through the two hundred years before Coleridge's birth. That it is a false picture; that elementary particles do not merely exist from eternity and keep on setting to partners; that the proposition "matter has no *inward*" [3] is a false proposition, was accordingly not simply an interesting metaphysical speculation, but a vital and neglected, or "lost," verity which he felt he had to re-establish before he could usefully say anything else to his contemporaries upon almost any subject, whether religion, politics, history, imagination[4] or life. Hence those "logical swim-bladders and metaphysical life-preservers" with which Carlyle had so much fun. They stem from one of the principal differences between Coleridge and those German philosophers with whom his thinking is most often associated—Kant, Fichte, Schelling, Hegel. It is a difference of circumstance. Speaking, as he had to do, to his already empirically minded English contemporaries, he had, so to speak, to lay down his track as he went along, and caterpillar wheels are slow compared with ordinary wheeled traction. But then they can go into much cruder places. If the German thinkers could count on at least a second-class road of understanding into the minds of their readers, Coleridge tried to penetrate where there was no longer a road at all; to awaken to active thought minds for which "the *conceivable*" had already been "reduced within the bounds of the picturable." [5]

What has been said in this chapter about the idea of change or transformation applies to the phenomenal world as a whole, not only to the
world of "living" organisms. One should ask, not: What is life? but
what is *not* life? "Remember, that whatever *is*, *lives*. A thing absolutely
lifeless is inconceivable, except as a thought, image, or fancy, in some
other being." [6] This leading principle in Coleridge's thought is one of
the two reasons why, surprisingly enough, it may be inaccurate and misleading to adduce his theory of poetry as an example of "organicism."
The other reason can be left to the next chapter.

Of course the word *life* is most commonly applied to organic phenomena. But that is only because it is in the realm of organic life that
the process of transformation is most rapid and therefore noticeable. All
nature is in a perpetual evolution, for which the words *change, life* and
growth become appropriate at one point and another. Vegetable growth
is merely the type in which we most readily recognise the idea. And it
was quite clearly for that reason, and not because of some horticultural
mystique, some "sentimental passion of a vegetable fashion," that Coleridge was fond of illustrating the nature of life, whether physical or
mental, by pointing to the phenomena of plant growth. As, for instance,
in the following striking passage from *Aids to Reflection*:

> . . . in the world we see everywhere evidences of a unity, which the
> component parts are so far from explaining, that they necessarily pre-
> suppose it as the cause and condition of their existing as those parts; or
> even of their existing at all. This antecedent unity, or cause and principle
> of each union, it has since the time of Bacon and Kepler been customary
> to call a law. This crocus, for instance, or any other flower, the reader
> may have in sight or choose to bring before his fancy. That the root,
> stem, leaves, petals, etc. cohere to one plant, is owing to an antecedent
> power or principle in the seed, which existed before a single particle of
> the matters that constitute the size and visibility of the crocus, had been
> attracted from the surrounding soil, air, and moisture. Shall we turn to
> the seed? Here too the same necessity meets us. An antecedent unity (I
> speak not of the parent plant, but of an agency antecedent in the order of
> operance, yet remaining present as the conservative and reproductive
> power) must here too be supposed. Analyse the seed with the finest tools,
> and let the solar microscope come in aid of your senses, what do you
> find? Means and instruments, a wondrous fairy tale of nature, magazines
> of food, stores of various sorts, pipes, spiracles, defences—a house of
> many chambers, and the owner and inhabitant invisible! [7]

In Coleridge's time the biological reference of the word *evolution* was itself beginning to undergo a transformation, which has since been completed. Its original significance was ontogenetic, not mainly phylogenetic as it is today. Its relevance was, not to the problem of how a new species came about in the first place, but that of how a single organism in any species habitually reproduces itself. Here the theory of "evolution," or "epigenesis" as it afterwards came to be called, had recently ousted an older theory of encapsulation, or *emboîtement,* according to which the future plant or animal, and all subsequent ones, are already encased, in miniature, in the germ. Against this the evolutionists maintained that the substance of the new organism, as it grows, is wholly derived from the world around it, by apposition or assimilation. Growth is not the unfolding of an actual ("I speak not of the parent plant"), but the "development" of a potential. The two problems, and therefore the two meanings of the word *evolution,* may look to us more like two different problems than two aspects of the same one. Moreover popular interest during the nineteenth century was to become concentrated entirely on the phylogenetic aspect—as is reflected in the predominantly current meaning of the word *evolution.*

It may be remarked in passing that it is somewhat odd that so many millions should have come to feel that the existence of, say, a poppy *as well as* a rose is a mystery deserving the closest attention, whereas the transformation of a minute poppy-seed into a full-blown poppy can be comfortably taken for granted. Coleridge at all events had no means of foreseeing that this would be the case. In the twentieth century it is advisable to bear all this in mind when we come to look at those reflections on the nature of organic life, which form part of the long posthumous essay called *Hints Towards a More Comprehensive Theory of Life.*[8]

This is a work which, like most of Coleridge's prose, repays very careful reading, though, like much of it, it suffers from his weakness not so much in expounding as in marshalling his materials. Because of its importance in our opinion and because it is comparatively rarely referred to, we shall not on this occasion be content with sporadic reference and quotation, but shall endeavour to give a brief, connected account of its content.

It begins, after a eulogy of the physician John Hunter, with a critique of various recent attempt to define life, such as "the sum of all the functions by which death is resisted"; "assimilation for the purposes of

reproduction and growth"; "nutrition by digestion"; "the power of re-
sisting putrefaction"; and it objects to them that they are all either
tautologous or inaccurate: tautologous when they merely "translate the
word Life into other more learned words" [560],* inaccurate when "a
single effect is given as constituting the cause" [562]. They all alike
presuppose

> the arbitrary division of all that surrounds us into things with life, and
> things without life—a division grounded on a mere assumption. At the
> best, it can be regarded only as a hasty deduction from the first super-
> ficial notices of the objects that surround us [559].

Coleridge regards the last of the attempted definitions given above as
superior to the rest, since at least it does not identify life with a single
one of its effects. Yet it still "confines the idea of Life to those degrees
or concentrations of it, which manifest themselves in organized beings,
or rather in those the organization of which is apparent to us" [563]
and thus "substitutes an abstract term, or generalization of effects, for
the idea, or superior form of causative agency" [563]. It would have
been better therefore to say: "a power which, during its continuance,
resists or subordinates heterogeneous and adverse powers" [563].

All this leads up to—or rather it partly leads up to and partly is
interwoven with—reflections on the true nature of definition; definition,
that is, of concretes: "real" definition, as distinct from the mere definition of a verbal abstraction. Above all (he has in effect been saying) in
the case of the word *life,* a verbal abstraction—that is a common noun
denoting all the properties observed in particular instances—must be
futile. For it can be no more than a generalization a posteriori from particular objects. Whereas the whole point of having such a word at all,
its very *raison d'être,* is to denote an antecedent somewhat that is not
merely derived from objects but is effective to produce them. What then
should we look for in a "real" or "physiological" definition? Such a
definition

> must consist neither in any single property or function of the thing to be
> defined, nor yet in all collectively, which latter, indeed, would be a
> history, not a definition. It must consist, therefore, in the *law* of the

---

* Numbers in brackets in this chapter are page references to *The Selected
Poetry and Prose of Samuel Taylor Coleridge* (see n. 8).

thing, or in such an *idea* of it, as being admitted, all the properties and functions are admitted by implication. It must likewise be so far *causal* that a full insight having been obtained of the law, we derive from it a progressive insight into the necessity and *generation* of the phenomena of which it is the law [562].

He goes on to distinguish between *accounting for* life and *explaining* it. In the former case "We are supposed to state something prior (if not in time, yet in the order of Nature) to the thing accounted for" [568–69]. But as regards life, this is *ex hypothesi* impossible. For life itself *is* the "something prior." Those, for instance, who assign any kind of phenomenon as the "cause" of life overlook the obvious difference between phenomenon and power; they overlook the fact that "visible SURFACE and *power* of any kind, much more the *power* of life, are ideas which the very forms of the human understanding make it impossible to identify" [568]. While those who assign structure or organisation as its antecedent "make A the offspring of B, when the very existence of B as B presupposes the existence of A [568]."

To *explain* a power, on the other hand, is "to unfold or spread it out," as the etymology of the word suggests. So that an explanation of life would consist in

the reduction of the idea of Life to its simplest and most comprehensive form or mode of action; that is, to some *instinct* or *tendency,* evident in all its manifestations, and involved in the idea itself . . . the tendency having been given in *kind,* it is required to render the phenomena intelligible as its different degrees and modifications [569].

And this is what his own explanation endeavors to achieve. But first he raises the question: what is the purpose of "generalizing the idea of life thus broadly"? And he answers, that, if no other use were conceivable, there would at least be *some* advantage in merely "destroying an arbitrary assumption in natural philosophy"; in "filling up the gap between physics and physiology" and justifying use of "the former as a means of insight into the latter" [572]. Since, in our own time, there is no lack of endeavour to fill up the "gap" between physics and physiology, it may be well to pause here and take a brief look at its history. For it was this presumed gap between the inorganic and the organic kingdoms of nature, and the passionate interest it had aroused, that set the stage, and determined the form, of Coleridge's Essay.

The use of the word *life* with that particular reference which Lewis identified as *life* (*biological*) is a comparatively recent habit. If we compare earlier with later contexts, we shall be left in no doubt that it arose only with that diremption of the world of experience into supposedly mental and supposedly extra-mental components, which was part cause and part effect of the scientific revolution. Before that the word certainly could, and generally did, include or imply this meaning, but never as a reference noticeably separable from other reference.[9] Descartes, who first adequately formulated the diremption, included animals, as well as plants, in the extra-mental component. But this contradicted common experience, which is sure that animals at least are "animate," and led to prolonged philosophical and scientific disputes. Apart from obvious signs, not only of sentience in all animals but also of intelligence in the higher species, there were difficulties in the way of accepting it even for the vegetable kingdom, since it appeared to leave unexplained the whole phenomenon of growth. For Descartes, and increasingly for the world of scientific thought as a whole, the extra-mental realm was, and always had been, exclusively answerable to the laws of mechanical causality; yet it is difficult, or rather impossible, to study plant growth and obtain either practical or theoretical results without retaining some concept of "form" or "pattern," which is incompatible with mechanism, especially if the mechanism is undesigned; without assuming, that is, that the end-pattern of the developed plant is present in some way in its patternless origin in the germ. In this respect not only animals, but plants also, appear to differ markedly from the mineral kingdom. The earliest recorded uses of the word *inorganic* (and of *organic* in the specific sense of its opposite) occur in the last third of the eighteenth century, after Coleridge was born. For the first time a word was needed as a class name for "inanimate matter" and bodies formed from it. For the first time *life* and *living* had become the correlatives, not of *death* and *dying,* but of *inorganic* or, in its later sense, *inanimate*.[10]

It is quite apparent from the disputes of that time, some of which Coleridge refers to in his essay, that the definition of life had become a bone of contention just because the concept in itself betokened the reappearance, or attempted re-appearance, of a half-way house between the mental and the extra-mental, which, for Descartes himself and for Cartesian science, had become simply an excluded middle between two contradictories. (That this concept of life is in fact performing much the same function in a great many minds today, and that, in doing so, it echoes a period in the history of thought before the dualism of mental and extra-mental had been enthroned in the general consciousness are two of the points made by Lewis in his essay quoted at the beginning of this chapter.) Very few made any attempt, as Coleridge did, to resolve the contradiction itself. Rather both parties to the disputes accepted it as axiomatic, but claimed "life" for their own side of the frontier. The materialists claimed it as exclusively material; the idealists and the religious claimed it as exclusively ideal. Thus, the materialists ostracised any reference to a teleological principle in living organisms as an impermissible "argument from design"; while the religious seized on it as evidence of the direct intervention of God in an otherwise admittedly clockwork universe. *Tabula in naufragio!* [11]

Perhaps this historical digression[12] may have helped to make it clear why Coleridge, whose whole system of thought, as we have seen, was rooted in, and must stand or fall with, his critique of the Cartesian dualism, was inevitably deeply interested in these debates about the nature of life. It was the bundle of hay which the two donkeys, whom that dualism had brought about, were each tugging the opposite way; and it was for him to show that the proper solution was to share it undivided between them.

We come back, then, to the *Theory of Life* at the point where Coleridge explicitly asks the question "What is Life?" and answers it with another question: "What is *not* Life that really *is?*" [571]. We need not pursue the intricacies of the argument, which leads to the conclusion that "since by the agreement of all parties Life may exist in other forms than those of consciousness, or even of sensibility, the *onus probandi* falls on those who assert of any quality that it is *not* Life." The work itself should be read. But Coleridge's own attempts at defining formulae must be mentioned. The most comprehensive one, we are told, would be "the internal copula of bodies," or "the *power* which discloses itself from within as a principle of *unity* in the *many.*" Again, life is *"the principle of individuation* or the power that unites a given *all* into a *whole* that is presupposed by all its parts." And there follows a passage on the connection, and the contrast, between life and mechanism, which calls for quotation in full:

Thus, from its utmost *latency,* in which life is one with the elementary powers of mechanism, that is, with the powers of mechanism, considered as qualitative and actually synthetic, to its highest manifestation (in which, as the *vis vitae vivida,* or life *as* life, it subordinates and modifies these powers, becoming contradistinguished from mechanism, *ab extra,* under the form of organisation), there is an ascending series of intermediate classes, and of analogous gradations in each class [573].

All this is summed up in a footnote, the content of which reverberates through the *Lectures on Shakespeare* (though there, of course, as the context demands, it is always the contrast, never the connection, that is stressed):

Thus we may say that whatever is organized from without, is a product of mechanism; whatever is mechanized from within, is a product of organization [573n].

Morever:

the unity will be more intense in proportion as it constitutes each particular thing a whole of itself; and yet more again, in proportion to the number and interdependence of the parts, which it unites as a whole.

But:

a whole composed, *ab intra,* of different parts, so far independent that each is reciprocally means and end, is an individual,

and:

the individuality is most intense where the greatest dependence of parts on the whole is combined with the greatest dependence of the whole on its parts; the first (namely, the dependence of the parts on the whole) being absolute; the second (namely, the dependence of the whole on its parts) being proportional to the importance of the relation which the parts have to the whole, that is, as their action extends more or less beyond themselves. For this spirit of the whole is most expressed in that part which derives its importance as an End from its importance as a Mean, relatively to all the parts under the same copula [574–75].

There follows a concise and classic statement of the principle sometimes rather vaguely alluded to, whether for the purposes of aesthetics, of psychology, or of ontology, as "organicism":

Finally, of individuals, the living power will be most intense in that individual which, as a whole, has the greatest number of integral parts presupposed in it; when, moreover, these integral parts, together with a proportional increase of their interdependence, as *parts,* have themselves most the character of wholes in the sphere occupied by them [575].

Having now reduced—or expanded—his definition of life to the *tendency to individuation,* Coleridge proceeds very briefly to illustrate from nature. His accompanying apology for brevity may be condensed by saying that he points out, in effect, what the title of his Essay already proclaims: that he is not establishing but "hinting." He has however already, a little earlier, claimed that the "proof of the probability" of his theory

is to be found in its powers of solving the . . . phenomena . . . more satisfactorily and profitably than has been done, or even attempted before [575–76].

It will be observed that there are imbedded in the foregoing account of the nature of "individuation" four distinguishable stages or gradations of the process: (1) absolute dependence of parts on whole; (2) additional dependence of whole on parts; (3) greatest number of integral parts presupposed in whole; (4) parts themselves possessing character as wholes, and this involving their increased interdependence. Referring to these, perhaps a little sanguinely, as "the preceding gradations, as above defined," he illustrates (1) with metals, (2) with crystals, (3) with the whole subject-matter of Geology, and (4) with vegetable and animal life.

Thus, gold, as a whole, has some sort of unity which an ingot, as ingot, has not. It has "the simplest form of unity, namely, the unity of powers and properties . . . the form of unity with least degree of tendency to individuation" [576]. In the crystal however there is "a union, not of powers only, but of parts." A crystal has not only unity, therefore, but also, in its simplest form, *totality.* The third illustration ("those vast formations, the tracing of which generically would form the science of Geology") is the first to bring him into direct conflict, with the overall theory then, and now, received; for he rejects an "inorganic" origin for *any* geological formations. Rather than holding up this already dubiously effective summary of a summary, we quote in full what he has to say on this in a note.[13] These formations are, he affirms, still connected with the present order of vegetable and animal Life, which constitutes the fourth and last step in these wide and comprehensive divisions [577].

In other words, with the lowest forms of vegetable and animal life—with the "organism," which, in a much more noticeable way than was the case at the previous stages, "maintains for itself a distinction from the universal life of the planet"—"we perceive totality dawning into *individuation*" [577].

He has now dealt with the tendency to individuation and detachment, and in doing so has shown, he says, that it cannot be conceived without the opposite tendency to connect:

> even as the centrifugal power supposes the centripetal, or as the two opposite poles constitute each other, and are the constituent acts of one and the same power in the magnet [578].

We have in fact (and we shall gain by keeping this particular formulation constantly in mind): *"the tendency at once to individuate and to connect, to detach, but so as either to retain or to reproduce attachment"* [578].

Thus, when Coleridge asks at the beginning of the next section: "The tendency having been ascertained, what is its most general law?"[14] it virtually follows, for us, from the previous chapter that he will reply:

> —*polarity,* or the essential dualism of Nature, arising out of its productive unity, and still tending to reaffirm it, either as equilibrium, indifference, or identity [578].

and that he will add:

> In its *productive* power, of which the product is the only measure, consists its incompatibility with the mathematical calculus [578].

What polarity *is* compatible with is, of course, imagination. But that is not here his topic, and he merely remarks in passing that no man who has "paralysed his imaginative powers" can be expected to see the necessity from without, nor learn the possibility from within,

> of interpenetration, of total intussusception, of the existence of all in each as the condition of Nature's unity and substantiality, and of the latency

under the predominance of some one power, wherein subsists her life and its endless variety . . . [584].

He now goes back to the beginning and traces the genesis of nature, proceeding from its origin in spirit as productive unity, under the law of polarity, through ascending gradations of reality; through time and space ("the oneness of space and time is the predicate of all *real* being"), length, breadth, depth, force, motion ("depth + motion = force"), to attraction and repulsion ("attraction + repulsion = gravitation"), in the synthesis of which "you have matter as a fluxional antecedent, which, in the very act of formation, passes into body by its gravity" [580–82]. But it will be better to leave this for the present, to omit the eristic digression,* and to continue from the point to which he had taken his exposition of the tendency to individuation, before he explicitly introduced the law of polarity; that is to say, to the vegetable and animal kingdoms and the principle of their "evolution."

If, at the inanimate level, magnetism is the "central phenomenon" for revealing to us the law of polarity, at the organic level the central phenomenon is reproduction. For there is clearly "separative projection" at work whenever like produces like. It will be recalled from Chapter 3 † that the constituent productive powers or forces are not extinguished by their synthesis in a structure—let us say in a body—but continue as that body's function. Another way of putting this is to say that polarities are themselves polarised; and that "life," so far as it is answerable at all to analytically ordered thought, is best conceived as this exponential process. It is at all events this conception that Coleridge seeks to elucidate in the *Theory of Life,* and which he illustrates most extensively, or least cursorily, in his account of organic life.

Every polarity, while being a duality from the point of view, so to speak, of either pole alone, is nevertheless a unity. It is in fact perpetually engaged in restoring, or rather renewing, the original unity, from which it springs. Thus, while *qua* duality it has already been polarised, yet *qua* unity this commencing polarity may again be polarised into two further opposites, and so *ad infinitum,* or rather *ad hominem sapientem*. It is by this proceeding that nature rises from stage to stage of complexity. Diagrammatically, if a commencing polarity is

* See n. 8.
† See p. 34.

represented by a line, then the two extremities of the line represent its
duality, its poles. But the whole line nevertheless remains a unity and
can itself be polarised. Its whole length then becomes the *axis* of a new
polarity; or, deserting the diagram for the reality, the original tension
itself becomes tensile. In terms of life, a new natural quality is engendered, and this genesis is symbolised on the diagram by taking it into
a second dimension. Thus, throughout the whole of life, not only as its
foundation but also as continuing agent, the principle of "productive
unity" remains paramount.

But so also does the "tendency to individuation," the "tendency to
detach but so as to retain or to reproduce attachment," which Coleridge
traces in ascending gradations, though the corals and conchylia ("characterised by still passing away and dissolving into the earth, which they
had previously excreted, as if they were the first feeble effort of detachment") through the molluscs and vermes, to the point in life which he
takes as the central phenomenon of his second-degree polarity, namely
irritability or (as he elsewhere suggests to be a better term) sensibility.

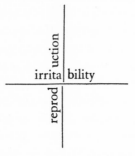

Nature, he comments:

> has succeeded. She has created the intermediate link between the vege-
> table world, as the product of the reproductive or magnetic power, and
> the animal as the exponent of sensibility . . . Had she proceeded no
> further, yet the whole vegetable, together with the whole insect creation,
> would have formed within themselves an entire and independent system
> of Life [594].

We will telescope the remainder of the section. Insects are a sort of
externalised version of something that is essentially *inward,* that is, of
sentience. That which is later to become a purely inward process is here
seen externalised in a spatial form. The morphology of the plant is an

expression of the principle of reproduction ("growth and identity of the whole, amid the change or flux of all the parts") [584]. The irritable antenna of the insect displays reproduction raised to another power. It reproduces *movement*. An insect is your perfect behaviourist. It immediately echoes in its own motion the external stimulus that excited it. Yet these subtly irritable organs are themselves only a sort of physical caricature of those far subtler motions that are proper to nature's next production—the animal and human soul. But first Coleridge pauses to point out the startling metamorphosis of outward form that characterises nature's transition to this next stage of animal existence. For the opposite forces of the one power, though they never act singly, and though they invariably interpenetrate, do alternate in the temporary *predominance* of the one over the other. The exuberant complexity of structure typical of the insect disappears altogether from the surface, having withdrawn to the interior parts of the body. The outlines of the fish are the simplest and severest that can well be conceived. Nature sinks back exhausted, as it were, from the line she has hitherto been following and in her repose gathers strength for her newest creation—consciousness. The insect's organ almost mechanically reproduces the external stimulus. The soul reproduces and retains, in the form of after-images, the impressions that come to it through the senses. This is the foundation on which later there is to be built the self-conscious life of the spirit.

This part of Coleridge's exposition makes the easiest, as it certainly makes fascinating, reading.[15] The above brief summary has been largely stripped of the illustrative detail that gives it its colour, and anyone not prepared to read the whole work is strongly recommended to read from page 589 to the end. We shall be referring in the next chapter to the culminating paragraphs depicting and characterising the ultimate "ascent" to human consciousness; but meanwhile the very word *ascent*, which is certainly not inappropriate to the theory, introduces another consideration. A modern reader can hardly peruse Coleridge's "explanation" of life without its continuing to grow on him that what he in fact has before him is a good deal more than an explanation. He suspects more and more definitely as he proceeds, and by the time he has reached the section on organic life the suspicion has become a certainty, that what he is really being fed is a full-fledged theory of evolution alternative to, and largely incompatible with, the one he has been taught to revere.

The conclusion is an inescapable one, and we shall return to some of its implications in a later chapter. Meanwhile however we should beware of assuming that Coleridge had clearly before his mind, in writing, that picture of a vast temporal process which has become so real to post-Darwinian minds. He speaks frequently of successive gradations, or stages, but rarely of *periods*,[16] in what he nevertheless alludes to as "the whole history of nature." The truth appears to be that his whole conception of time past was less quantitative than ours, and this for two reasons, one of which he probably shared with most of his contemporaries, while the other was more peculiar to himself. As to the first, he was thinking and writing in the early dawn of that new dimension of consciousness, for which perhaps the most satisfactory name is "historicism," though there are certain grave objections to it;[17] and to which we partly owe the radically altered meaning of the word *evolution*. In this respect he was in advance of, and leading,[18] his contemporaries. The *Philosophical Lectures,* for instance, show an awareness, of the evolution, not now of nature, but of consciousness itself, which has rarely been evinced before our own time. As to the second, our whole arithmetically calibrated image of a remote, pre-human past of indefinite extension would appear to stem from the Cartesian dualism.[19] Experience, or Fancy, in that mode has been increasing, and was still steadily increasing in the minds of those around him, but Coleridge deliberately rejected it and, in that respect, may indeed be regarded as *behind* his contemporaries. Change in the concept of "evolution" went hand in hand with change in the concept, and image, of "matter"; for if one takes the older picture of *emboîtement* and looks it steadily in the face, it becomes evident that, in order to be barely credible, it requires a far less antiseptically spatial, and notionally visible, idea of matter than mechanistic theory entails. In a word the older perspective was radically different. Ontogenesis was the reality, was the knotty problem; while phylogenesis was no more than its telescoped and shadowy background—rather as the opening genealogical pages of a Victorian novel, covering perhaps several centuries, are the telescoped and shadowy background to the story we are really interested in, covering a few months or years. As to the mysterious relation between the two, it was not in issue, since the whole process was viewed as substantially one. It is only as general attention has increasingly focussed on the phylogenetic component, and lost interest in the ontogenetic, that the fact of the persistent "recapitulation" of the former by the latter has turned into an important, but unaccountable, freak of nature.

Coleridge was in fact writing out of the old perspective into the new; and this comes out especially clearly at the point where he seeks to substitute the image of the ladder for that of the chain. A chain is suspended from above, but a ladder rises upward from below, and "It has before been noticed that the progress of Nature is more truly represented by the ladder, than by the suspended chain . . ." [591]. Yet this need not signify a merely linear ascent, for he continues: "and that she expands as by concentric circles." [20]

For the reasons just advanced caution must be exercised in characterising the *Theory of Life* as a teleological one. It depends what we mean by *teleological*. In the perspective of time quantitatively measured—clock time—a teleological explanation entails design and the argument from design[21]—a sort of anthropomorphic "planning"—but this is something quite different from that relation between potential and actual, between the lower kingdoms of nature and the higher, between parts and whole, between efficient cause and final cause, and thus between past and future, which Coleridge envisaged. For this he sometimes used the term *irradiation;* and we shall be returning to it in a subsequent chapter.

This one has already perhaps grown too long. But it should not be closed without a few observations on the relation between the concept of *life,* as it is built up in the *Theory of Life,* and Coleridge's concept of *nature,*[22] which is a term he used far more frequently in his other prose writings. The word *nature,* he pointed out, had been used in two different ways, one of them active and the other passive; "energetic (= forma formans), and material (= forma formata)." [23] We have seen how he himself adopted an older distinction between *natura naturans* and *natura naturata.* When the topic is nature itself—the nature of Nature—it is of the utmost importance to distinguish these: and we have seen that he censures Aristotle for confounding them. In other contexts, where for instance the topic is the distinction between *man* and nature, the former distinction does not need to be maintained, and Coleridge himself does not always maintain it. What matters *then,* is that in nature, whether *naturans* or not, "there is no origin." [24] It is "self-organizing," but not, as is the case with a willed act, "self-originating."

As far as science and philosophy are concerned, the prevailing tendency among his contemporaries was to lose sight of, or to deny altogether, the former of the two distinguishable senses of *nature* and this tendency, as we know, he set himself to combat. There seems no need to regard *life* and *natura naturans* as other than virtual synonyms, or to doubt that in the *Theory of Life* we have his most extensive, and most nearly systematic, treatment of what he elsewhere called *natura naturans*—but sometimes also by other names: *forma formans, vis vitae vivida* and so forth. The only difference is that none of these technical terms has ever become part of our common vocabulary. It is otherwise with *life,* and, as we saw at the beginning of this chapter, contexts abound today in which, if *life* does not mean *natura naturans,* it would be difficult to say what, if anything, it does mean.

⋙ 5 ⋘

Outness

I<small>T WAS</small> observed in the preceding chapter that it can be inaccurate and misleading to adduce Coleridge's thought as an example of "organicism." This is certainly so if by "organic" is meant a structural principle only to be found in the vegetable and higher kingdoms of nature. But it may also be the case, and it usually is, even when the word is taken in the wider sense of a structural principle underlying the world as a whole. Professor M. H. Abrams, for instance, defines organicism as "the philosophy whose major categories are derived metaphorically from the attributes of living and growing things" [1] and describes it later as "implicitly asserting that all the universe is like some one element in that universe." [2] It is, for him, one of those "metaphors of mind," whose "mutations" during the eighteenth and nineteenth centuries he has traced so ably in an earlier chapter.

But this is not at all what Coleridge's organicism meant to Coleridge, or for that matter Schelling's to Schelling; and yet neither of these two men would appear to have been incapable of distinguishing a metaphorical from a literal statement, that is, from a statement that is figurative only because and to the extent that *all* language is figurative. "Metaphor of mind" signifies an extra-mental process described because it is separate from, but analogous to, a mental one, which latter it may therefore lead us to apprehend. Now not only is this not what Coleridge himself thought he was giving us in his psychology and his critical theory; it is what he spent a substantial part of his time and energy explaining that he was *not* giving us. The greater part, for instance, of Chapter XII of the *Biographia Literaria* consists of a laborious endeavour to make it clear to the reader that, in speaking on the one hand of nature and on the other of what he terms the "act of consciousness," he is not depicting process B in terms of process A, but is describing one single homogeneous process. It seems odd to overlook[3] these efforts altogether and find it, as Professor Abrams does, "astonishing how much of Coleridge's critical writing is couched in terms that are metaphorical for art and literal for a plant."

If Coleridge is to be understood, we must first be able, at least for the purpose of argument, to treat his concept of nature, not as a picturesque metaphor for his concept of mind, but as an integral component of his concept of mind. That of course does not signify that he saw mind as emergent from nature by evolutionary development, or as one part of a whole which is nature. This last is the erroneous assumption that underlies Walter Pater's complaint,[4] that his theory of creative imagination involves determinism. A fairly pardonable error, since Coleridge's nature is as much determined as any biologist's. What he seeks to show in the *Theory of Life* and elsewhere is, that it is determined by other laws in addition to those of mechanical causality, and further that those laws cannot be grasped unless through the seminal concept of polarity. But it is still determinate.

> Whatever is comprised in the chain and mechanism of cause and effect, of course necessitated, and having its necessity in some other thing, antecedent or concurrent—this is said to be natural; and the aggregate and system of all such things is NATURE. It is therefore a contradiction in terms to include in this the free-will, of which the verbal definition is— that which originates an act or state of being.[5]

By and large, up to the point to which it was followed in the previous chapter Coleridge's concept of nature could just possibly be interpreted as one variant of the familiar, if hazy, notion of a "life force" or Shavian "evolutionary appetite" at its work of producing, first, solid but inanimate matter, then life, then animal sentience and finally *homo sapiens.* Why then is his concept of "life," as *natura naturans,* at all stages, so important not only to Coleridge himself but also (as the length of that chapter must have suggested) for the proper understanding of what Coleridge thought, and thought not only about nature but about pretty well everything else?

There are many passages in his prose writings to which we could go for an answer to this question, but we will choose one from the *Friend,* where he points out that

> the productive power, or *vis naturans,* which in the sensible world, or *natura naturata,* is what we mean by the word, nature, when we speak

of the same as an agent, is essentially one (that is, of one kind) with the intelligence, which is in the human mind above nature.[6]

Moreover the conviction that this is so is, he maintains, one that is *ultimately* ineradicable from the mind of a self-conscious being; for

> so universally has this conviction leavened the very substance of all discourse, that there is no language on earth in which a man can abjure it as a prejudice, without employing terms and conjunctions that suppose its reality, with a feeling very different from that which accompanies a figurative or metaphorical use of words.

He goes on to draw the distinction, referred to in the previous chapter, between teleology as planning and teleology, or goal-directedness, as denoting that relation between a whole and its parts which is intrinsic to all organic structures, where, in the mere act of contemplating them as wholes, "whether as integral parts or as a system, we assume an intention as the initiative of which the end is the correlative." In other words, "without assigning to nature as nature, a conscious purpose," we yet "distinguish her agency from a blind and lifeless mechanism." [7] And we not only do so, but we cannot help doing so.

The productive power, then, which *in* nature acts *as* nature, is nevertheless "essentially one (that is, of one kind) with the intelligence, which is in the human mind above nature." This is where Coleridge's concept of nature, and of evolution, differs so sharply from the one we are accustomed to that its usual fate with his commentators is to be ignored. For, after all, how can it be so? How can the life-force operative out there in nature—how can *any* "force"—be of one kind with the intelligence in the human mind?

One rather schematic way of delineating his answer to this question would be as follows. We have three distinct concepts, three undoubted realities, which we can distinguish, though we cannot normally divide them from one another: (1) *Natura naturata*, (2) *Natura naturans* or "life," and (3) Intelligence or mind. Of these, 1 is, by definition, sensuous, while 2 and 3 are, by definition, supersensuous. But it is also the case that 1 and 2 are one indivisible whole, the entire operation of *natura naturans* being to produce and sustain *natura naturata*. Now in the same way it is the case that intelligence and *natura naturans* are one indivisible whole. One may concentrate on *that* unity—and that way lies whatever is to be said about poetic or creative imagination, which was to have been the fundamental topic of the unwritten Chapter XIII, and *is* the topic of what there is of it. But if A is one with B and B is one with C, it follows that A is one with C. Alternatively therefore one may eliminate B from one's reflections and concentrate on the unity of C and A, that is, the unity of intelligence with *natura naturata* or with nature as *natura naturata,* that is, with sensuous nature—with the phenomenal world. And that way lies epistemology or, in Coleridge's vocabulary, "transcendental philosophy"; and therewith the philosophic imagination, which is the fundamental topic of Chapter XII.[8]

Now to speak at all of the unity of intelligence and nature is of course flatly to contradict Descartes. Accordingly, if one intends to do so, it must be made very clear at the outset that one differs from Descartes. Coleridge does make this very clear indeed. In particular, he makes it clear in the *Biographia Literaria,* both in Chapter VIII (apart from the critique of Hartley, the first of its philosophical chapters) and again, as we have seen, in the opening paragraph of Chapter XIII.[9] But there is another and a more formidable difficulty. The dualism of mind and matter, of the mental and the phenomenal, which Descartes netted in his philosophical formula, is not just an abstruse philosophical theorem, difficult to grasp. It is everyman's everyday experience. It is "common sense." At least it was so in Coleridge's day and, with some slight modifications, it is so still. You may call this otherness of things from ourselves, made palpable to our senses by their "outness" in space, "Cartesianism," if you wish, and it is historically not altogether incorrect to do so. But it is also—well, it is obvious. Indeed it is, for most people, almost what the word *obvious* means. Seeing is believing. In characterising Coleridge's concept of the relation between subject and object as the *pons asinorum* of his system, as we did in Chapter 1 (page 13, above), it was by no means intended to suggest that all who shy upon that bridge are asses.

Chapter XII of the *Biographia Literaria,* which is one of the only two really long chapters in the book, bears the somewhat crotchety title: "A Chapter of requests and premonitions concerning the perusal or omission of the chapter that follows." When the reader recalls that the chapter that follows was, in effect, never written and consists, as it stands, of only about six pages;[10] and when, moreover, he finds that Chapter XII itself does *not* consist of requests and premonitions but, in the main, of closely knit and by no means easy philosophical argument, his reaction may be one of pardonable irritation. As to that . . . Coleridge was Coleridge. We must take him as we find him, if we are to take him at all. Unfortunately, in practice, the reader is apt to take the "requests and premonitions" as applicable, not to Chapter XIII, but to Chapter XII itself and, after a few pages of perusal, to opt for omission.

It is very unwise to do so; for odd as it may be, this is the place where, more than anywhere else, the dynamic philosophy is brought together in epitome. It is impossible to master the chapter without becoming substantially seised of what Coleridge thought. But that is difficult and is likely to be attempted by comparatively few. If it were otherwise, there would be the less need for such a book as this.

In *form* Chapter XII may be said to consist of four main divisions; first, an opening one, which contains the "requests and premonitions" including the important maxim stated at the outset: *until you understand a writer's ignorance, presume yourself ignorant of his understanding;* but which also contains a great deal more, inadequately marshalled, matter of importance; secondly, a discussion of the "outness" of phenomena; thirdly, ten numbered "Theses" containing, very closely packed, the philosophical statement of Coleridge's position; and lastly a final section in which he again grows eloquently discursive over the difficulties of the task he has set himself and, in particular, "the obstacles which an English metaphysician has to encounter."

In *substance* the chapter may perhaps best be seen as consisting of two interwoven threads, one of them being this obvious outness of the material world, and the other the existential consequences of reflecting on it. A detailed exposition of the whole would be out of place, since the intention is that its content should be allowed to transpire from this book taken as a whole. But because the second of the four sections, into which we have ventured to divide it, is particularly relevant at this point, and is moreover in our view crucial to the issue of validity, it will be well to describe that part of the chapter in some detail and to summarise its argument. He points, then, to the presence in every human mind of two absolute convictions, or certainties, neither of which requires demonstrating, and both of which are in fact indemonstrable, because they are the twin constituents of human consciousness itself. Perhaps we may call them "awarenesses." The first is the awareness "that there exist things without us," [11] in other words, naïve realism, not as doctrine but as common experience and common sense. The second is the awareness that I am perceiving the things.

Coleridge calls them both, to start with, "original and innate prejudices" and the reason for his choice of the noun transpires, as he proceeds to show the respect in which they differ from one another. It is this. The former "prejudice," while it inevitably remains, or returns, *as experience,* nevertheless disappears upon reflection, *as doctrine.* For the mind, the solid world of familiar "objects" dissolves upon analysis. This is a fact that is borne out by the whole history of philosophy and science. But the second "prejudice" does not so dissolve. That which is doing the analysing remains aware that it is doing it, however far the analysis has been carried. Even if it ends by purporting to deny that it is doing it, the very act of denial affirms the contrary.[12] This awareness, this certainty, therefore, "cannot so properly be entitled a prejudice";[13] for this one remains a certainty "equally for the scientific reason of the philosopher as for the common sense of mankind at large." [13]

There is only one conclusion, Coleridge continues, which can be drawn from these premises; only one solution of

> the apparent contradiction, that the former position, namely, the existence of things without us, which from its nature cannot be immediately certain, should be received as blindly and as independently of all grounds as the existence of our own being,

and that is "the supposition that the former is unconsciously involved in the latter."

It is essential at this point that we should realise *all* that this conclusion means. It acknowledges not only that

> but for the confidence which we place in the assertions of our reason and our conscience, we could have no certainty of the reality and actual outness of the material world.[14]

It acknowledges further, that the certainty *is* the outness; that the outness, as he goes on to say at the point where we interrupted the penultimate quotation, "is not only coherent but identical, and one and the same thing with our own immediate self consciousness." [15]

It should not be difficult to grasp that this is something quite different from the substitution of idealism for realism; but Coleridge, aware that it would be so misinterpreted, expends a paragraph pointing out that it is not only *not* that, but is its opposite. It is the substitution of actual realism for a bastard and *soi-disant* realism, which is in fact a form of idealism in disguise.[16] The outness of the material world is not explained away by, it is built into *this* realism. It is therefore, says Coleridge, "the truest and most binding realism." With the sophisticated realism of both philosophy and science, and we may add of psychology, he contrasts, in the following passage, his own "true and original realism":[17]

> For wherein does the realism of mankind properly consist? In the assertion that there exists a something without them, what, or how, or where they know not, which occasions the objects of their perceptions? Oh no! This is neither connatural nor universal. It is what a few have taught and learned in the schools, and which the many repeat without asking themselves concerning their own meaning. The realism common to all mankind is far older and lies infinitely deeper than this hypothetical explanation of the origin of our perceptions, and explanation skimmed from the mere surface of the mechanical philosophy. It is the table itself, which the man of common sense believes himself to see, not the phantom of a table, from which he may argumentatively deduce the reality of a table, which he does not see. If to destroy the reality of all, that we actually behold, be idealism, what can be more egregiously so, than the system of modern metaphysics, which banishes us to a land of shadows, surrounds us with apparitions, and distinguishes truth from illusion only by the majority of those who dream the same dream. "I asserted that the world was mad", exclaimed poor Lee, "and the world said, that I was mad, and confound them, they outvoted me".

On another occasion Coleridge gave precise and gnomic expression to the existential bearing of his first "prejudice," when he wrote: "the sense of outwardness as a sense of reality, is a law of our nature, and no conclusion of our judgment." [18] And it was of course his view that the cardinal error of Descartes lay in attempting to show that it was *both* a law of our nature *and* a conclusion of our judgment. The law of our nature is that by which

> in every act of conscious perception, we at once identify our being with that of the world without us, and yet place ourselves in contra-distinction to that world,[19]

and we acknowledge, in obeying it, that the existence of things without us is "one and the same thing with our own immediate self consciousness." It follows that of all we see, hear, feel and touch the substance is and must be in our-selves; and therefore there is no alternative between the dreary (and thank heaven! almost impossible) belief that every thing around us is but a phantom, or that the life which is in us is in them likewise . . .[20]

Now, in stating his conclusion concerning the relation between the two "original and innate prejudices," it will be recalled that Coleridge does not merely put it that "the former is involved in the latter"; he writes: "the former is *unconsciously* involved in the latter." In other words, although the outness of phenomena is a law of our nature, we are not conscious of it *as* law. We are merely conscious of their outness. The first prejudice may properly be called a "prejudice" because it dis-solves on analysis. It ceases to be a prejudice only when we become conscious of it as a law; when we transcend it, not by a sophisticated and unreal realism of appearances-of-things *versus* things themselves, but by that *actual* realism, which understands and accepts the law. In doing so, we become aware that reality, although it is indeed real, is also appearance; and that appearance, although it is indeed appearance, is also reality. We emerge from what was essentially a sleeping relation with phenomena into a waking one; and it was this awakening, into which, paradoxically, the unhappy opium addict was mainly concerned to rouse his contemporaries and posterity, confident that, once that has been effected, the fact that nature is essentially one with the intelligence in us, will no longer seem a wild and incredible speculation, or a pa-thetic fallacy, but will become a self-evident fact.

It must have become sufficiently apparent that the distinction be-tween *man* and *nature,* as Coleridge drew it, is by no means one with that other important distinction, with which it is so commonly equated, between a psychosomatic organism enclosed within its own cuticle on the one hand and, on the other, the rest of the world outside that bit of space. But, even when that is clear, there still remains his distinction between *subject* and *object.* And it has to be realised that this is not *merely* co-extensive even with his own, less crass, distinction between man and nature. Not every object is a natural object. *Anything* we think about becomes, by definition, "object" and, since it is a fact that we can think even about thinking, we know experientially that mind is a subject which can become its own object—though, unlike natural objects, it is then "an object of which itself is the sole percipient." [21] This first-hand knowledge we ought not simply to jettison, when we go on to place our interpretation on all that we observe in nature and in life.

But all this is only another, more technical, way of stating the *conclusion* arrived at from the discussion of outness, which we endeavoured to summarise first. Although the intelligence in us is "essentially one, that is, of one kind," with *natura naturans,* yet it is not simply another name for *natura naturans;* for it is also true that intelligence "is in the human mind above nature." [22] While therefore we can say, of the two awarenesses, that we know that the former (outness) is unconsciously involved in the latter (I am),[23] we cannot also say we know the latter is involved in the former. On the contrary, we know it is not. The proposition of "involvement" is reversible between a subject and "its own" objects; but not between a subject and natural objects, not between man and nature. Nature is always a "becoming." A subject that can become its own object is our immediate experience; natural objects are our immediate experience; but of *an object that can become its own subject* (which is the alternative "theory of life" to Coleridge's) we have no experience. Nor could we ever have.[24] If we choose to suppose it, we do so at our own risk; which is the risk of erecting an ever more elaborate inverted pyramid of judgments upon that very outness, which itself disappears in the light of judgment.[25]

What then, in these terms of subject and object, is the basis of Coleridge's own theory of life? "*Life* is a subject with an inherent tendency to produce an object, wherein and whereby to *find* itself . . ." [26]

We only understand the "tendency to individuate," on which life is based throughout, when we see it as this potentially self-conscious subject, operant, as the agent of process, at every stage of the process; from the origin of matter itself, through the evolution of matter into vegetable life, of vegetable life into sentience, and of animal instinct into understanding. Of that process—the process wherethrough life "becomes a subject by the act of constructing itself objectively to itself" [27]— outness, as the law of self-conscious nature, is the end product; but it is difficult so to regard it, while we remain obsessed with outness as it is for merely somnolent experience. Therefore it seemed best to reserve the conclusion of the *Theory of Life* until the conclusion of the present chapter. The tendency "at once to individuate and to connect, to detach, but so as either to retain or to reproduce attachment" could only culminate in one way; only in a combination of "the most perfect detachment with the greatest possible union"; only in "things without us" at the one pole and "us," self-conscious, at the other; yet with the two so related that the one extreme is "identical and one and the same thing" with the other.

> The class of Vermes deposits a calcareous stuff, as if it had torn loose from the earth a piece of the gross mass which it must still drag about with it. In the insect class this residuum has refined itself. In the fishes and amphibia it is driven back or inward, the organic power begins to be intuitive, and sensibility appears. In the birds the bones have become hollow; while, with apparent proportional recess, but, in truth, by the excitement of the opposite pole, their exterior presents an actual vegetation. The bones of the mammalia are filled up, and their coverings have become more simple. Man possesses the most perfect osseous structure, the least and most insignificant covering. The whole force of organic power has attained an inward and centripetal direction. He has the whole world in counterpoint to him, but he contains an entire world within himself. Now, for the first time at the apex of the living pyramid, it is Man and Nature, but Man himself is a syllepsis, a compendium of Nature—the Microcosm! Naked and helpless cometh man into the world. Such has been the complaint from eldest time; but we complain of our chief privilege, our ornament, and the connate mark of our sovereignty.
> *Porphyrigeniti sumus!* [28] In Man the centripetal and individualizing tendency of all Nature is itself concentred and individualized—he is a revelation of Nature! Henceforward he is referred to himself, delivered up to his own charge; and he who stands the most on himself, and stands the firmest, is the truest, because the most individual, Man. In social and political life this acme is inter-dependence; in moral life it is independence; in intellectual life it is genius.[29]

We are so minded today that it is difficult for us to envisage anything as real, unless we can also see it as having gradually evolved to be what it is. It is clear from the *Theory of Life* that, although he did not consider this the most important thing about it, Coleridge did in fact hold that the relation between nature and the human mind, as we have it, is one that has gradually evolved to be what it is today. It is hoped therefore that the approach we have adopted, by way of that Essay, may, for some readers at least, have helped to make his "subject" and "object" something more than the brain-cracking conundrum too many literary men appear to have found them in the past.

Imagination and Fancy (1)

I F WE ask of something, a rainbow for instance, the question: What
is it?, we may mean one of two very different things. We may be asking simply: How is it identified? How do I know when I am in the
presence of this thing as distinct from other things more or less like it?
In the actual case of an appearance as easily identified as a rainbow
that is perhaps unlikely to be a problem. But in many cases it is. A man
who has many times observed a diffused glow in the sky may enquire:
What exactly is the Aurora Borealis? because he suspects that sometimes that is what he has seen, while at other times it was merely the
day's after-glow or the lights of a distant city reflected from the clouds.
He suspects moreover that his inability to distinguish shows there are
things about the Aurora Borealis which he has been too careless to notice. And he is right.

On the other hand the question may mean, not, how is a rainbow
to be identified when it appears? but, of what nature is a rainbow?
And this question again may be subdivided into two questions. We
may be asking: How is it brought about? or we may be asking: what
is its ontological status? Where does it stand in terms of such categories as real and unreal, mental and physical, natural and supernatural, human and non-human? These three questions are closely connected. The second is normally preceded by the first and the third
arises out of the second. Thus, in the case of the rainbow, three possible answers, based respectively on Newton's optics, on Goethe's theory
of colour and on the Book of Genesis, are all of them answers to the
second question which many would regard as being at the same time
the only possible answer to the third. The fact remains however that
they are three different and clearly distinguishable questions.

One peculiar feature about the mind of Samuel Taylor Coleridge
is that the question: What is imagination? appears to have assailed

him simultaneously, and upon a sharp encounter, in all of its three different senses. He was critic, poet and philosopher—in that order, not because that is the order of their importance or of his abilities, but because in any contemporary enquiry that is the natural order in which the three questions occur.

He himself has told us how he encountered the first question while he was still at school. His schoolmaster, the Rev. James Boyer,* used to point out to his pupils that "Poetry, even that of the loftiest and, seemingly, that of the wildest odes, had a *logic of its own,* as severe as that of science." [1] He was to spend much of his later life justifying, in depth, the four words we have italicized; but it is clear that Bowyer was mainly concerned with training his pupils to *recognize* genuinely "poetic" language and to distinguish it ostensively from its spurious imitations. Probably it was only a good deal later that Coleridge associated this distinction with the word *imagination;* but poetic utterance, as he already felt, and later understood it, *is* imagination appearing, as surely as the coloured arch in the sky is a rainbow appearing. The question: Is this a rainbow or not? is the same question, whether we use the word *rainbow* or some other word.

Among young men with any love of literature, and particularly of poetry, these exercises in identification go on almost of their own accord and are one of the principal delights of friendship. We know how Coleridge saw, or thought he saw (later he was a good deal less certain) the rainbow of imagination in Bowles's sonnets and the eagerness with which he sought to share his discovery. His correspondence for a few years from about 1796, particularly perhaps with Charles Lamb and Robert Southey, is full of similar literary exchanges. Lamb, with his delicate literary taste and literary gusto but without any marked desire to proceed from the first question to the other two,[2] was surely an ideal friend for this purpose. The term *exercises* is of course misleading. It may be quite proper for a biographer to see them in that light, in retrospect, but the experience at the time is more like that of sheer high spirits. Your friends are reading poetry—and trying to write it. You are reading poetry—and trying to write it. You delight in your friends and they in you. You are all young and all things are still possible. It is glory beyond all glory, but it is also a private joke

---

* Coleridge refers to him as "Bowyer."

between you. It is the halcyon time when you post off the latest effu-
sion with an intentionally idiotic doggerel note beginning:

> In stale blank verse a subject stale
> I send *per post* my *Nightingale;*
> And like an honest bard, dear Wordsworth,
> You'll tell me what you think, my Bird's worth . . .[3]

and, when you are not exchanging verses of your own, you are arguing
about the merits of accepted classics, such as Gray's *Elegy,* or contend-
ing "with unfeigned zeal for the honour of a favourite contemporary." [4]

In this way, in the sometimes easy-going and sometimes strenuous
exchanges of literary friendship, the first question merges inevitably
into the second. It would be the same with rainbows if, besides identifying them, men could create them. In Coleridge's case it was through
his friendship with Wordsworth, above all others, that he encountered
the second question: How does imagination come about? It would
almost be truer to say that it encountered *him*.[5] It is a moving experience to contemplate, in the pages of the *Biographia Literaria* and in
Coleridge's correspondence throughout his life, his unfaltering admiration, if not adoration, of Wordsworth's genius and his love of the
man. But this book is not a biography; still less is it a history of English literature; and it is not within its purview to show how Coleridge's
encounter with that other genius was a major formative influence in
his life, or how the contact between the genius of Wordsworth and the
genius of Coleridge himself (perhaps, in spite of the adoration, the
greater of the two) set up reverberations which have continued ever
since, and have largely determined the course not only of "Romantic"
but largely also of anti-Romantic literature and poetic theory.

We have introduced the word *genius* and, in doing so, have reached
and passed the boundary, such as it is, between the second question
and the third: the ontological status of imagination. But it would be
a mistake, as already indicated, to imagine that this was the point in
Coleridge's life at which he himself first advanced to a consideration
of the third question. The ontological status of imagination turns on
the relation between the mind of man and his environment; particularly on the relation between mind on the one hand and nature on the

other; and this was a matter with which Coleridge's own mind had begun concerning itself at a very early age indeed. "He was a metaphysician," writes Shawcross, "long before he studied the German philosophers . . ." [6] And one may add: "and long before he began to ponder what his contemporaries called *imagination* or *fancy*." Lamb's vignette of "the inspired charity boy" unfolding in the cloisters of Christ's Hospital "the mysteries of Iamblichus and Plotinus," is too well known to require citation.[7]

If that may be suspected of exaggeration, we have Coleridge's own word for his "early study of Plato and Plotinus, with the commentaries and the *Theologia Platonica* of the illustrious Florentine [Marsilio Ficino]." [8] In other words, before he was out of his 'teens he was familiar with a view of the relation between mind and nature, to which the mental habit of tacitly presupposing the Cartesian duality presented no problem, since it had not been collectively acquired, when that view was formed. Arrived at Cambridge, he went on to read Jakob Böhme, whose seminal influence on German philosophy and indeed on Western thought in general, is becoming increasingly, but is perhaps still inadequately, appreciated.[9] He was a free man, so to speak, of that philosophical and theosophical stream of thought which has not ceased to irrigate the culture of the West, and in particular its literature, art and theory of art, since it first began to flow, though it has percolated underground for much longer periods than those during which it has watered the surface.[10] He had already absorbed a Neo-platonic and hermetic philosophy of "beauty" before he began to think about "imagination"; and it was upon a mind so predisposed and shaped and stored, as well as on a tremulously delicate sensibility, that the beauties of nature and of poetry opened themselves afresh in early manhood. And it was with a mind so shaped, disposed and stored, and after that opening and the *annus mirabilis* in his own career as a poet to which it led, that he travelled to Germany and began his study of German philosophy.

All this is reflected in that tantalising, and certainly unsatisfactory, product of genius, the *Biographia Literaria*. The reminiscences in the early chapters concerning, for instance, his excitement over the appearance of Bowles's sonnets, reflect his encounter with the first of the three questions: How do I identify imagination, when I see it? So also does his account in Chapter IV of the appearance of Wordsworth's *Descriptive Sketches* in 1793, when he himself was still at Cambridge;

but it is noticeable that this is immediately followed by a remark on "the poetic Psyche, in its process to full development . . . ," and it is this remark, not the *Descriptive Sketches,* that leads in to "the sudden effect" produced on his mind a few years later by hearing Wordsworth recite a manuscript poem.[11] The whole of the Wordsworth *motif,* from its first appearance in Chapter IV to its culmination in the memorable nine chapters (XIV–XXII) analysing, criticising and praising Wordsworth's poetry, are saturated with Coleridge's response to the second question: How does imagination work? But it is not perhaps surprising that, in dealing with Wordsworth's poetry in critical detail, his mind sometimes harks back to the old days and the first question. Thus, there is force in some of the objections that have been raised against these chapters; Coleridge, it is said, does not always apply his own principles[12] and even echoes those Aristotelian and Johnsonian categories with which he must have been familiar when the *Descriptive Sketches* first attracted his attention. It has also been observed that some of the particular examples he selects of Wordsworth's excellence are not those we should have chosen ourselves. In such cases it is probable that he was remembering the shock of his first youthful encounter with the passage he quotes—into which all sorts of accidents no doubt entered. The "manuscript poem" already referred to[13] is not one many of us would choose for the purpose of emphasising Wordsworth's pre-eminence in what Coleridge means by "imagination." No. But, as a matter of history, it happens to have been that particular poem that lit the spark in his friend. It happens to have been that one that goaded Coleridge from the first question on to the second and, through that, to the third.

We have seen that his was a mind acutely aware of its own *activity;* and it is precisely out of such an awareness that the philosophical problem of "beauty" turns readily into the psychological and philosophical problem of "imagination." It is this problem that forms the central substance of the *Biographia Literaria* as it stands. It may well be that, had Chapter XIII ever been written, the intellectual emphasis would have rested finally on poetic rather than "philosophic" imagination. As it is, however, systematic argument is abandoned before that point is reached. Chapter XII is concerned almost exclusively with the philosophic imagination,[14] and above all (as we have seen) with establishing its ontological status. But its last paragraph begins: "I shall now proceed to the nature and genesis of the imagination," and it is fairly clear that Chapter XIII was to have dealt with the psychology (the second of our three questions), rather than the philosophy, of imagination and in that way to lead over from philosophy to poetry. It would also, presumably, have made clearer the distinction between the two aspects, and thus the two uses of the word *imagination,* which, as it is, we are left to infer as best we can from occasional hints, such as the remark in Chapter VII, to which we shall be returning:

> In philosophical language, we must denominate this intermediate faculty in all its degrees and determinations, the IMAGINATION. But, in common language, and especially on the subject of poetry, we appropriate the name to a superior degree of the faculty, joined to a superior voluntary control over it.[15]

If we confine the word to this latter sense, Professor Appleyard is justified in saying that "Coleridge promised to deduce the imagination, but he never did so." [16] It is certainly true that he never did so in the *Biographia Literaria,* because he never wrote Chapter XIII. But that is not to say that we cannot deduce it ourselves from what there is of Chapter XIII, taken with the rest of the book and the rest of Coleridge's work.

With the first and longest part of Chapter XIII we have already dealt at some length. If now we look again at the concluding paragraphs, giving, as Coleridge says, "the main result of the Chapter," we find they comprise, firstly, the well-known distinction between primary and secondary imagination.

> The IMAGINATION then, I consider either as primary, or secondary. The primary IMAGINATION I hold to be the living Power and prime Agent of all human Perception, and as a repetition in the finite mind of the eternal act of creation in the infinite I AM. The secondary Imagination I consider as an echo of the former, co-existing with the conscious will, yet still as identical with the former in the *kind* of its agency, and differing only in *degree,* and in the *mode* of its operation. It dissolves, diffuses, dissipates, in order to re-create; or where this process is rendered impossible, yet still at all events it struggles to idealize and to unify. It is essentially *vital,* even as all objects (*as* objects) are essentially fixed and dead.[17]

And, secondly, the equally well-known distinction between both of these on the one hand and fancy on the other:

Fancy, on the contrary, has no other counters to play with, but fixities and definites. The Fancy is indeed no other than a mode of Memory emancipated from the order of time and space; while it is blended with, and modified by that empirical phenomenon of the will, which we express by the word Choice. But equally with the ordinary memory the Fancy must receive all its materials ready made from the law of association.

The following chapter is devoted to considering each of these paragraphs in turn.

⊰ 7 ⊱

Imagination and Fancy (2)

T HE nature of primary imagination, and therefore of imagination
as a whole, as Coleridge presents it, can really only be understood in
terms of that relation between the act of thinking and its product,
thought, which formed the subject of our own first chapter. Between
the act of thinking, the "act of self-consciousness" [1] and the "act of
imagination" no very sharp distinction transpires. This is because the
act, as such, is one and the same, while the name chosen for it is varied
according to which one of its several effects is being expressed in the
context. Mathematical lines, points and surfaces, Coleridge avers in his
Treatise on Logic, are "acts of the imagination that are one with the
product of those acts." [2] If then, being first thoroughly seised of the
reality of the act distinguished as an act, we accept, for the purpose of
further contemplation, its 'oneness' nevertheless with its own product,
we shall then see imagination as a varying interplay between active
and passive elements in the *relation* between self and world, of such a
nature that the two elements themselves may change, the one into the
other. Or, we may say, between man and nature. Only, in using those
terms, we must remember that the boundary here presumed between
man and nature is by no means the currently fancied one. It is not the
boundary of a fixed "outness." Within *that* schema the only possible
mental interaction between active man and passive nature occurs at or
within the skin. Whereas the interplay, which is imagination, though
it is involved with body and space, is not their creature; and it would
be as true to say that it occurs in nature as to say that it occurs in man. [3]
We have seen that the life of nature is at all levels a power of "separa-
ive projection," and separative projection ("the eternal act of creation")
is what the act of self-consciousness—what the act of imagination—is.
The underlying reality (sub-stance) of things is thus not matter, nor
any equivalent inanimate base, but immaterial relationship. [4] For Cole-

ridge, because man did not create himself, there is indeed an actual (I–Thou) relation between subject and natural object; but, since man is to be free, it is also a genetic and progressive one. Phylogenetically that progressive relation is nature. Ontogenetically it is imagination.[5]

Primary imagination, then, is an act, but it is an act of which we are not normally conscious. It becomes secondary, whether philosophically or poetically, when it is raised to, or nearer to, the level of consciousness and therewith becomes expressible. Whereas the only thing that could be called the "expression" of primary imagination as such is the familiar face of nature herself. The "rules" of secondary imagination are, however, still "the very powers of growth and production," [6] for that is what they were already at the primary stage, when they were simply the laws of nature. In other words, they are not rules at all, though critics had been trying to turn them into rules. They are powers. Nor is it very difficult to see what sort of powers Coleridge had in mind, and would have written further of, had he actually composed the chapter whose "main result" he summarised in the two paragraphs we are now considering. We have already seen (in Chapter 3, above) that the part of Chapter XIII that *was* written, that is the opening paragraphs, is an attempt to introduce the reader to those two forces of the one power, and the relation of polarity between them, on which his theory of life itself is constructed. It is these forces which are "the very powers of growth and production" and the deduction of imagination, which he promised, must needs have taken the form of showing how these forces may operate, not only unconsciously and half-consciously as life in nature, but also self-consciously as the same life in human nature. "They and they only," he had written in the previous chapter:

> can acquire the philosophic imagination, the sacred power of self-intuition, who within themselves can interpret and understand the symbol, that the wings of the air-sylph are forming within the skin of the caterpillar; those only, who feel in their own spirits the same instinct, which impels the chrysalis of the horned fly to leave room in its involucrum for antennae yet to come. They know and feel, that the *potential* works *in* them, even as the actual works *on* them.[7]

We have observed in some detail, in previous chapters, what it meant to Coleridge to say that the potential (that is, *natura naturans*) "works" whether as formation or at the later stage of unself-conscious instinct. Let us place alongside of that one of the earliest passages on the psychology of imagination to be found in the *Biographia Literaria,* taking the liberty to italicize in order to bring out the point now being made:

> Now let a man watch his mind while he is composing . . . Most of my readers will have observed a small water-insect on the surface of rivulets . . . and will have noticed how the little animal wins its way up against the stream, by *alternate pulses of active and passive motion,* now resisting the current, and now yielding to it in order to gather strength and a momentary *fulcrum* [original italics] for a further propulsion.

But the point here is, not merely the fact that imagination is an interplay between active and passive elements in the relation between man and nature, but also the further fact that that interplay may be consciously experienced. The water-insect, he continues,

> is no unapt emblem of the mind's self-experience in the act of thinking. There are evidently two powers at work, which relatively to each other are active and passive; and this is not possible without an intermediate faculty, which is at once both active and passive. In philosophical language, we must denominate this intermediate faculty in all its degrees and determinations, the IMAGINATION. But, in common language, and especially on the subject of poetry, we appropriate the name to a superior degree of the faculty, joined to a superior voluntary control over it.[8]

In referring to "common language, especially on the subject of poetry" it is fairly clear that Coleridge had in mind the *lingua franca* of literary criticism and aesthetic theory, in which the word *imagination,* under the influence of Addison, Akenside and others, had recently been coming to play a more and more important part. But it should be equally clear by now that "the mind's self-experience in the act of thinking" was, for Coleridge, by no means the exclusive affair of poets and poetry. In philosophy, and indeed in science, it entails a new freedom to select and apprehend the "central phenomenon"[9] in nature, as in poetry a new freedom to select and apprehend the relevant symbol. It gives in fact the possibility of "secondary" imagination.

In the many and scattered passages where Coleridge, in his capacity

as a literary critic, addresses his mind to the topic of poetry and drama
and through that to the nature of imagination, there are two predominant themes. In poetry and drama it is a special quality in the relation
between the whole and its parts; in imagination it is the principle of
"unity in multeity." [10] Looking first at the latter, we shall find that the
various distinctions with which he operates, such as that between imi-
tating and copying, between genius and talent, between imagination
and fancy, between Shakespeare's "universal" characters and the abstract stereotypes of inferior dramatists, between principles or laws and
mere 'rules,' are all of them applications of that root principle of an
antecedent unity in all natural variety, which it was the purpose of the
Theory of Life to "explain." They are all based on "the power which
discloses itself from within as a principle of unity in the many." [11]
They all tend to demonstrate how the imagination acts chiefly by cre-
ating "a oneness, even as nature, the greatest of poets, acts upon us,
when we open our eyes upon an extended prospect." [12] They conceive
imagination as the process of "separative projection" at work in an
individual mind; and the individual mind in which this process occurs is what Coleridge means by "genius." Shakespeare was his favourite example of genius, and when he describes Shakespeare as "a nature
humanized" Coleridge is not speaking metaphorically:

> Nature, the prime genial artist, inexhaustible in diverse powers, is
> equally inexhaustible in forms. Each exterior is the physiognomy of the
> being within . . . And even such is the appropriate excellence of her
> chosen poet, of our own Shakespeare, himself a nature humanized, a
> genial understanding directing self-consciously a power and an implicit
> wisdom deeper than consciousness.[13]

Today, when we read of "a power and an implicit wisdom deeper than
consciousness," we are in danger of jumping to conclusions and identifying it over-hastily with "the unconscious" of modern psychology,
safely ensconced somehow or other within the cuticle of an individual
organism. Still more so, perhaps, when we read, in the essay *On Poesy
or Art,* that "there is in genius itself an unconscious activity; nay, that
is the genius in the man of genius"; and of the conscious having to be
"impressed on the unconscious." Was Coleridge, then, a depth-psy-
chologist in advance of his age? Yes and no. We need to read the
whole essay[14] to see what *he* meant by "the unconscious."

> In the objects of nature are presented, as in a mirror, all the possible elements, steps, and processes of intellect antecedent to consciousness, and therefore to the full development of the intelligential act; and man's mind is the very focus of all the rays of intellect which are scattered throughout the images of nature . . .

It is the function of art

> to make the external internal, the internal external, to make nature thought, and thought nature . . . body is but a striving to become mind . . .

Genius therefore must "master the essence, the *natura naturans,* which presupposes a bond between nature in the higher sense and the soul of man." It is its business to acquire

> living and life-producing ideas, which shall contain their own evidence, the certainty that they are one with the germinal causes in nature . . . For of all we see, hear, feel, and touch the substance is and must be in ourselves.

This is certainly depth-psychology; but it is a depth-psychology which twentieth century theory has not yet overtaken.

"The power which discloses itself from within as the principle of unity in the many," the "productive unity" of nature, results in a manifold of parts having an "organic" relation with the whole and, through that (*totus in omni parte*) with each other. In apprehending this we are moved by the *beauty* of nature. The same power, at the level of imagination, creates another manifold having a similar relation between parts and whole; and in apprehending it we are moved by the imagination of the poet. In the *Theory of Life* we saw "totality dawning into individuation" and, following that, an increasingly complex and increasingly reciprocal, part-whole structure. It is this element that Coleridge stresses in his treatment of poetry and drama, and occasionally of art in general. Only now the "tendency to individuation" has been replaced by the power to give pleasure or delight.

> A poem is that species of composition, which is opposed to works of science, by proposing for its *immediate* object pleasure, not truth; and from all other species (having *this* object in common with it) it is dis-

criminated by proposing to itself such delight from the *whole,* as is compatible with a distinct gratification from each component *part.*[15]

Or, as he had phrased it a little earlier; "by the production of as much immediate pleasure in parts as is compatible with the largest sum of pleasure in the whole." [16] A work of art will be "rich in proportion to the variety of parts which it holds in unity." [17] The unity in multeity, the *totus in omni parte,* of nature herself grows

> more intense in proportion as it constitutes each particular thing a whole of itself; and yet more, again, in proportion to the number and inter-dependence of the parts which it unites as a whole.[18]

And hence:

> Nature itself would give us the impression of a work of art, if we could see the thought which is present at once in the whole and in every part; and a work of art will be just in proportion as it adequately conveys the thought, and rich in proportion to the variety of parts which it holds in unity.[17]

While, then, imagination at its primary stage empowers experience of an outer world *at all,* at its secondary stage it both expresses and empowers experience of that outer world as the productive "unity in multeity," which results in a whole and parts organically related to one another.

There remains the second of the two paragraphs at the close of Chapter XIII: the distinction between Imagination and Fancy. This is a concept about which, over the years, there has been a great deal of controversy.[19] The question always is whether or no there is really a difference in kind between fancy and imagination (as Coleridge is taken to have held) or whether they are after all merely different degrees of the same power. It is doubtful however whether it has often been noticed that, precisely in connection with this question of fancy and imagination, Coleridge himself had a good deal to say on the true significance of "degree" and "kind" in general.

The distinction between imagination and fancy was one that meant much to Wordsworth, who used it extensively in his 1815 Preface. Now Coleridge's own original apprehension of it was inextricably involved with the impact upon him of Wordsworth's poetry. Wordsworth, he had written in 1804, in a letter to Richard Sharp, is

> the only man who has effected a compleat and constant synthesis of Thought and Feeling and combined them with Poetic Forms, with the music of pleasurable passion and with Imagination or the *modifying* Power in that highest sense of the word in which I have ventured to oppose it to Fancy, or the aggregating power.[20]

And some twelve years later he recalls, in Chapter IV of the *Biographia Literaria,* "the immediate impression on my feelings, and subsequently on my judgement" made by the union, in Wordsworth,

> of deep feeling with profound thought; the fine balance of truth in observing, with the imaginative faculty in modifying the objects observed . . . This excellence, which in all Mr. Wordsworth's writings is more or less predominant, and which constitutes the character of his mind, I no sooner felt, than I sought to understand. Repeated meditations led me first to suspect, (and a more intimate analysis of the human faculties, their appropriate marks, functions, and effects matured my conjecture into full conviction,) that fancy and imagination were two distinct and widely different faculties, instead of being, according to the general belief, either two names with one meaning, or, at furthest, the lower and higher degree of one and the same power.[21]

Here is a clear enough statement that the difference between fancy and imagination is a difference, not of degree but of kind. Nevertheless it appears that Wordsworth, with whom he had had "frequent conversations on the subject," had made too much of it. Referring to the observations on fancy and imagination in the latter's 1815 Preface, Coleridge comments:

> The explanation which Mr. Wordsworth has himself given will be found to differ from mine, chiefly perhaps, as our objects are different . . . it was Mr. Wordsworth's purpose to consider the influences of fancy and imagination as they are manifested in poetry, and from the different effects to conclude their diversity in kind; while it is my object to investigate the seminal principle and then from the kind to deduce the degree.[22]

What are we to say? Here, only a page or so after the passage previously quoted, is an almost equally clear statement that fancy and imagination differ, *not* in kind, but only in degree!

The object of this book is, not to contend that Coleridge invariably expressed himself in the way least calculated to confuse his readers, but to disclose, if possible, what he in fact thought. And for this purpose we do well to turn to a later passage in the same work, where (in a different context altogether) he addresses himself for a moment to the relation between "kind" and "degree" as such:

> The first lesson of philosophic discipline is to wean the student's attention from the DEGREES of things, which alone form the vocabulary of common life, and to direct it to the KIND abstracted from *degree*. Thus the chemical student is taught not to be startled at disquisitions on the heat in ice . . .[23]

The naïve man, he appears to be saying, sees all *obvious* differences as differences in kind. It is only when we go more deeply into it—only when we get down to the *real* "kind"—that we discover his error. And now, if we return to the former passage, the implication transpires that Wordsworth, in his Preface, had taken imagination and fancy as differing in kind in *the same way* that the naïve man takes "hot" and "cold" as differing in kind. Further that he had done this because he was first and foremost a poet and no psychologist. He was, as I. A. Richards has observed, "more interested in the products [poems] than in the process." [24] "My friend," Coleridge continues:

> has drawn a masterly sketch of the branches with their *poetic* fruitage. I wish to add the trunk, and even the roots as far as they lift themselves above ground, and are visible to the naked eye of our common consciousness.

In fact his own purpose, as he has just said, was "to investigate the seminal principle, and then from the kind to deduce the degree." [25]

Thus, in terms of the three questions (or three forms of the one question: What is imagination?) distinguished at the beginning of the last chapter, one could perhaps say that, for the purposes of the first question, fancy and imagination are different in kind, but for the purposes of the second, and still more certainly of the third, question they must be seen as differing only in degree. It is unfortunate that, at the point where he told us that his own object was "from the kind to deduce the degree," Coleridge did not specify more precisely *what* kind it is that includes both fancy and imagination as degrees. For that we have to jump on from Chapter IV to Chapter XII, where we learn that the "kind" in question is the intelligence present both in nature and in man, from which may be "deduced" not only poetic fruitage but all forms of consciousness and indeed of life:

> Bearing . . . in mind, that intelligence is a self-development, not a quality supervening to a substance, we may abstract from all *degree*, and for the purpose of philosophic construction reduce it to a *kind*, under the idea of an indestructible power with two opposite and counter-acting forces. The intelligence in the one tends to *objectize* itself, and in the other to *know* itself in the object.[26]

This, then, is clearly the direction in which he would have developed the topic in Chapter XIII, where (he tells us): "it will probably appear . . . that deeming it necessary to go back much further than Mr. Wordsworth's subject required or permitted, I have attached a meaning to both fancy and imagination, which he had not in view." [27]

That is said at the end of Chapter XII, where Coleridge reverts for a moment to the issue between himself and Wordsworth. Look deep enough and the alternative: *either* kind *or* degree becomes unreal. Indeed one who was inclined to consider too curiously might say that, in Chapter IV, he has hardly ceased opting for "kind" rather than "degree" as marking the difference between fancy and imagination, before he goes on to raise, at least implicitly, the question whether the difference between kind and degree is itself a difference in kind or only in degree! What matters is of course the actual nature of the relation between the two. Or rather, assuming that we already understand fairly well the nature of imagination and its place in Coleridge's system, the question is: what is fancy, and what place does *that* occupy in it? And if, at the end of our enquiry, there shall still remain an element of doubt or ambiguity about fancy, which we do not feel about imagination, it may transpire that that is not entirely Coleridge's fault but is due rather to a quality inherent in fancy itself.

In the first place, if, in the light of the foregoing, we regard fancy also as being, after all and in the deeper sense, a "degree" of intelligence as "seminal principle," we are granting her a place in that "ascending series of intermediate classes" between the lowest degree of the principle and the highest, of which life itself consists. That Coleridge regarded fancy in this light is suggested by a good many of his observations. It is a series in which each lower degree, or intermediate class, has the higher degrees potential in it or, as Coleridge sometimes put it, is "irradiated" by them. "Nature in her ascent leaves nothing behind, but at each step subordinates and glorifies:—mass, crystal, organ, sensation, sentience, reflection." [28]

> Potential sensibility in its first epoch, or lowest intensity, appears as growth: in its second epoch, it shows itself as irritability or vital instinct. In both, however, the sensibility must have pre-existed, or rather pre-inhered, though as latent: or how could the irritability have been evolved out of the growth . . . or the sensibility out of the irritability . . . ? [29]

Animal, vegetable and mineral differ in kind, if any things do; yet they are all degrees of the one "seminal principle"; which is the kind of kinds. And, above the level at which consciousness begins, the same principle continues to apply as between the lower faculties or manifestations of intelligence and the higher. So, Wordsworth's deficiency in fancy sometimes lamed the expression of his imagination and in the *Table Talk* we find Coleridge expressly remarking that:

> Genius must have talent as its complement and implement, just as in like manner imagination must have fancy. In short the higher intellectual powers can only act through a corresponding energy of the lower.[30]

In short, fancy is given an indispensable place, and thus an honourable status, in "the world of intelligences with the whole system of their representations," which Chapter XIII promised it would "cause to rise up before you." [31]

But now let us place over against this some of the other things said about fancy. And first, as we have seen, it was not only Wordsworth, but Coleridge also who at first suspected, and then became convinced, that fancy somehow differs from imagination in kind, and *not* only in degree. Moreover it was this conviction that originally prompted him to go deeply into the whole subject. So far—in view of Coleridge's observations on the philosophical reduction of naïvely apprehended differences in kind to actual differences in degree (*heat* in ice)—the difficulty can perhaps be met by phrasing the argument somewhat in this way: 'On the analogy of the natural world, the difference between fancy and imagination is more like the difference between one natural kind and another than it is like the difference between two species of one kind or genus. It is true that even the former difference is ulti-mately to be seen as a difference in degree only; true also that the rela-tion between nature and mental operation is not in fact merely one of analogy—that they are themselves ultimately of one kind: but let that pass, since at the moment it is more important to stress the divergence between fancy and imagination than the unity.'

Does this make it all plain sailing? Not quite. Let us take one more look at the two paragraphs at the close of Chapter XIII. Whereas the secondary imagination "dissolves, diffuses, dissipates in order to re-create," fancy "has no other counters to play with, but fixities and definites." What is it, then, that imagination dissolves and dissipates? Clearly, the same fixities and definites which fancy can only rearrange. Fancy is the *aggregating* power; it combines and aggregates given units of already conscious experience; whereas the secondary imagina-tion "modifies" the units themselves. Moreover, in doing so, it shows itself to be "identical in the *kind* of its agency" with the primary imagination, on which all conscious experience is based. It is *one with* the primary imagination (that is, the seminal principle) in a way that fancy, distinguishingly, *is not*. For it modifies "sense" itself,[32] that com-mon sense, or koenaesthesis, which fancy must take, and leave, as it finds it. "You may conceive the difference in kind between the Fancy and the Imagination in this way, that if the check of the senses and the rea-son were withdrawn, the first would become delirium, and the last mania." [33] It was because Wordsworth had so little idea of all this that he managed to make at once too much and too little of the difference between the two.

But, besides its characteristic activity, fancy also has a merely pas-sive role. For, in his three chapters on Hartley's associationist psychol-ogy, Coleridge speaks of "the universal law of the passive fancy and the mechanical memory." [34] Schemes which promise an artificial *mem-ory*, "in reality can only produce a confusion and debasement of the fancy." [35] And again, our fancy is "always the ape, and too often the adulterator and counterfeit of our memory." [36] This linking of it with *memory* indicates fancy's playing a part in the genesis of consciousness at an altogether earlier stage than literature could be concerned with. Besides "playing with" the fixities and definites that are given to it, fancy has evidently taken a hand in producing them—in rendering them the very fixities they are. And, especially in his references to this stage, the pejorative vocabulary (*dead, mechanical, artificial, ape, adul-*

terator) strongly suggests, no longer a natural degree within the one ascending series that manifests the seminal principle of mind or intelligence, but an almost hostile interference with it from a source outside itself.

Here, then, is the final ambiguity. Our attempt at resolving it will take the form of a general account of the nature of fancy, as we suppose Coleridge to have conceived it, taking into consideration, not only his specific observations on that subject, but the important place it occupies in the *Biographia Literaria,*[37] and bringing to bear on it our whole understanding, for what it is worth, of Coleridge's system.

In the first place, then, fancy has its proper and beneficent place in the genesis of consciousness as a whole and, particularly, in the conversion of perceptions into memories. But it is easily debased. In its debased form it is, as *passive* fancy, more or less identical with precisely those characteristics of human perception, which it is the function of imagination (by modifying perception) to overcome, namely: "the film of familiarity and selfish solicitude," in consequence of which "we have eyes, yet see not, ears that hear not . . ." or, more shortly, "the lethargy of custom." [38] The mind is in thrall to the lethargy of custom, when it feeds solely on images which itself has taken no active part in producing. But there is more to it than this. For the debasement of *active* fancy carries this process further. Where the mind deliberately *chooses* to feed only upon such images, there you have the debasement of active fancy; and there the lethargy of custom becomes that deliberate practice of reducing "the *conceivable* within the bounds of the picturable," at which Coleridge never tired of pointing his warning finger.[39]

The significance of active fancy thus extends far beyond the limits of literature, in which indeed it is least likely to occur in a debased form, and where its debasement perhaps does least harm. Fancy is at work, for instance, wherever the unobservable in nature is converted, for handling, into supposed observables. Instances of it therefore would include, not only the *Rape of the Lock* and Mercutio's speech in *Romeo and Juliet,* but also the epicycles of Ptolemaic astronomy (so far as they were not conceived as pure geometry), the psychology of Locke and Hume, Hartley's "vibratiuncles," phlogiston, the ether of classical physics, the Rutherford-Bohr planetary atom, and all other scientific hypotheses not distinguishable from some fancied 'model.' [40]

Passive fancy and passive memory are closely allied, if not indistinguishable. But active fancy involves a certain "emancipation" from the order of time and space,* and it is this very emancipation that makes possible the higher faculty of *understanding*. Nevertheless it is a very different sort of emancipation from time and space than the one which *reason* (in Coleridge's sense) alone makes possible. This however is to anticipate. Moreover it would appear to be this memory-cum-fancy that gives rise to "fixities and definites"; and it follows from the whole tenor of Coleridge's thought that these latter include objects themselves ("all objects [*as* objects]"), the "deadness" of natural objects as such being that very "outness" of theirs which memory-cum-fancy has helped to project.

Lastly, active fancy is exercised by a personally biased will ("the empirical phenomenon of the will, which we express by the word CHOICE")* and not by the absolutely free will, which (again anticipating) is one with reason, nor by an individual will acting in accord with reason.

Imagination *is,* and fancy is *not,* "the very power of growth and production";† and we have seen how it is *this* power which, as its own two opposite forces, works at all stages of the process, at first of nature and then of consciousness leading to self-consciousness. And yet the "outness" of objects is or has been, itself, an essential element in that process at its later stages! It is even described as "a law of our nature." ‡ It would seem then that fancy *is* part of the process; and there is much in Coleridge to suggest that it is. But in that case why should fancy be so very decidedly *not* a power of growth and production? The process is the whole process that constitutes nature and man, so that, if fancy is no part of the process, its provenance must lie somehow outside of nature and of man; and again there is a good deal in Coleridge to suggest that it does. There *is* ambiguity[41] then; but it could be argued that it is an inevitable one, and we shall be less inclined to fix the blame on Coleridge's system, if we reflect that there is a similar ineluctable ambiguity about the cosmic status of evil. The specific relation he detected between fancy and death points up such a parallel without pressing it. Matter itself (which is the *violent* "out-

---

* See Chapter 6, p. 75, above.
† See p. 77, above.
‡ See Chapter 5, p. 65, above.

ness" of objects—outness congealed into absolute and idolatrous detachment) is evil as entailing the agonies of death and bereavement, but beneficent as enabling the maximum individualization of detached spirits—and, therewith, the birth of freedom and of love.

We might well leave it at that. But we are tempted to essay one further step towards a resolution of the ambiguity, or the paradox—a resolution that is perhaps implicit in Coleridge's system, though we believe he never explicitly propounded it. We have seen something of the nature of those "two opposite and counteracting forces" [42] in looking at the *Theory of Life* and the *Biographia Literaria,* and we may recall from the first paragraph of Chapter XIII of the *Biographia* that the one of them "tends to expand infinitely, while the other strives to apprehend or *find* itself in this infinity," and again, from the previous Chapter XII, that "The intelligence in the one tends to *objectize* itself, and in the other to *know* itself in the object." [42] Now imagination is precisely an advance of the mind towards knowing itself in the object. We have seen also that it is characteristic of the relation of polarity that, although one pole, one force, cannot be without the other, yet there is always also a *predominance* of one over the other; further, that it is upon these varying and alternating predominances that all evolution, and indeed life itself depends. But how could such predominances occur, if the two forces were not "oppugnant" as well as "opponent"—if it were not that each force—from its own point of view, so to speak—*is* literally *"striving"* for total ascendancy over the other—in blind ignorance, or ruthless disregard, of the inevitable consequence: that, if it 'had its way,' polarity, and with it life itself, would cease.[43]

Can we say then that, in the case of fancy, or in some cases of it, there is an *undue* predominance of the (centripetal) force that seeks to apprehend or find itself by "objectizing"; whereas, in the case of imagination, the two forces are working in harmony, that is to say, with the necessary, but without any undue, predominance of the one over the other? And is this the "irremissive though gentle and unnoticed control (*laxis effertur habenis*)" which is "retained by the will and understanding," when the poet

> brings the whole soul of man into activity, with the subordination of its faculties to each other, according to their relative worth and dignity. He

diffuses a tone and spirit of unity, that blends, and (as it were) *fuses,*
each into each, by that synthetic and magical power, to which we have
appropriated the name of imagination.[44]

Imagination is, or it is striving to become, the ultimate polarity of self
and world experienced *as such.* In its fullness that experience would be
the reconciliation of the two forces, not their cessation. But the finite
activity of poetry, like every other motion, still requires a predominance,
however slight, of the one pole over the other. This is exemplified in
the fine contrast which Coleridge detected between Shakespeare and
Milton—"his compeer, not rival":

> While the former darts himself forth, and passes into all the forms of
> human character and passion, the one Proteus of the fire and flood; the
> other attracts all forms and things to himself, into the unity of his own
> IDEAL. All things and modes of action shape themselves anew in the
> being of MILTON; while SHAKESPEARE becomes all things, yet for ever
> remaining himself.[45]

But it is also exemplified in the contrast, which at the same time
deepened the affinity, between Wordsworth on the one hand and Coleridge himself on the other. They are both of them "nature-poets" and
both of them also "mind-poets," if the expression may be allowed. But
for Wordsworth, although the sub-title of his longest and perhaps
greatest poem is "The Growth of the Poet's Mind," it was nature that
was the predominating factor in the polarity between mind and nature.
He looked for, and found, inspiration in nature considered, or certainly *felt,* as another being altogether rather than as counterpoint to
his own mind. Coleridge also looked for, and sometimes found, inspiration in the same way. But his was a mind in which the opposite
factor predominated—which was more inclined therefore to consider,
and certainly to *feel,* how

> We receive but what we give,
> And in our life alone does Nature live.*

It was out of this subtle difference of emphasis, discovered, explored
and fruitfully mated by the two poets during those walks in the Quan-

---

* *Ode to Dejection.*

tock hills, that the *Lyrical Ballads* came into being. In that volume, Coleridge says

> it was agreed, that my endeavours should be directed to persons and characters supernatural, or at least romantic; yet so as *to transfer from our inward nature* a human interest and a semblance of truth . . . Mr. Wordsworth, on the other hand, was to propose to himself as his object, to give the charm of novelty to things of every day, and to excite a feeling analogous to the supernatural, by awakening the mind's attention from the lethargy of custom, and directing it to *the loveliness and the wonders of the world before us* . . .[46]

The conversations, we are told, "turned frequently on the two cardinal points of poetry," which are on the one hand "the power of exciting the sympathy of the reader by a faithful adherence to the truth of nature," and on the other "the power of giving the interest of novelty by the modifying colours of the imagination." [47] But the poems were nearly all by Wordsworth, and we believe it does no disservice to Coleridge's own greatness as a poet (with which this book happens not to be concerned) to suggest that what Wordsworth illustrated by his poetry for poetic experience Coleridge demonstrated in his thought for all experience: namely that the two cardinal points of poetry are such because they embody the two cardinal and constitutive principles of the human spirit itself, antagonists indeed and poles apart, yet still, and somehow in spite of themselves, two forces of the one power.

◆§ 8 §◆

Understanding

"WE MUST seek," wrote Coleridge in the *Friend*, "for some general law, the action of which is such, as (if it remained untempered and uncounteracted) would prevent or greatly endanger man's development and progression. But this we shall find in that law of his understanding and fancy, by which he is impelled to abstract the changes and outward relations of matter and to arrange them under the form of causes and effects." [1]

Here is a good example of one of those pregnant passages—pregnant with the whole structure of his thought—which require some of that background to be filled in, if they are to be more than superficially understood. In this chapter we shall endeavour to perform that office for one particular phrase, namely the apparently casual reference to "the law of his understanding and fancy." And, since the previous chapter has already dealt at some length with fancy, we shall now be principally concerned with understanding. It will be well however to preface with a few observations that apply not only to understanding, but to fancy also, as well as to some of the other key words in Coleridge's psychology. Perception, imagination, fancy, understanding etc. are not separate "faculties." In making use of them a man is not "exerting different faculties"; he is "exerting his faculties in a different way." [2] Although this must already be clear from the previous chapters, if they have been at all understood, yet there has been so much misunderstanding over it that it is probably best to state it definitely, as Coleridge himself did on more than one occasion. We are in less danger of being misunderstood if we call them "powers," but it is not always convenient or advisable to ignore the term in common use, and Coleridge himself by no means always did so.

There is another consequence, more important than nomenclature, which follows from dismissing any fiction of separate faculties; and that is, that we shall not be exasperated when attempted definitions of them are found to overlap one another. This is inevitable, because the powers themselves interpenetrate one another. They can and must be *distinguished* from one another, but that does not mean that they are *divided:*

> Distinct *notions* do not suppose different *things*. When we make a threefold distinction in human nature, we are fully aware, that it is a distinction not a division, and that in every act of Mind the *Man* unites the properties of Sense, Understanding and Reason. Nevertheless, it is of great practical importance, that these distinctions should be made and understood . . .[3]

The difference between dividing and distinguishing is a point we have had before.* It is rather remarkable that the type of Coleridge critic, who will ignorantly accuse him in one breath of adopting an old-fashioned psychology of "faculties," will sometimes be the very one to complain in the next of inconsistency because the components of his terminology are not kept sufficiently distinct. It is the nature of inseparable powers not to be separate, and we are in a realm of discourse where one subject not only interpenetrates another, but is quite likely to be in process of actually changing into it. We may, if an analogy will help, have defined very precisely the difference between "pushing" and "throwing," but how many contexts will remain in which what we must say of the one would be equally applicable to the other? Thus, imagination, "as soon as it is fixed upon one image, becomes understanding; but while it is unfixed and wavering between them, attaching itself permanently to none, it is imagination." [4] Even sensation is already intelligence in process of constructing itself,[5] and that process is essential in the psychology both of instinct and of fancy. Nevertheless we must fix and use names, if we are to think and speak at all—or, as Coleridge himself put it, "unless we would make an end of philosophy, by comprizing all things in each thing, and thus denying that any one power of the universe can be affirmed to be itself and not another." [6]

Coleridge both defined and described the understanding on a number of different occasions and in a number of different contexts.[7] He was much more definite about it indeed than he ever succeeded in being about fancy. We must select some one definition to start from, and we will take the one found in the original (1812) version of the *Friend*:

---

* See Chapter 1, pp. 18–20.

the Understanding or regulative faculty is manifestly distinct from Life and Sensation, its *function* being to take up the *passive affections* of the Sense into Distinct Thoughts and Judgments. These Forms however, as they are first awakened by impressions from the Senses, so have they no Substance or Meaning, unless in their application to Objects of the Senses . . .[8]

A few sentences further on he emphasises the difference between this and "reason," as he himself uses—and again has frequently defined—that word. The distinction between understanding and reason* is, for the comprehension of Coleridge, an all-important one, and its importance is a matter about which he never had any doubt. Moreover he was deeply convinced that the failure of most people in his time to grasp the distinction was the very sleeping-sickness of the age. He said in later years that the *Friend* was the one of his prose works to which he attached the greatest importance and he said in the *Friend* itself that, once his readers had grasped that distinction, they would have little difficulty in comprehending anything else. The habit of using reason and understanding as virtual synonyms has however not ceased; so that any reader acquainted neither with Kant nor with Coleridge finds the dice loaded against him. He starts off on the wrong foot, because in many modern contexts the vaguer connotations of the two words are actually the opposite of those implicit in Coleridge's use of them. *Reason,* with its derivatives and parallels, *reasoning, reasonable, ratiocination,* often sounds to us the shallower of the two; *understanding* the deeper because more sympathetic. The first thing to do therefore, while we are reading Coleridge, is to jettison these more familiar associations.[9]

Reason will form the subject of the ensuing chapter; but partly because the contexts in which Coleridge has most frequently defined and delineated the understanding are just those in which he meticulously distinguishes it from reason,[10] and partly because of the very nature of the relation between the two, some anticipation is inevitable and there will be not a little said about reason in the present chapter also.

If the understanding is to be strictly called, not a faculty but a "power," it must be said of reason, speaking with equal strictness, that it is not even a power.[11] It is not *a* power, though, as "the power of Ideas," [12] it is in one of its aspects, the source of all powers. "Without

---

* As to the use, or not, of the initial capital, see Chapter 9, below.

being either the sense, the understanding, or the imagination, it contains all three within itself, even as the mind contains its thoughts, and is present in and through them all; or as the expression pervades the different features of an intelligent countenance." [13] "All reason is above nature" [14] and reason is therefore *really* different "in kind" * from all those degrees of nature and from all those degrees of the human psyche, correlative to nature, which we call functions and faculties. Psychologically therefore it is to be apprehended not as a power, but rather as a gift[15]—a gift which the human understanding enjoys, and by virtue of which it is human.

But, though reason is present *to* the understanding alone, it is present *in* the whole process of nature. This appears to contradict (to any reader's own unawakened understanding it *does* contradict) the previous proposition that all reason is "above" nature; and that contradiction is perhaps the principal difficulty in the way of comprehending what Coleridge meant by it. It is one that is simply not removable, unless we are prepared to treat his whole cosmology as an *alternative* to the Cartesian dichotomy, and not simply as an interpretation of it. For the present we must leave it at that. It is for instance, because reason is present in nature that sensation is potential instinct, and that instinct itself is potential understanding—which will then be open to the ideas of reason; so that it is not merely metaphorical to say, as Coleridge does in Chapter XII of the *Biographia Literaria,* that those who possess the philosophic imagination "feel in their own spirits the same instinct, which impels the chrysalis of the horned fly to leave room in its involucrum for antennae yet to come. They know and feel that the *potential* works *in* them, even as the *actual* works *on* them." [16]

It is because reason is present in nature, and *not* merely because of repressed physical appetites, or of physically "inherited" memories, that we can speak fruitfully of a "*consciousness,* which lies beneath or (as it were) *behind* the spontaneous consciousness natural to all reflecting beings," [17] and that it nevertheless makes sense to call this consciousness-beneath-consciousness "philosophic." [18] Indeed the best way of approaching the relation between reason's "presence in" nature and its "presence to" the understanding, may well be to think in terms of "the unconscious" and consciousness, or, more simply, of sleeping and waking: "Plants are Life dormant; Animals = Somnambulists; the mass of

---

* Cf. Chapter 7, pp. 83 ff., above.

Mankind Day-dreamers; the Philosopher only awake." [19] What was present but asleep as life in nature becomes, when present to the understanding, the awakener. It begins the awakening process in all men, but it can only bring it to completion when it has been discerned and, in being discerned, becomes aware of itself as reason. That is why the distinction between understanding and reason is so important. Meanwhile, for the mass of mankind, "the understanding sleeps in order that the fancy may dream." [20]

Some of the terminological distinctions Coleridge makes, he does not (as we have seen) himself invariably observe, occasionally perhaps from carelessness or haste but more often for the reasons already given. In a dynamic philosophy "faculties" are "powers," and "kinds" themselves are ultimately "degrees." The distinction between understanding and reason however is not in this category. Moreover Coleridge not only made it explicit many times over; in any context in which it was at all relevant, he almost invariably observed the distinction himself, though, because of the intimate relation between the two, it is not always easy to do so. That may have already become apparent from the present chapter, the object of which is to build up the concept of understanding in artificial isolation from that of reason.

In doing so it will be best to begin with the gamut, or scale, he himself drew up in one of his marginal notes:

> Reason
> Imagination
> Understanding
> _____
> Understanding
> Fancy
> Sense

And first it must be emphasised that what appears on the page as linear succession must be imagined in the mode of polarity. That this is so is not only evident from the rest of Coleridge's thought, but it is also underlined by the fact that the whole series is written out twice, the two lists appearing side by side but in reverse order; so that reason appears next and opposite to sense and imagination next and opposite to fancy.* Another way would have been to link the polarities together and we should then get:

---

* See pp. 101 and 219, below.

"Extremes meet" was, as is well known, one of Coleridge's favourite maxims; but we also see here that the point where the two extremes most gradually and observably encounter (though they were of course meeting and interpenetrating throughout) is precisely the understanding. There is a polarity between understanding and understanding, a tension within the understanding itself. Keeping this in mind will help us to apprehend in depth some of Coleridge's other pronouncements on the topic of the understanding, for instance:

> For the understanding is in all respects a medial and mediate faculty, and has therefore two extremities or poles, the sensual, in which form it is St. Paul's φρόνημα σαρκός* and the intellectual pole, or the hemisphere (as it were) turned towards the reason.[21]

This polarity, which constitutes the understanding, is, in accordance with the essential character of polarity, a relation between an active component and a passive one, either of which may predominate. It is active as bringing down the upper half of the series, passive as bringing up the lower half; active out of reason, and passive out of sense.[22] So to divide it—to treat the passive understanding, and all below it, in notional isolation from the active and all above it, is of course an artificial disentangling from one another of "two forces of one Power." It is none the less necessary for the purpose of fully conscious apprehension; and accordingly the remainder of this chapter will concern itself as exclusively as possible with the lower half of the series, reserving the upper for the ensuing chapter on *Reason*.

'Mere' understanding—understanding conceived as unirradiated by reason—is a faculty man shares with the higher animals; in whom it is the further development of instinct. It is in fact Bertrand Russell's "animal inference." So considered, but only so considered, it is not different in kind from the "instinctive intelligence manifested in the ant, the dog,

---

* *Phronēma sarkos*. Romans, 8.7, translated "carnal mind" in the A.V.

the elephant etc." [23] For instance, it is subject to the physical laws of heredity.[24] The progress of evolution in fact from sense to passive understanding is an unbroken one in both man and animal. But in *man* there is also its polar opposite, active understanding. Moreover, although it is convenient to use the stage of understanding for pointing it out, this difference between human and animal psychology is also present at *all* stages in the series. It is present, for example, in the faculty of "attention" which was considered in Chapter 1; and, if we were to proceed further downward into the "sense" pole, we should no doubt have to begin distinguishing the element of "intentionality" in human perception, as marking the operation already, at the extreme of passivity, of that opposite pole of activity, which is the act of consciousness itself *in potentia*.

The animal however does not perform any *act,* which entails withdrawal from, and contemplation of, the natural process of which its intelligence remains a part:

> . . . the Understanding wherever it does not possess or use the Reason, as another and inward eye, may be defined the conception of the Sensuous, or the faculty by which we generalize and arrange the phaenomena of perception: that faculty, the functions of which contain the rules and constitute the possibility of outward Experience.[25]

The word *rules* is important here. Coleridge uses it frequently when writing of the understanding. Understanding is "the adaptive power." [26] Rules, unlike principles or laws, grow out of experience. They are inventions, whose mother is necessity. Understanding is "the faculty of suiting measures to circumstances" [27] or of "adapting means to proximate ends." [28] And it is in this sense that Coleridge is thinking when he contrasts understanding as "the faculty of rules" with reason as "the source of principles." [29] From life to instinct to instinctive intelligence to understanding, the progression is one without sharp breaks, and the true contrast is not between instinct and understanding (which differ only in degree), but between both of them and reason.[30]

One consequence that ensues from this, for dynamic philosophy though not for a theory of merely emergent evolution, is the following. Just as understanding cannot be explained without our seeing it as developed instinct, so instinct itself cannot be explained without our seeing it as potential understanding. "The lower derives its intelligibility from the higher." [31] At the same time the absence of any sharp break does not mean simply a linear progression from the one to the other. It is not incompatible with substantial *change*. It is the same here as it is with the evolutionary change from vegetable to animal life. "We are not to seek in either for analogies to the other, but for counterpoints . . . the nearer the common source, the greater the likeness; the farther the remove the greater the opposition." [32] Polarity is a parameter within which 'the more there is of mine, the less there is of yours'; and therefore "the Understanding appears (as a general rule) in an inverse proportion to the Instinct," [33] of which it is none the less a true development.

This brings us naturally to the mental process known as "abstraction." [34] Understanding is "the faculty judging according to sense" [35] and "judging" entails abstraction. A rule of behaviour—as contrasted with a blind instinctual drive in lower organisms, or in some particular organ of a more complex creature—is already potential abstraction; but in *human* psychology abstraction involves something more; for it entails the power not merely to behave by rules, but also to formulate them—to know, in fact what the word *rule* means. For what renders understanding human is precisely this ability to identify by naming. It is this that gives the possibility of the distinctively human acquirement of speech. No abstraction, no language. But for human understanding, and therefore for the coming forth of language, the presence of reason is essential—its presence, not yet the apprehension of it *as* reason. Thus, there is probably no better illustration of this 'dreaming' presence of reason to the human understanding than the birth of language, whether in the history of humanity or in the mind of a growing child.

Coleridge defines the proper function of the human understanding as "that of generalizing the notices received from the senses in order to the construction of names." [36] The generalising is done by animals also; but from the absence of reason, they do not go on to abstraction proper and, with that, to the construction of names; they do not achieve the stage "of referring particular notices (that is, impressions or sensations) to their proper names; and, *vice versa,* names to their correspondent class or kind of notices—" [37] Hence the significance of the part played by language in the development of human understanding out of instinctive intelligence. Reason participates in language as the element of grammar; and it is this that "gradually raises into acts and objects of distinct consciousness what Nature and the alone true natural state of Man had previously called forth as instinct." It is grammar that

> reflects the forms of the human mind, and gradually familiarises the half-conscious Boy with the frame and constitution of his own Intellect, as the polished Glass does the unconscious infant with the features of his own countenance . . . bringing about that power of Abstraction, by which as the condition and the means of self-knowledge, the reasoning Intellect of Man is distinguished in *kind* from the mechanical Understanding of the Dog, the Elephant, the Bee, the Ant, and whatever other animals display an intelligence that we cannot satisfactorily reduce to mere Instinct . . .[38]

Abstraction therefore is the distinctive mark of the human understanding; and we have already seen the high importance Coleridge attached to it (Chapter 1, pp. 20–21, above). But it is important as a means, not as an end in itself; and the ends towards which it should be employed are imagination and the ideas of reason. The abstract, that is the human, understanding is not only concerned with names; it is concerned *only* with names.

> in all instances, it is words, names, or, if images, yet images used as words or names, that are the only and exclusive subject of understanding. In no instance do we understand a thing in itself; but only the name to which it is referred.[39]

Whereas, in instinct, we are still united with nature; and whereas in imagination we are re-united with it; by understanding we are detached from it. If therefore we make of understanding an end in itself, we become "a race of animals, in whom the presence of reason is manifested solely by the absence of instinct." [40]

> falling prostrate before lifeless images, the creatures of his own abstraction, [man] is himself sensualized, and becomes a slave to the things of which he was formed to be the conqueror and sovereign.[41]

We begin to comprehend more fully perhaps what was at the back of Coleridge's mind when he wrote in the *Friend* of man being "impelled" by the law of his understanding and fancy to abstract the outward relations of matter and to arrange them under the form of causes and effects; and when he went on a little later to refer to this impulsion as a "temptation." [42] Idols are means which we have been tempted into revering as ends. To idolize the understanding, instead of being active to awaken the reason dreaming within it, is to corrupt or pervert our part in reason. The abstract understanding has two gifts to bestow: accuracy, or the elimination of error;[43] and that detachment from the whole process of life which the existence of an individual spirit presupposes. All beyond that depends on imagination and stems from reason. Understanding, alone, gives "outness," accuracy and the experience of unity; but this unity is not unity in multeity; it is unity by the exclusion of multeity. Understanding, alone, assures us that we exist as separate and distinct points; but only *as* points, only as the nothings of a Sartre-type existentialism. It is by virtue of reason and imagination that we exist substantially as very beings, and it is only through reason and imagination that we can even be sure that anything exists outside of us. Through understanding we experience the culmination of our detachment; through imagination and the gift of reason we realise, in polarity, that very culmination as the possibility of a different and higher order of attachment.[44]

Thus, to ignore the distinction between understanding and reason is to lose sight of the essential difference between man and beast. It is to commit existential suicide. And this, Coleridge tried to show, was exactly what had been happening with the spread of English empiricism and the technologising of science—submitting, as the Sophists had done long ago, "all positions alike, however heterogeneous, to the criterion of the mere understanding." "The understanding was to be corrupted by the perversion of the reason" [45] and what was called "the Enlightenment," as is not uncommon with cant labels, was mainly the opposite of what the label signifies. It was the deliberate shuttering of the understanding from the light of reason.

It may help at this stage to look once more at the psychological scale, this time as Coleridge himself in fact wrote it down:

lowest	*highest*
Sense	Reason
Fancy	Imagination
Understanding	Understanding
Understanding	Understanding
Imagination	Fancy
Reason	Sense

The fundamental break (emphasised by the line) lies between the two opposite directions that can be taken by the understanding itself, and it is this that originates the growing divergence between the contrasted pairs in the series. The difference between fancy and imagination is an easier one to spot than a difference between understanding and understanding, between understanding as passive and understanding as active. At the moment when the tide turns it is difficult to say whether it is going out or coming in; but choose a moment five minutes before or five minutes after the turn, and you can be pretty certain. We have tried, in the two previous chapters, to watch Coleridge's mind stumbling, as it were, on the fact of those divergent directions after they have reached a wider and more conspicuous stage. It was the task of the present one to observe the finesse with which he afterwards probed the divergence to its origin in the understanding; or rather to its commencement there, since its origin lies of course in the will.

If we would now venture to express, in terms of his own gamut, the light in which he beheld the intellectual climate of his age, we should have to set against the series just quoted the following altered and truncated version of it:

Fancy (active)
Understanding
Fancy (passive)
Sense

Refusal to distinguish understanding from reason is "the omission to notice what not being noticed will be supposed not to exist." [46] To the understanding apart from reason the Peripatetic maxim *Nihil in intellectu quod non prius in sensu* does apply. Its forms, as we have seen, "as they are first awakened by the senses, . . . have . . . no substance or meaning, unless in their application to the objects of the senses" (p. 94, above). Concepts without perceptual content *are* "empty." But it is really only understanding, with *denial* of reason, that adds and adopts the legal maxim, *De rebus non apparentibus et non existentibus eadem est ratio.* [47] It is only understanding, with denial of reason, that falls under the despotism of the eye; with the result that the faculty of abstraction, which affords access to the ideas of reason, is turned back, in its search for content, upon the impressions of sense. If you will not acknowledge the "downshine" of imagination and reason into the active understanding, you will have nothing to set over it but fancy all over again.

And this, in Coleridge's eyes, was just what had long been happening. This is what he has at the back of his mind when he affirms that "the Present is the Epoch of the Understanding and the Senses";[48] or when he refers to "abstract knowledge, or the science of the mere understanding," which "leads to a science of delusion";[49] or when he speaks of "Imagination excluded from poesy; and fancy paramount in physics; the eclipse of the ideal by the mere shadow of the sensible."[50] It is what lies at the back of his mind when he coolly pronounces that "Incredulity is but credulity seen from behind, bowing and nodding assent to the habitual and the fashionable."[51]

There will be more to say of this, when we come to the bearing of what Coleridge thought on the development of science. But first of all it is clearly necessary to endeavour to treat at some length of what has already, and unavoidably, been frequently referred to in this chapter; that is, reason and the ideas of reason.

❧ 9 ❧

Reason

IT WAS pointed out in the last chapter that the fundamental difference between human and animal psychology is effective, not only in the understanding, but at all stages of consciousness. In other words, reason, which appears at the top of Coleridge's scale of mental powers, nevertheless irradiates the human psyche at all stages of its natural evolution. Since this is both an unfamiliar and, in this "epoch of the understanding and the senses," * a difficult notion, it may help at this point to construct an analogy, though it is one which must not be pressed too hard.

If we were to replace the parameter of psychology, to which Coleridge's scale applies, with that of sexual relationship; and if we were to substitute "law" for "reason," then understanding could be taken as corresponding to something like "mating." Permeated by law, mating becomes the human mating called marriage; and, as such, it may 'rise' into the sphere of law itself (dynasty, nationality, status, contract, property-rights etc.). But the difference between marriage and mating is also effective below the "mating" level, even down into the moment of copulation (corresponding with Coleridge's "sense"), where it appears as, for instance, the possibility of a sacramental dimension, different in kind from that of 'mere' copulation. The fact that the category of sacrament is 'higher' than that of social and municipal law improves rather than mars an avowedly imperfect analogy. Extremes meet; and we shall be noticing later that from one point of view reason, at the top of the 'scale,' has a greater affinity with its octave, sense, than it has with the understanding, which it enters only to sharpen it to the point of nullity; or even with the imagination, into which it is ever willing to be transformed.

---

* Chapter 8, p. 103, above.

Professor Muirhead has observed that Coleridge added to the dynamic theory of reality "the conception of the principle of that activity as the nisus towards individuality." [1] We have already traced this in his *Theory of Life,* and have seen how, above the human level, the nisus is from consciousness towards self-consciousness; which is another name for individuality. It is against this background that we are bound to interpret the scale; and, in doing so, we find that the mystery, or problem, of self-consciousness can be effectively confronted as the mystery or problem of the relation between understanding and reason; and, above all, in the circumstance that reason may be present to the understanding in two different modes, one of which we characterised as 'dreaming' and the other as 'waking.' In the former mode reason is present to the understanding, but without being realised or apprehended as reason. In the latter mode it is both present and consciously realised as present; it is "conscious self-knowledge." [2] And progress from the former mode to the latter is the final stage of the nisus.

Coleridge found, or adopted, several different ways of formulating the distinction between the two modes: as for instance conceptual reason and ideal reason; negative reason (*lumen a luce*) and positive reason (*lux intellectus*).[3] But when he speaks more generally of the "irradiation" of understanding by reason, he does not always specify which of the two modes he is referring to. Nor is this very surprising, when we reflect that the very act of *talking about* negative reason is a step towards converting it into positive reason, since it involves becoming to some extent conscious of reason. The same must be said of his use of the capital letter. It would be pleasant if we could say comfortably: "*Reason,* yes, that is positive reason or *lux intellectus; reason,* yes, that is negative reason, or *lumen a luce*"; but it will be found impossible to do so. Coleridge's free and irregular use of the initial capital for all sorts of words (including *Understanding*), to which he wishes to draw particular attention at the moment, is well known and has already become manifest from quotations, where we have preserved it intact. Elsewhere we have thought it wiser for the most part to cut out the capital, though in the particular case of "Reason" the decision was reached only after considerable hesitation. Even there however it is doubtful whether on the whole it would help, and it might even hinder the important thing, which is this: while remaining immovably aware of the difference between reason and understanding, to sit rather loosely to the *word* "reason" in Coleridge. It was not always relevant, or even possible, for him to maintain the distinction between positive reason and negative reason; not only so, but, where occasionally the word is used in the sense of reason-*ing*—ratiocination—it amounts to no more than the active human understanding.[4] This is in fact the sense in which it is most commonly used in current speech, and Coleridge himself could so use it in contexts outside of philosophy and psychology, in his political writings for example.

Reason, in its proper sense, specifies the mere understanding into distinctively human understanding. And this in two ways, or by two stages. As negative, it brings about the total detachment which individuality presupposes. As positive reason, it is the being of the individual so detached. The ideas of reason "are of higher origin than the notions of the understanding, and by the irradiation of which the understanding itself becomes a human understanding."[5] (Because it is being, reason itself has no plural. We can speak of the "understandings" of a number of people, but not of their "reasons." So, too, Platonizing philosophers spoke of superhuman, or divine "Intelligences"; never of divine "Reasons." The only plural of reason is "ideas of reason," to which we must come in the following chapter.) But "when this light shines downward into the understanding . . . it is always more or less refracted, and differently in every different individual."[6] The light of reason is thus both the origin and the abiding basis of individuality. Without the positive presence of reason to the understanding, there is no individuality, only the detachment which individual being presupposes. Reason, in both its negative and its positive aspect, is the individualiser.

And yet—and this is where the difficulty occurs for most people—reason is, not only "supersensuous," but also, as has just been seen, "superindividual."[7] Not only so, but its whole characteristic is to *be* superindividual. It individualises because it is, and by being, superindividual; by being *totus in omni parte*—"entire in each and one in all."[8] There is abundant evidence of how well aware Coleridge was that this irreducible contradiction was at once the most unacceptable and the most important truth he had to deliver. How often, and how very hard he tried! We may look in particular at the disquisition on two passages from Leighton and Harrington in *Aids to Reflection*,[9] or to the corresponding one on Harrington in the *Friend*,[10] or to the *Statesman's Manual* with its long Appendix B.[11] But in one place and another he was always at it. As to its importance, we have already heard him insisting that, if the *Friend's* readers would only grasp it, all else would follow. More emphatically, when he comes to read through the *Statesman's Manual* some time after it has been printed, he adds in ink:

> Let not the Reader imagine that this distinction of the Understanding from the Reason is optional, or a mere refinement in words. It is either false and mischievous: or it is a most radical and necessary truth. I know indeed of but one other truth of equal worth and pregnancy—and that is the Primacy of the Will, as deeper than and (in order of *thought*) antecedent to Reason. See St. John's Gospel 1.18.[12]

These are only two examples, from many, of the heavy stress he laid on this (to many people) almost hair-splitting distinction. It should not be difficult to see why. The line drawn *between understanding and understanding,* in that 'scale' of mental powers, was no abstraction to him. It represented the stage on which the whole drama of the human mind, and with it of human destiny itself, is being played out. For it is at that point in the scale that the will may turn either way: back to negative reason and, through that, to the mere understanding, and through that, to sense; or on to positive reason.[13] But that involves, first of all grasping that there *is* such a thing as positive reason. It involves *knowing* the reason as directly present to the understanding. Here, if anywhere, then it may accurately be said that "Truth is self-restoration."[14]

For the other way amounts in the end to existential suicide. This is the truth which he saw so clearly and from which nearly all around him, including the representatives of the Churches, were sedulously looking away—with disastrous consequences.[15] Perhaps, looking or attempting to look through his eyes, we may say that he saw the relation between understanding and reason, not as a piece of wire-drawn psychology, but rather as the relation between the tiger and the lady in the old limerick. Understanding had gorged reason, instead of being ridden by it, and the brash complacency left over from the Enlightenment was "the smile on the face of the tiger."[16]

Something has now been said of Coleridge's views on the nature of reason, as well as on its peculiar relation to the understanding in man. But of course he did not merely affirm these things as *ipse dixits.*[17] He believed he had demonstrated them. If we are now to try and follow the lines of his demonstration, it will be well to revert in the first place to the topic of Chapter 1, where the point was made that thinking is not something that simply happens to us, but is our own act; and further that everyone, who has the will to do so, can convince himself of this fact. To apprehend the nature of reason, however, I have to take the further step of realising that, although thinking is my act, it is not "mine" in the sense that understanding uses the word *mine*.[18] This follows from the very nature of reason, which determines the nature of thought as such. My concept, although it is my act, is thus not my private property.[19] An inveterate assumption to the contrary is at the heart of the common difficulty, already referred to, of grasping the reality of reason. Yet it is an assumption which is at once removed by candid reflection on the nature of thought; reflection, that is, on its nature as immediately experienced and actually used; not of course reflection on hypothetical causes, whether physical or otherwise, since these are already products, posterior to and now remote from, the act that produced them. But such reflection is not a very popular pastime. Coleridge himself on one occasion beautifully christened our unspoken but obsessive, presumption that the same concept in two minds is two concepts and not one, as "the queen bee in the hive of error." [20]

It may be recalled from Chapter 1 that, in addition to reflecting upon it, Coleridge maintained that it is possible, though for most of us not easy, to *experience* the nature of thought, or rather of thinking as an *act,* by raising it from its normally unconscious function into a conscious one; and possibly the idea of an unconscious act of thought, becoming raised to consciousness, is less of a stumbling block to us than it was to his contemporaries. Indeed one way, for us, of approaching his whole conception of reason, is to think of it as "the unconscious"; with a corollary to the effect that the true significance of that word has been partly limited and partly distorted out of all recognition by various schools of psycho-analysis, to whom however (no small debt) we owe the widespread recognition of it as a reality. Coleridge's "consciousness, which lies beneath or (as it were) *behind* the spontaneous consciousness natural to all reflecting beings," * was not, like theirs, based on an initial presumption of fixed "outness" and all that flows from that by way of fancying ultimately physical sources.[21]

Exposition of the paradoxical, or self-contradictory, essence of reason was a task that by its very nature could do with all Coleridge's acuteness of logical analysis on the one hand and all his subtlety of psychological

---

* Chapter 8, p. 95, above.

experience and psychological analysis on the other; and he bestowed them liberally, his main point of attack being precisely this distinction between reason and understanding. We should perhaps remember the difficulty of the task, when we are minded, as we sometimes are, to criticise the means he adopted. Thus, it may annoy, but need not madden us, when we find him introducing his disquisition on Reason and Understanding in *Aids to Reflection* by quoting an Aphorism from Bishop Leighton, in which the Bishop says that "faith elevates the soul above reason" and speaks of "natural reason judging according to sense"; and when we find Coleridge not only pointing out that by "reason" here Leighton meant what he (Coleridge) calls "understanding," but, in order to drive the point home, making use of a sentence adapted from James Harrington in which Coleridge has first substituted the terms *understanding* and *reason* for the terms (*reason* and *religion*) which Harrington himself had actually employed.[22]

Always, and however laboriously, he is aiming to bring out (*a*) the two different *modes* in which reason operates; and (*b*) the two contradictory *aspects* of reason (on the one hand its individuality and on the other its universality, or superindividual nature).

The two aspects do not respectively correspond to the two modes; on the contrary both of them apply to both. In one mode reason is, positively, the act of self-consciousness; it is "conscious self-knowledge";[23] it is the I AM. In the other mode, it is present only negatively, or unself-consciously, to the understanding. In both modes however it is the superindividual so acting as to individualise.

Thus, as we saw in the previous chapter, reason, via the understanding, enables a mind's total detachment from 'nature,' that is, it enables subjectivity. But it does this by making possible *abstraction,* that is generalising, that is, experiencing objects in terms of 'universals.' The power to generalise and abstract depends in its turn on the power to *compare,* that is, the power to analyse a vague impression of 'likeness' into the clear concepts of *difference* on the one hand and *sameness,* or identity, on the other. And, in the terminology of logic, that is to apprehend the fact of *contradiction*. A is A; and it is not B. It is at all events not "not-A." For the two conceptions contradict and exclude one another, and "reasoning [negative reason in the understanding] consists wholly in a man's power of seeing, whether any two conceptions, which happen to be in his mind, are, or are not, in contradiction with each other." [24]

Hence man's experience of detachment—and thus of himself as

autonomous unit—varies directly with the development of his understanding. But the development of his understanding also brings about another result. It reduces his knowledge of nature to knowledge of the mechanical in nature. This was a principal part of Coleridge's message to his contemporaries, with the addition that, in so far as nature is mechanical, it is *natura naturata;* it is nature without life—a truth which has become a good deal more widely realised since his time.[25]

But Coleridge also saw that this epistemological limitation of the mere understanding, properly understood, actually compels us to go a step further and realize that the human understanding is *not* 'mere.' If we pause to *contemplate* the absoluteness, for the understanding, of the principle of contradiction, we begin perforce to become aware of the "unindividual and transcendent character of the Reason" [26] that informs it. We become aware that rational understanding does indeed give us our subjectivity, our detachment; but that, by itself and untranscended, it gives no assurance of an external world,[27] and thus excludes the very possibility of knowledge. It tells us that the act, by which we have abstracted and combined, is *one* act;[28] but it tells us nothing else. Any actual knowledge of nature does in fact, whether we are fully aware of it or not, bring to bear, "the intelligence which is in the human mind above nature"—and therefore also above mere understanding.[29]

For what does the principle of contradiction, without more, offer to a mind? What does the mind obtain by "submitting all positions alike . . . to the criterion of the mere understanding"? * Quite literally nothing. The principle of contradiction tells us nothing of what nature, or anything else, *is.* It tells us only what it is *not;* and, in doing so, clenches our absurd detachment from it—which we perhaps choose to call our "analytical unity." Actuality escapes it altogether; this was the discovery of the Eleatic school, and the weapon of the Sophists. What does it mean to say a car "begins to move"? As far as the understanding is concerned, it is either already moving, or it is at rest. Beginning, change, motion itself, development, evolution, life—anything whatever that is *naturans* as well as *naturata*—eludes the rigorous *either:or* of the mere understanding plus the senses.[30]

The "step further" which Coleridge was calling on his contemporaries to take was, once again, to pass on from the product to the producent. Now the immediate product of reason in the understanding

---

* Chapter 8, p. 101, above.

is the principle of contradiction. But only that which itself transcends two contradictories can have produced them. Thus, if we do not remain wilfully blind, our attention is drawn, by the truth in contradiction itself to "the truths of reason." It is indeed a "test and sign" of any truth of reason that *"it can come forth out of the moulds of the understanding only in the disguise of two contradictory conceptions."* [31]

Thus, by contemplating contradiction, the mind is propelled from "the outward sense" to "the mind's eye"; from superficial accuracy about the unknown to the depth of actual knowledge. And what is it that is known? The producent of products in contradiction with one another. But that is only a rather more Latin way of saying: "One Power manifesting as two forces." The first step towards apprehending reason, as active, is thus the apprehension of polarity; it is to apprehend reason as "productive unity," as "separative projection," as "the tendency at once to individuate and to connect, to detach, but so as either to retain or to reproduce attachment." Such, or of such a nature, is the background-thinking of which we should be aware when, for example, we hear Coleridge drily affirming that the ideas of reason are "constitutive" and not (as Kant held) merely "regulative." [32]

The moonlight of reason negative in the understanding can prompt the mind's eye to turn towards the positive sunshine, of which it is the pale and the dead reflection.[33] To do so is to proceed from *natura naturata* into *natura naturans;* it is to pass on from fancy's business of arranging and re-arranging the "products of destruction, the *cadavera rerum*," [34] to imagination's business with "the existence of absolute life," which is "the correlative of truth." [35]

Polarity, being "incompatible with the mathematical calculus," is not graspable by the understanding, but only in the imagination; in fact we have already had occasion to specify it as the basic act of imagination.* The present chapter and the preceding one are really only a fuller statement of that position. Separative projection "comes forth out of the moulds of the understanding" as the absurd equation, $1 = 2$; imagination as its converse, $2 = 1$.[36] It is perhaps worth pausing here to remark that the interest, steadily increasing over the last fifty years, taken by those who have a feeling for imagination in poetry and in language generally, in the nature of simile and metaphor seems to indicate a dawning awareness of this. It is realised, though not always explicitly,

---

* Chapter 3, p. 36, Chapter 4, p. 52, above.

that the meaning-content of a metaphor is destroyed if we look in it, as Aristotle did, for a *tertium comparationis;* that is to say, if we force it into the moulds of the understanding by analysing the likeness, on which it is based, into sameness on the one hand and difference on the other. To experience metaphor *as* metaphor, on the other hand, is to experience likeness as a *polarity* between sameness and difference;[37] and there is a similar contrast underlying the distinction between allegory and symbol, or allegory and myth.[38]

The place of imagination, between reason and understanding in the gamut of mental powers, becomes more clearly evident. "Even in France," wrote Coleridge on a copy of the 1818 recension of the *Friend,* "I see more to *hope,* than in Britain. It is wonderful, how closely Reason and Imagination are connected, and Religion the union of the two." While, from the other direction, "The completing power which unites clearness with depth, the plenitude of the sense with the comprehensibility of the understanding, is the imagination, impregnated with which the understanding itself becomes intuitive, and a living power." [39] Swallowed up by the understanding, positive reason becomes the negative reason of logic, which is however still necessary, which is indeed the ground we stand on, which is still reason. *Linked* to it through imagination, reason retains, or recovers, her manage and mastery as positive reason; and the understanding is then "employed in the service of the pure reason." [40] A year or two earlier he had observed in the *Statesman's Manual* that "The histories and political economy of the present and preceding century partake in the general contagion of its mechanic philosophy, and are the product of an unenlivened general understanding. In the Scriptures they are the living educts of the imagination"; and it is at this point that he continues with what Professor W. J. Bate has called "perhaps his most specific definition" of imagination:[41]

> that reconciling and mediatory power, which incorporating the reason in images of the sense, and organizing (as it were) the flux of the senses by the permanence and self-circling energies of the reason, gives birth to a system of symbols, harmonious in themselves, and consubstantial with the truths of which they are the conductors.[42]

Reason then is one power, of which the forces in any manifestation are inevitably two. We are endeavouring to reserve Coleridge's theology for a subsequent chapter, but, as already observed, the nature of his system is such that absolutely serial treatment is impossible to maintain. He is so frequently depicted as having most ingeniously and artificially, even a little dishonestly, combined what, without the help of a smoke-screen, it is almost impossible to keep separate: for example, the concept of the Logos, or creative Word, which was never very far from his mind, and the substantially un-Darwinian, because un-Cartesian, concept of evolution that found embodiment in his *Theory of Life*. Reason is being; but that is another way of saying that reason is God;[43] and indeed the polarity, God)(Man, is the basis of all polarity, in nature and elsewhere.[44] Just as, psychologically, it is reason which enables the experience of unity, but it is also reason which enables the experience of absolute contradiction, so God is the ground of the unity between God and man, but also of the distinction between them; and that distinction is itself the ground of all other distinctities—including the distinctities, whether of so-called 'kind' or 'degree,' in nature; since the process of psychology and the process of nature are not in fact two separate processes, but one and the same, namely: "the increase of consciousness in such wise that whatever part of the *terra incognita* of our nature the increased consciousness discovers, our will may conquer and bring into subjection to itself under the sovereignty of reason." [45]

In the same way, we have endeavoured both here and in Chapter 1 to state absolutely the paradox of individuality (it is *my* act) and universality (*it is superindividual*) inherent in thinking itself.[46] But there would be a certain artificiality—it is after all the separation, not the combination that is artificial—in isolating this idea from that of the incarnate word, from the wisdom, in the Christian tradition, of John and Paul. There is a certain artificiality in demonstrating that "I" am also "not I," without so much as a reference to St. Paul's "I live, no longer I, but Christ lives in me." [47] Within this frame of reference "the Word or Logos is life, and communicates life" (the entire life-process culminating in the individual understanding); but it is also "light, and communicates light"; and this light is positive reason; whereas the negative reason, which alone the understanding can be said to "possess," is only "the capability with which God had endowed man of beholding, or being conscious of the divine light." Yet that capability is, itself also, the light[48]—though not immediately; and although the darkness of the mere understanding in which it resides may fail to comprehend and use it.[49]

Here, at the close of two relatively abstract chapters, it may be well to listen as well to another way Coleridge found of portraying the nature of reason; a way more in tune with the shy approaches to these matters that win approval in the twentieth century. It is his interpretation of the myth of Prometheus:[50]

The generation of the *nous,* or pure reason in man. 1. It was superadded or infused, *a supra* to mark that it was no mere evolution of the animal basis—that it could not have grown out of the other faculties of man, his life, sense, understanding, as the flower grows out of the stem, having pre-existed potentially in the seed: 2. The *nous,* or fire, was 'stolen'—to mark its *hetero-* or rather its *allo-*geneity, that is, its diversity, its difference in kind, from the faculties which are common to man with the nobler animals: 3. And stolen 'from Heaven'—to mark its superiority in kind, as well as its essential diversity: 4. And it was a 'spark'—to mark that it is not subject to any modifying reaction from that on which it immediately acts; that it suffers no change, and receives no accession, from the inferior, but multiplies itself by conversion, without being alloyed by, or amalgamated with, that which it potentiates, ennobles, and transmutes: 5. And lastly (in order to imply the homogeneity of the donor and of the gift), it was stolen by a 'god', and a god of the race before the dynasty of Jove—Jove the binder of reluctant powers, the coercer and entrancer of free spirits under the fetters of shape, and mass, and passive mobility; but likewise by a god of the same race and essence with Jove, and linked of yore in closest and friendliest intimacy with him. This, to mark the pre-existence, in order of thought, of the *nous,* as spiritual, both to the objects of sense, and to their products, formed, as it were, by the precipitation, or, if I may adopt the bold language of Leibnitz, by a coagulation of spirit.

In other words this derivation of the spark from above, and from a god anterior to the Jovial dynasty—(that is, to the submersion of spirits in material forms)—was intended to mark the transcendency of the *nous,* the contra-distinctive faculty of man, as timeless, and, in this negative sense, eternal. It signified, I say, its superiority to, and its diversity from, all things that subsist in space and time, nay, even those which, though spaceless, yet partake of time, namely, souls or understandings. For the soul, or understanding, if it be defined physiologically as the principle of sensibility, irritability, and growth, together with the functions of the organs, which are at once the representatives of these, must be considered in *genere,* though not in degree or dignity, common to man and the inferior animals. It was the spirit, the *nous,* which man alone possessed.

Ideas, Method, Laws

Aт one point in Coleridge's remarkable Address to the Royal Society of Literature on the *Prometheus of Aeschylus,* from which we quoted at the conclusion of the preceding chapter, he sums up his interpretation of the myth as follows: "the groundwork of the Aeschylean *mythus* is laid in the definition of idea and law, as correlatives that mutually interpret each the other." This principle is one that is nearly central to Coleridge's cosmology, and an expansion of it may prove the best approach to the meaning of the word *idea,* as he habitually employs it.[1]

It was further observed in Chapter 9 that the only plural of reason is ideas of reason. To this it may now be added that *all* ideas are "ideas of reason" in Coleridge's terminology. For the other senses in which the word is most commonly used he himself employs the terms *notion, conception* and occasionally *maxim.* It needs also saying that the ideas of reason are not the plural of reason in the ordinary sense, whereby the particular components of a collective noun might be thought of as its plural reference; in the sense, that is, that the plurality of "crowd" is the persons who compose the crowd. An idea is not a component part of reason, because reason, the whole, is present and effective in each idea. Alternatively, we may speak of ideas as "parts" of reason, only if we are prepared to let the term connote *that* relation between a whole and its parts, whereby the particular and the universal are one—*totus in omni parte.* Coleridge himself sometimes uses the term *constituent.*

> . . . as constituents of reason we necessarily contemplate unity and distinctity. Now the latter as the polar opposite to the former implies plurality: therefore I used the plural, distinctities, and say, that the distinctities

considered apart from the unity are the ideas, and reason is the ground and source of ideas.[2]

We need, once again, to be able to distinguish without dividing; and that very ability is itself reason.

It follows that much, if not most, of what has already been said of reason will also apply to the ideas of reason, or any one of them. In neither case is it possible to "account for," or even fruitfully to discuss, the paradox of singular plurality or of identity in difference. It must be accepted because, on examination, we find that it is itself the experiential ground on which all intellectual acceptance and rejection are based. Reason "affirms itself." [3] It is understanding that thinks "of" or "about" things. Reason is the thinking.[4] Itself the creative polarity that engenders many from one, it "comes forth out of the moulds of the understanding" only as the invincible contradiction, the insoluble 'problem,' of the one and the many.

By the same token the understanding as such can have nothing to say about the relation between reason and the ideas of reason. All it can do is to take note of the fact that to be at once universal and particular is the very nature of the act of thinking, the act of consciousness itself; and this has already been dealt with at some length in the previous chapter.*

The like consideration applies to the relation between the ideas of reason and the phenomenal world. Seeking an explanation of the "multeity" of nature, we are driven, first, to eliminate our inveterate fancy of a fixed and anterior "outness" of phenomena; secondly, to the discovery that understanding points us back behind itself to reason, to reason as at once the source of living opposites and the lightning-flash that arrests them at the entrance to the understanding and reveals them as a stony landscape of logical contradictions bounded by its horizon; thirdly, and consequently, to the presence of reason as the *ground* of the understanding. It would be absurd, or more strictly speaking preposterous, to look 'behind' reason for some fancied source, either ("as monkeys put their hands behind a looking-glass")† in the phenomenal world, which is itself the product of reason, or in the understanding, of which reason is the ground. A thing cannot be the

---

* Chapter 9, pp. 107–108, above.
† Shedd I, 465.

product of that which it has itself produced; "that the *very* ground, saith Aristotle, is groundless or self-grounded, is an identical proposition." [5]

And so with imagination: having been told that it is characteristic of imagination to apprehend unity in multeity, or the all in each, we can ask why this should be so; and we can be answered: Because that is the nature of reason, and imagination is the mind's approach towards self-knowledge, and thus towards a fuller awareness of the presence of reason within us. But there we must stop. It is meaningless for the understanding to go on and ask: why should, or how can, that be the nature of reason? All the understanding can hope to do is to remove the obstacles which its own confused conceptions have interposed; and that is just the task that Coleridge set himself. When they *are* removed, we may participate in reason; but not by understanding it, only by awakening it within us as we contemplate its effects; or, if it is preferred, by meditating it. *Meditation* is a word Coleridge introduced more than once when he was emphasising the "all in each," the universal human nevertheless particularised, which we find in Shakespeare's presentation of his dramatic characters.[6]

It follows then from the nature of reason, and of its relation to the ideas of reason, that nearly everything we can say about an idea is also being said about reason; and vice versa. To ask: how do we apprehend an idea? is to ask: how do we participate in reason? And there is the same difficulty about answering the one question as about answering the other; a difficulty not really met by using carefully chosen words like *participate* (which already transcends the conceptions of the understanding). Nor is it met (though all this may contribute something to the "pointing back") by going farther and attempting to define participation as, let us say, "a felt union with the inner origin of outward forms." Moreover, assuming that it has been apprehended, any attempt to *express* it will involve those "blank misgivings of a creature | Moving about in worlds not realised" of which Wordsworth wrote. It follows in fact from the whole nature of the relation between reason and understanding that "an idea, in the *highest* sense of that word, cannot be conveyed but by a *symbol*";[7] that is to say, so far as language is concerned, in figurative language.

Here again a modern reader of Coleridge may find that he derives some assistance from the now familiar, though dim, mental image of an unconscious, or subconscious, mind—an image, which itself, of course, flouts the conceptions of the mere understanding, since it amounts to saying "unconscious consciousness." It is significant that Freud, who was avowedly determined to limit himself to a body-bound notion of the unconscious, was nevertheless obliged to rely, via the dream, almost wholly on symbolism.[8] It may also be useful at this point to look at one of Coleridge's own attempts to convey, in figurative language, something of what is involved in the apprehension of an idea. He compares it with the experience of listening to music:

> Music seems to have an *immediate* communion with my Life; . . . It converses with the *life* of my mind, as if it were itself the Mind of my Life. Yet I sometimes think that a great Composer, a Mozart, a Beethoven must have been in a state of Spirit much more akin, more analogous to, mine own when I am at once waiting for, watching, and organically constructing and inwardly constructed by, the *Ideas,* the living Truths, that may be re-excited but cannot be expressed by Words, the Transcendents that give the Objectivity to all Objects, the Form to all Images, yet are themselves untranslatable into any Image, unrepresentable by any particular Object, than I can imagine myself to be a Titian or a Sir C. Wren.[9]

To apprehend an idea is to be aware of at once constructing and being constructed by it; it is to be aware, in the same act and moment, of myself and the source of my selfhood; for it is to participate in reason, to become one again with the living opposites that created me and, as growth-forces, sustain my own creative being.

It is perhaps, then, by equating reason with "the unconscious," though in a non-Freudian sense,[10] that we can approach most sympathetically Coleridge's numerous references to the "dimness" of ideas, at least on their first appearance in the mind.[11] Clearness is founded on shallowness.[12] It is for the conceptions or notions of the understanding to be clear, and it is when they lack that saving virtue that they become dangerous; for then they filch some of the strength of growth, and of feeling, which belongs by right to ideas, since it is ideas that actually "constitute" our humanity.[13] And that is why deep thinking necessarily entails strong feeling.[14] It will be best to return to this later in the chapter. But we may note here its bearing on the station occupied by imagination between reason and understanding. Whether we think of the mind as in the first place understanding,[15] but ascending towards reason; or of ideas as in the first place "the permanence

and self-circling energies of the reason," * but descending[16] towards
the understanding, we shall not be surprised to find them often enough
"in that shadowy half-being, that state of nascent Existence in the Twilight of Imagination, and just on the vestibule of Consciousness . . ."
where feeling also has its roots.[17]

In apparent contrast with these references to the dimness of ideas
lies the fact that it is precisely on the apprehension of ideas, as distinct
from mere conceptions or maxims, that Coleridge bases his important
concept of "method." In this volume we are attempting to outline what
Coleridge thought, in accordance with a particular selected plan. It
would have been possible to choose a different plan altogether and to
work outwards, so to speak, from the little group of Essays in the
Friend in which he himself outlines what he understands by method.[18]
Because ideas are the permanence and self-circling energies of reason,
they are also in an almost literal sense "the prophetic soul | of the wide
world dreaming on things to come" and it is therefore only *their*
presence in the mind that can give rise to a knowledge effective for the
future as well as analytical of the past; and (which is much the same
thing) only that which can produce any radically *new* knowledge. The
conceptions of the understanding, "like lights in the stern of a vessel,
illumine only the path that has already been past over." [19] Coleridge
himself once adduced the literary example of Polonius;[20] but perhaps
the best analogy to mere understanding is the idea of the perfect computer. Raise the computer to absolute perfection: reduce the understanding to absolute "mereness": and there need be no significant
difference between the two instruments.

Coleridge develops his own idea of method by contrasting it with
classification—which is arrangement for the convenience of memory or
communication. In the sphere of natural science he takes as an out-
standing example of classification the system of Linnaeus in botany.
After praising the illustrious Swede warmly for his services to the
study, he points out that the system amounts nevertheless to "little
more than an enormous nomenclature; a huge catalogue, *bien arrangé,*
yearly and monthly augmented in various editions, each with its own
scheme of technical memory and its own conveniences of reference!" [21]
Linnaeus "invented an universal character for the Language of Botany
chargeable with no greater imperfections than are to be found in the

---

* See Chapter 9, p. 112, above.

alphabets of every particular Language";[22] and alphabetical arrangement is the *terminus ad quem* of non-methodical (in Coleridge's sense) arrangement. It was in fact as the introduction to an Encyclopedia, the topics in which were to be ordered otherwise than alphabetically, that he evolved his *Treatise on Method*.[23]

A *methodical* order must be based, he held, not on notions but on ideas. Above all it requires, in any particular field, the "initiative idea," which Linnaeus lacked.[24] For the plurality of ideas is not a merely numerical one; "there is a gradation of Ideas, as of ranks in a well-ordered State, or of commands in a well-regulated army." [25] And in the case of natural science it is on *this* order that any ultimately fruitful method will need to be based, since this is the actual order of *natura naturans,* and thus the natural order in the mind.[26] Yet the received scientific method—with a few important exceptions—was ignoring it altogether. Coleridge held that the latter was in fact no method at all, but a typically Linnaean, or encyclopedic, classification of disjointed fragments of *natura naturata.* The result was, not the reality of nature, but an arrangement projected upon the phaenomena by memory and fancy. Whereas a genuine method must stem from the participating apprehension of related ideas, and thus of that timeless articulation of ultimate reality, out of which *natura naturans* emerges to become ("quenched" now "in the product" *) the static multeity of *natura naturata.* It is at this stage that method reveals itself as resulting from "the due mean or balance between our passive impressions and the mind's own reaction on the same." [27] And we may think of that mean indifferently as "organisation" in nature or as "imagination" in man.

For there is no getting away from the fact that in Coleridge's system we cannot, in the long view, divide the one from the other, though we can distinguish them sharply enough. Nature is all that is objective, but the relation between mind and nature remains an inseverable polarity. Thus the emergence of ideas from the dimness of instinct, which we have already considered; the fact that the idea then "commences the process of its own transmutation . . . and . . . finishes the process as the understanding";[28] the fact that "organisation ceasing, mechanism commences"; the fact that "an idea conceived as subsisting in an object becomes a law" [29]—none of these are to be taken as exclusively psychological events or processes.

---

* Chapter 2, p. 24, above.

The most carefully considered formulation of the relations between *idea* and *law* is probably the one that will be found near the beginning of *Church and State*:

> That which, contemplated objectively (that is, as existing externally to the mind), we call a law; the same contemplated subjectively (that is, as existing in a subject or mind), is an idea. Hence Plato often names ideas laws; and Lord Bacon, the British Plato, describes the laws of the material universe as the ideas in nature. *Quod in natura naturata lex, in natura naturante idea dicitur.*[30]

True, there are other ideas besides those that coincide with the laws of nature. In the *Treatise on Method* Coleridge distinguishes Metaphysical Ideas, which "relate to the essence of things as possible," and which "continue always to exist in and for the Mind alone," from Physical Ideas, or "those which we mean to express, when we speak of the *nature* of a thing actually existing and cognizable by our faculties, whether the thing be material or immaterial, bodily or mental."[31] The Essays are closely reasoned and require to be studied at first hand. Here it may suffice to say that, for the relation between ideas and laws, it is physical ideas that are significant. From that point of view metaphysical ideas are mainly of importance because reflection on them— for example on the idea of a perfect circle in geometry—or upon a law of thought, such as the principle of contradiction—may develop our capacity for that "inward beholding" which is our only access to the ideas of reason, whether metaphysical or physical. They can help us to overcome

> the difficulty of combining the notion of an organ of sense, or a new sense, with the notion of the appropriate and peculiar objects of that sense . . . the organs of spiritual apprehension having objects consubstantial with Themselves (ὁμοουσία), or being themselves their own objects, that is, self contemplative[32]

and thus to preserve the all-important distinction between a genuine law of nature and a mere hypothesis evolved by fancy for the purpose of saving the appearances.[33]

We may now conveniently complete the quotation from the address on the *Prometheus of Aeschylus,* with which this chapter opened:

the groundwork of the Aeschylean *mythus* is laid in the definition of idea and law, as correlatives that mutually interpret each the other,—an idea, with the adequate power of realizing itself being a law, and a law considered abstractedly from, or in the absence of, the power of manifesting itself in its appropriate product being an idea.[34]

Fortunately however we are not limited to pondering definitions; for in Essays VIII and IX of the *Friend,* Section 2, Coleridge has taken up and expanded these definitions in a careful study of the relation between Plato and Bacon. And these two Essays are important for two more reasons: because they survey the relation between law and idea in the light, as Coleridge observes, of the General History of the Human Mind,[35] and because, in doing so, they solve, or should solve, the difficulty which many have found in perceiving the actual relation— the difference as well as the resemblance—between Plato's doctrine of ideas and Coleridge's.

There is yet a fourth reason why these two Essays should be studied. They suggest that a substantial revision, or at all events readjustment, is called for of the popular image of Bacon's place in the history of science. His view of what constitutes induction is indeed adversely criticised (on the basis, incidentally, of a misunderstanding of which Coleridge makes short work); but he is still, for most, an admired leader of a merciful escape from the leading-strings of Plato, Aristotle and the Middle Ages. To describe him as "the British Plato" is in fact pretty startling in view of his own loudly proclaimed contempt for all three. Coleridge was well aware of this, and the Essays are a carefully documented response to the obvious challenge his judgment invokes. In the first of them (VIII) he briefly reviews the current misunderstanding of what Bacon in fact endeavoured to assert concerning the relation between nature and mind and considers the extent to which Bacon himself was responsible for it, stressing heavily in this regard the latter's brutal rejection of his predecessors. It is this unthinking, and unjustified, rejection, he says, which has been hailed with joy as a great step forward in the growth of science, not the actual teaching, which is in fact very closely allied to Plato's. There *was,* at this point, a step forward in "the education of the mind of the *race*," [36] as he will show in Essay IX, but it was a different and far subtler one than is commonly assumed. But there is also another, a semantic, reason why Bacon is misunderstood; and Coleridge concedes, towards the end of Essay VIII, that

> it will be no easy task to reconcile many passages in the *De Augmentis* and the *Redargutio Philosophiarum* with the author's own fundamental principles, as established in his *Novum Organum;* if we attach to the words the meaning which they *may* bear, or even, in some instances, the meaning which might appear to us, in the present age, more obvious . . .[37]

We shall not reproduce the arguments and supporting quotations from the *Novum Organum,* of which Essay IX consists. Its two principal contentions are, firstly, that the "lux intellectus" or "lumen siccum," on which Bacon lays repeated emphasis, is not, as had been generally supposed, the shallow clarity of understanding, but is identical with Plato's *nous* or Coleridge's reason; while the famous "idols," on whose correction he was so insistent, are precisely "the limits, the passions, the prejudices, the peculiar habits of the human understanding, natural or acquired . . . the arrogance, which leads man to take the forms and mechanism of his own mere reflective faculty, as the measure and nature of Deity." [38] Bacon's real point is that

> our understanding not only reflects the objects *subjectively,* that is, substitutes for the inherent laws and properties of the objects the relations which the objects bear to its own particular constitution; but that in all its conscious presentations and reflexes, *it is itself only a phaenomenon of the inner sense* [reason], and requires the same corrections as the appearances transmitted by the outward senses [italics not in original].

The second, and more particular, contention he summarises in the following passages:

> Thus the difference, or rather distinction between Plato and Lord Bacon is simply this; that philosophy being necessarily bi-polar, Plato treats principally of the truth, as it manifests itself at the *ideal* pole, as the science of intellect (i.e. *de mundo intelligibili*), while Bacon confines himself, for the most part, to the same truth, as it is manifested at the other, or material pole, as the science of nature (i.e. *de mundo sensibili*).

Plato's *main* concern therefore was with metaphysical ideas—"those objective truths that exist in and for the intellect alone," whereas Bacon's was with those which

> have their signatures in nature, and which (as he himself plainly and often asserts) may indeed be revealed to us *through* and *with*, but never *by* the senses or the faculty of sense.

And hence, Coleridge concludes,

> it will not surprise us, that Plato often calls ideas LIVING LAWS, in which the mind has its own true being and permanence; or that Bacon, vice versa, names the laws of nature *ideas;* and represents . . . *facts of science* and *central phaenomena,* as signatures, impressions and symbols of ideas.[39]

Plato's gaze was turned in one direction, Bacon's in the other; but both were agreed, and it is "often expressed, and everywhere supposed" by Bacon, not only

> that there is potentially, if not actually, in every rational being, a somewhat, call it what you will, the pure reason, the spirit, lumen siccum, intellectual intuition etc. etc.

but also

> that in this are to be found the indispensable conditions of all science, and scientific research, whether meditative, contemplative, or experimental.[40]

It was the shift of emphasis, the change of direction of the gaze, that constituted an actual "step" in the general history of the mind, not (as has been very widely assumed) the adoption of a new scientific *method;* most certainly not so, if that method is taken to be a wilful limitation of science to the mere understanding and the senses.[41]

It is, then, in connection with these two Essays on Method, and his remarks on method elsewhere, that the difference between Coleridge's doctrine of ideas and Plato's can be best discerned. Here too it is a difference of emphasis or direction rather than of substance. Plato's *nous,* we may say, is Coleridge's reason; for both of them, the hierarchy of ideas which constitutes that *nous* or reason is the articulation of ultimate reality and for both of them these ideas are also the powers that produce and sustain the natural world.[42] But Plato never spoke of an "initiative idea"; he never equated an idea with the *act* of reason individualised, and thus with an individual human thinker.[43] All that Coleridge has to say of the relation between reason and *will*[44] is foreign to him. There is really no word in Greek that corresponds to what we mean by will, and none to what we mean by "subject." That polarity between subject and object, which is at the base of Coleridge's system, is nowhere to be found in Plato. It is only in Coleridge therefore that we find such a concept as that of an "initiative idea,"[45] on which method depends. Plato's method was his dialectic. It is only for Coleridge that the articulation of ideas can be itself at the same time method; that it is indeed the only reliable method, since we cannot in the last resort divide the objective ordering of nature from its ordering in and by human reason; since "the mind of man in its own primary and constituent forms represents the laws of nature."[46]

That which functions in nature as the principle of "productive unity," is necessarily at the same time functioning in nature's ideal pole, spirit, as that principle of "unity with progression," which is the principle of method.[47] It is always so functioning potentially and is felt, when it first begins to be felt, as instinct.[48] What we call "discovery" is the raising of it from potential to actual by becoming fully conscious of it; and that is the proper, the *methodical,* function of the understanding. ". . . every idea is living, productive, partaketh of infinity, and (as Bacon has sublimely observed) containeth an endless power of semination."[49] "From the first, or initiative Idea, as from a seed, successive Ideas germinate."[50] We are entitled to designate Coleridge's system "organicism" only if, in doing so, we are aware that "semination" and "germinate" here are not mere *metaphors*—unless, of course, by the word *metaphor* we merely allude loosely to the fact that all words referring to the ideal pole of reality have, or at one time had, reference also to the phenomenal pole.[51] Coleridge's organicism is definitely not "a metaphor of mind" in the ordinary sense of the word; it is not "an implicit assertion that all the universe is like some one element in that universe." *

"Hypotheses non fingo." Newton refused to seek "behind" the law of gravitation for causes or explanations acceptable to a human understanding boggling at the impossible contradiction of "action at a dis-

---

* See Chapter 5, p. 59, and note 3, above.

tance." He left that to inferior scientists;[52] and the law of gravitation is one of Coleridge's favourite illustrations of a "law of nature," as distinct from theory or hypothesis. Law differs from hypothesis, as idea differs from abstraction; just as an idea is not a notion "of" or "about" something other than itself, so a true law of nature is not a rule generalized from particular observations of natural behaviour; it is nature behaving. An idea is neither an abstraction nor a thing, but a physical idea *is* at the same time a law of nature. We must still therefore distinguish the idea or law itself from any uncontemplative notion of it. It is the *notion* of a law of gravity which degenerates into fancied invisible string.[53] The very law itself is also the power.[54] Science went astray in its dealings with both matter and space when, instead of accepting gravitation as at once a law of nature and an idea of reason, it began to devise hypotheses which would render it acceptable to the understanding. Where Newton was content to think of, and to quantify, the link that holds the earth to the sun as a vector, the lesser fry in an age of the understanding and the senses must fancy their piece of invisible string or something like it. They could never accept, because they could never understand, that the ultimate explanation of phenomena cannot itself be phenomenal.[55] In the *Treatise on Method* Coleridge put it as follows:

> Every Physical Theory is in some measure imperfect, because it is of necessity progressive; and because we can never be sure that we have exhausted the terms or that some new discovery may not affect the whole scheme of its relations . . . the doctrines of vortices, of an universal ether, of a two-fold magnetic fluid, etc., are *Theories* of Gravitation: but the Science of Astronomy is founded on the *Law* of Gravitation, and remains unaffected by the rise and fall of the Theories.[56]

The true object of science is "that knowledge in which truth and reality are one and the same, that which in the ideas that are present to the mind recognises the laws that govern in Nature if we may not say the laws that are Nature." [57]

Of course the mental activity of forming theories and hypotheses may lead the mind to the apprehension of laws. In fact a sound theory will prove to have been an anticipation of one; it "becomes an IDEA in the moment of its coincidence with an objective law." [58] And here lies the clue to the true function, and the value, of *experiment*. There is naturally much on this subject in the Essays on Method and the *Treatise,* but it is not there alone that Coleridge has dealt with it, and in particular one of the Notebooks contains a fairly extensive treatment of the whole relation between idea, law and theory.[59] There are a good many minor difficulties, and it might be worth someone's while to investigate as fully as the records permit such topics as Coleridge's later substitution of *theorems* for metaphysical ideas,[60] his occasional, but only occasional, distinction between *theory* and *hypothesis,*[61] and his more frequent, but not invariable, distinction between *laws* and *rules.*[62] Instead of attempting anything of the sort we shall simply try to outline in our own way, and on our own responsibility, the general scheme of the relation between ideas, theories and laws which appears to result from a general survey of the many and scattered observations of Coleridge relevant thereto. It was on that relation that his methodology was founded.

For this purpose it will be necessary to begin by reverting once more to that "order of the Mental Powers," to which we have already alluded in previous chapters:

> Reason
> Imagination
> Understanding
> —————————
> Understanding
> Fancy
> Sense

It will be recalled that the scale is meaningful only if it is conceived in the mode of polarity. So conceived, it may be used, before we proceed farther, to illuminate a little the difficult issue of the peculiar relation between ideas and mind. We have used such terms as *apprehend, contemplate, participate, meditate.* Coleridge himself on one occasion, and in one particular context, went so far as to say that idea *is* mind.[63] But more often he makes the relation equivalent to a perceptual one.[64] This is in accord with the scale, since the mode of polarity involves a relation between the two extremities that is closer to identity, though it is greater in distance, than that between any two other points in the scale or process. Thus, the closer one is to reason, the closer also has one come to its octave, sense, "Reason indeed is much nearer to Sense than to Understanding; for Reason (says our great Hooker) is a direct aspect, an inward beholding, having a similar relation to the intelligible or spiritual, as Sense has to the material or phenomenal." [65] The distinction is that, in the case of reason, we are in a realm where an act may be "one with the product of the act"; we are dealing with "a subject which becomes its own object." And it is for that reason that, as previously mentioned,* reflection on metaphysical ideas is a valuable aid. For there we are *obliged* to combine "the notion of an organ of sense . . . with the notion of the appropriate and peculiar objects of that sense." Contemplating *any* idea, the mind contemplates its own energies; contemplating a metaphysical idea, "the mind *exclusively* contemplates its own energies." [66] Reason is "an organ of sense, or a new sense," † but it is an organ of *inward* sense and moreover "an organ identical with its appropriate objects." [67] Human reason, as organ, perceives or contemplates the ideas of reason which constitute it, but are nevertheless its own act. Perception of an idea is therefore self-apprehension or self-contemplation; but then so would physical sense-perception be, given full self-consciousness.[68]

Just as the understanding *without* the light of reason, or without the use of reason as an organ turned inward, is a very different matter from the understanding when properly related to reason (a difference Coleridge expressed by the line drawn between understanding and understanding), so is what is ordinarily meant by a law of nature very different from the true law, which is at the same time an idea. We may venture accordingly to parallel Coleridge's gamut with another of our own construction:

> Reason (as "the source and birthplace of ideas")
> Idea
> Law
> ———
> Law
> Theory
> Sense

We believe that, seen within such a framework, many of Coleridge's observations become more meaningful or at all events less mystifying; such observations, for example, as that "in the infancy of the human mind all our ideas are instincts";[69] or that the scientist, in forming a

---

* P. 121, above.
† P. 121, above.

theory, is instinctively labouring to extract a law, and further, that "This instinct [note: *not* the theory] is itself but the form, in which the idea, the mental correlative of the law, first announces its incipient germination in his own mind." [70] It would be well to consider also, in this framework, his many allusions to the necessary relation between deep thinking and strong feeling, into which we shall not closely enter. Attention has often been drawn to them. "Ignorance seldom *vaults* into Knowledge, but passes into it through an intermediate state of obscurity . . ." [71] "deep feeling has a tendency to combine with obscure ideas . . ." [72] We shall not well understand them, unless we are keeping in view the fact that Coleridge always has at the back of his mind the idea; that the idea is at the opposite pole to, but not detached from, sense; and that knowledge and acknowledgment of an idea "requires the whole man, the free will no less than the intellect." [73]

At the moment however we are concerned with that all-important line between law and law, which parallels the line between understanding and understanding; the difference—and of course the relation— between the law of nature, which is at the same time an idea, and the so-called law (more properly a "rule") which may be arrived at by generalising the notices of the senses.[74] Must it not have been on that very line that the real function of experiment, and with it the whole conception of scientific method, balanced and faltered in the mind of Francis Bacon? If Coleridge was convinced that the future of mankind depends on its success in grasping the former distinction, he was no less convinced that the future of science depends on its success in grasping the latter.

In the former case we endeavoured to elucidate the consequences of *failure* so to distinguish, by presenting an alternative scale, decapitated by eliminating reason.* If we tried the same experiment in the latter, we should get something like the following:

> Fancies (= hypostatized notions)
> Laws   (= rules)
> Hypotheses
> Sense

and this is in fact ("fancy paramount in physics")* what we have largely got.

---

* Chapter 8, p. 102, above.

For that reason Coleridge has not a great many examples to offer of his genuine laws of nature. On one or two occasions he placed beside the law of gravity the principle of Archimedes and Kepler's laws of the planetary motions.[75] He believed that John Hunter was on the verge of arriving at a law of life, as universal as the law of gravity,[76] and it distressed him to see this true *principle* of life (the tendency to individuation) being gratuitously supplemented by the hypostatized notion of a "fluid," just as the true principle of gravitation was being supplemented by the fancied "ether." [77] Above all, however, there was his own discovery, or re-discovery, of polarity as another law of nature no less universal than that of gravitation.* The law or idea of polarity was one he had evidently been feeling towards for a long time; the more so, because in this case the artificial split between law aspect and idea aspect cannot so successfully be maintained. In this case understanding and fancy cannot so easily have it their own way. It might indeed be said that a certain "tragic" element in the relation, in the very identity, between idea and law, which he laboured to expose in his paper on the *Prometheus of Aeschylus,* is *most* evident in the law of gravity, *least* so in the law of polarity. Much in his letters, and many unpublished notes, show that in his latest years he devoted a good deal of attention to the contrast and relation between the two. But it will be best to consider this in its bearing on the relation between what Coleridge thought and the world of modern science.

---

* See Chapter 3, above, and especially the long passage from the *Friend* quoted on pp. 38-39.

Coleridge and the Cosmology
of Science

THE relation between a physical idea and a law of nature, or rather the coincidence of the one with the other, was, as we have seen, a central feature of Coleridge's system. Laws of nature however are the special province, not of the philosopher and still less of the poet, but rather of the scientist; and we have seen that Coleridge did not hesitate to apply his principles in that province, when the occasion called for it. So much so that anyone who has decided to take Coleridge seriously will be shirking the issue if he fails to consider the relation between what he thought, on the one hand—and 'Science' on the other. When the word is half-personified in this way, as it so often not unjustifiably is, it may be taken to signify the way in which laws of nature are in fact handled by those whose business is with research or technological applications, together with the results of that handling— the broad body of theories, and particularly of theories taken as long proven, and crystallised into presuppositions, that are acted on by the scientific establishment as a whole and are accepted by the great mass of mankind (including most, though not all, scientists themselves) as matters of fact. Instances of such a matter would be: that the solidly physical structure of the earth is many millions of years old; that the sun is—or perhaps "is only"—a ball of gas, with certain electro-magnetic and other properties not yet fully ascertained, emitting light, heat and other radiations taking about eight minutes to reach the earth.

The question now is: how is the thought of Coleridge, and how are many particular observations of his, related to that whole intellectual corpus? One possible answer would be, and sometimes has been,[1] that they are simply dismissed by it—that as soon as they are brought into contact with what is actually going on in the real world of science, they explode into ingenious fantasies.

There are good grounds for regarding this answer as, to say the least of it, an over-simplification. The relation of Coleridge's dynamic philosophy to science may conveniently be considered under two separate aspects. There is, as we have just seen, a logical relation (compatible or incompatible); but there is also a historical relation. We believe it is important to keep the one quite distinct from the other, and for that reason we shall deal with them separately, considering the logical relation first.

The natural sciences may, at least for the purpose of classification, be divided into organic and inorganic. Strangely perhaps, the *historical* relation of our "organicist" to science is to be found only in the latter division. But this turns out to be convenient for our purpose, since, in dealing in the first place with his relation to the science of *organisms,* we shall also be dealing almost exclusively with the logical relation. The very absence of any historical link or influence—the almost total gulf, between, for instance, the content of the *Theory of Life* on the one hand and natural history, or evolutionary biology, as we have it, on the other, serves to bring out the sharpness of the logical opposition between Coleridge as scientist and 'science' as above defined. If therefore we shall have looked, first, at the relation between his organicism and the contemporary science of living organisms, we shall be the less likely, when we come on to physics, to fall into the tempting error of assessing the significance of his contribution by criteria that are not really applicable to it. We shall indeed be emphasising that contribution, if only because it appears up to now to have been almost entirely overlooked, but we shall not forget that the *main* feature of Coleridge's relation to science is his critique of method (to which may be added his detection of the failure of conventional method to preserve the distinction between speculative maxims and empirically ascertained facts).

Thus, it was pointed out in Chapter 4 that what is in fact offered in the *Theory of Life* is "a full-fledged theory of evolution alternative to, and largely incompatible with" the received theory. The incompatibilities hardly need stressing. But before we dismiss it on that ground we must reflect that the central premise on which *his* interpretation of *any* particular fact of observation is based is different from the received premise. "In order to *comprehend* and *explain* the forms of things, we must imagine a state *antecedent* to form." But all form is engendered "organically"; it is only as "organisation ceases" that "mechanism commences." This is directly counter to the premise on which the teachings of, for example, nineteenth and twentieth century geology and palaeontology are based; for it presupposes that what is accepted as true of the secondary formations (organic origin) is in fact true of the earth as a whole; and this in turn necessarily presumes "the original fluidity of the planet." [2] That is really enough to be going on with; it is enough to show that there is not much point in selecting pronouncements from the *Theory of Life,* placing them beside modern developments in the study of natural history or evolution, and then either ridiculing Coleridge for the discrepancy or patting him on the back if he has once or twice let fall something that seems to fit in.[3]

The conclusion is at first sight obvious: current theory, at least in its general outline, is by now so incontrovertibly established that there is no point in taking this aspect of Coleridge seriously—except for noticing that, for some curious reason, it enabled him to evolve a rather profound theory of poetry. There remains however the question whether such a conclusion would be correct; and it is a question that cannot be examined without unearthing certain strata in the history of science, and of Western thought in general, which are usually left undisturbed. We have spent some time in examining Coleridge's premises, and his justification of them. What, by contrast, are the premises on which the conflicting, and incontrovertibly established, theories are based?

We will start the enquiry from a position which no-one is likely to dispute, and which Coleridge himself stated in the following terms: "It is of the highest importance in all departments of knowledge to keep the Speculative distinct from the Empirical. As long as they run parallel, they are of the greatest service to each other: they never meet but to cut and cross." [4]

That being accepted, Coleridge's case is that, at the foundations of conventional science, the speculative and the empirical have in fact intersected; they have *not* been kept distinct; and that that is one of the principal reasons why an alternative method is called for. There are two glaring instances, the first of which had already taken place long before he began to think and write, while the second, which flowed from it, was beginning in his time and has developed since his death. The first is of course the presumption, on which all conventional science is based (with the possible exception of a certain trend in advanced physics), and that is the absolute dichotomy between mind and

matter, or subjective and objective, or the observer and the phenomenon observed, or however it is put—in a word, the "outness" that was
the subject of Chapter 5. Coleridge's position is quite clear. It is that
this is itself a speculative and not an empirical principle. It is a maxim
of interpretation, not a truth of fact. It is an extremely useful (in the
strict sense, *use*-ful) "fiction of science," which Descartes, "in contempt
of common sense" propounded as a truth of fact.[5] This, as we have
shown, he claims to have demonstrated.

The second instance of a "meeting, cutting and crossing" of the
speculative and the empirical has affected mainly the more restricted
scientific field of natural history—geology, palaeontology, biology. It
had not crystallised during Coleridge's life, though James Hutton's[6]
Theory of the Earth with Proofs and Illustrations was published in
1795. It is the maxim of interpretation which was formerly known as
"uniformitarianism"—namely, the doctrine of the continuity of natural
causes, or the maxim that the past is only to be interpreted by what
can be seen to be the present order of nature. In this case, the fusion
between speculative and empirical took longer to accomplish, as the
very word *uniformitarianism* suggests. It was current during the
second half of the nineteenth century, when the alternative option of
"catastrophism" had not yet disappeared from sight. Sir Charles Lyell
was perhaps the last who found it necessary to *affirm* the dogma "that
no causes whatever have, from the earliest time to which we can look
back, to the present, ever acted, but those now acting, and that they
never acted with different degrees of energy from which they now
act." [7] Since his time it has crept into, and become part of, the general
body and structure of 'science.'

This second maxim is of course corollary to the first and the "causes
now acting" (which are to be presumed therefore to have been acting
from the earliest time) have nothing in common with Coleridge's
"powers" and antecedent unities. They are the fundamentally mechanical causes recognised by post-Cartesian scientific method. But what is
important for deciding whether or not to reject out of hand Coleridge's
views on method and all the hints and suggestions he based on it, is
to realise that both maxims *are* speculative. No doubt most of us tend
to assume, if we entertain the question at all, that, even if they must
be technically classified as theoretical, they are theories that have become firmly established by a steadily accumulating pile of corrobora-
tive observations. That however is not the case. They cannot even

claim the status of scientific *theories* at all; for that would require them to be, if not verifiable, at least falsifiable by experiment or predicted observation; which is ruled out, where it is not the present or future but the past that is being notionally constructed. They are thus not theories but selected maxims of interpretation.

Now Coleridge denied them both. He said they were both errors; and he was well aware that, in saying so, he was joining battle not simply with error but with error inveterate and entrenched.[8] It may be that John Stuart Mill had a dim inkling of this, when he affirmed in 1840, in his essay on Coleridge: "the class of thinkers has scarcely yet arisen by whom he is to be judged." It is for the most part useless to take seriatim the numerous hints and suggestions to be found in his writings on such subjects as geology, biology, physiology, chemistry, and contrast them with the pronouncements of contemporary science on the same subjects. The minor collisions are subsumed under the major collision between his cosmology and the cosmology of science. The facts are the same, but even the immediate interpretations are different, because the maxims are different on which all interpretation is based. Of course discoveries have been made, and palpable errors of fact refuted, since his day; but broadly speaking the record of the rocks, for example, was the same for Coleridge as it is for a modern geologist. Only it is a record that will play a different tune according to the needle of interpretation that is inserted in the observer's mind.

The major collision is perhaps most succinctly delineated by pointing out that, if Coleridge is right, then for cognition (however the case may be for immediately technological purposes) physical process cannot be isolated from mental process, nor natural science from human and ethical psychology. The contrary assumption is of course implicit today in every observation, every choice of experiment, every laboratory, every scientific textbook on which the young are reared. If, because of that, we are not prepared even for a moment to think it possible that that contrary assumption may nevertheless be mistaken,[9] we can have no use for the detail in the *Theory of Life,* or other and similar material to be found in Coleridge's prose. If we are, we may think twice before we dismiss as merely amusing such a passage as the following from a MS note in the British Museum:

1. In the plant each part is capable of passing by metamorphosis, progressive and retrogressive, into every other—while yet each remaining bears

or supports the higher, the root bearing the stem, the stem the leaves, all the calyx and flower. In the insect each antecedent form makes way for the higher—and perishes in giving it birth; the Egg is sacrificed that the Larva may appear, and the Imago, or mature Insect, takes the place of the Larva.

2. The Plant is the nuptial Garland of Earth and Air—their equation of Carbon, Oxygen and Hydrogen. Or as Carbon as the negative factor of Life is common to all the realms of organic Nature, we may better call the Vegetable Tribe the equation of Oxygen and Hydrogen—not the neutralization, which is water, and therefore the product of quantitative combination: but the *potentization,* or endlessly varied proportions eliciting the inner spirit of the two Gases by communication of qualities.— Now as in powers the three great Co-efficients of Nature are Gravity and Light with Warmth, as the Indifference, so in bodies, which necessarily contain, each body all three, yet under the predominance of some one, Carbon most represents Gravity, Oxygen Light, and Hydrogen Warmth.

3. Accordingly, in the Flower, the Crown of mature vegetation, we have the qualitative product of Oxygen = Light in the outness and splendour of Colours, the qualitative product of Hydrogen = Warmth in the inwardness and sweetness of Fragrance. All offering that is truly sacrificial, i.e. hallowing, sanctifying, proceeds from and is preceded by and the act of a *Yearning,* desiderium, πόθος [pothos], στοργή [storgē]—what will not the Mother sacrifice when her bowels are yearning for her children . . .[10]

It may be that we have somewhat overstated the case against Coleridge as a possible contributor to the contemporary science of organisms. It may be that, even without abandoning the cherished "dis-animation of nature," there are some lines of interpretation and enquiry which could be pursued with advantage by it—for instance, his confident contention that the true relation between vegetable and animal is one, not of analogy but of contrast or counterpoint; that the relation of the two kingdoms to each other is not that of linear progression but of corresponding opposites; and that, consequently, "the resemblances would be as the proximity, greatest in the first and rudimental products of vegetable and animal organization" . . . (The nearer the common source, the greater the likeness) . . . "Whereas, according to the received notion, the highest and most perfect vegetable, and the lowest and rudest animal forms, ought to have seemed the links of the two systems, which is contrary to fact." [11] We suggest this because, in the inorganic realm, as we shall be seeing in a moment, the idea of polarity has not proved wholly indigestible nor wholly fruitless.

But that is a minor issue. The real issue is, quite simply, whether Coleridge's argument, which we endeavoured to summarise in Chapter 5, ought to be accepted or not; whether he was right or wrong in all he had to say about "outness." This book is about Coleridge; but of course he is not the only thinker whose just valuation depends on the answer to that question. The contributions to knowledge of the *Natur-philosophen,* his contemporaries—Hegel, Schelling, Jacobi, Steffens, Oken, Blumenbach and others—would also have to be pulled from under the carpet and looked at again. Above all, Goethe's scientific writings (to which Goethe himself attached greater importance than he did to his poetry—and he was, after all, not altogether a fool) would cease to enjoy the comfortable oblivion to which they have been con-signed.[12] Nor is it only Germans, nor only Coleridge's contemporaries, who would call for drastic reappraisal; whose works have sunk almost without a trace, following a collision with one or other of the two maxims or with theory originally based on them and later embalmed as fact.[13]

Putting it succinctly, uniformitarianism presupposes the fixed "out-ness" of phenomena. If outness goes overboard—if, however deeply it may be a law of our unthinking nature, it is untenable as a conclusion of our judgment*—then the whole Laplace-Lyell-Darwin, closed-sys-tem universe (together with its fancied billions of earth-years and millions of "light-years") can go overboard with it; for a system is *not* part of our unthinking nature, but a series of logical conclusions dependent on each other. It is astonishing how many of those who in the last hundred and fifty years have been called idealist philosophers have declined to draw this simple inference.

The story of the relation between what Coleridge thought and what 'science' thinks alters in a striking way when we turn from the organic to the inorganic, from biology and the historical sciences to chemistry and physics. Here its relevance no longer depends on a man's willing-ness to entertain a position "directly the reverse of all I had ever been accustomed to consider as truth." [14] Or in other words there is, as we have already said, an historical relation in addition to the logical

---

* Chapter 5, p. 65, above.

one. This appears up to now to have been very little realised. Professor Jackson Bate, for instance, remarks (1968) that, when Coleridge defined a *thing* as a *synthesis of opposing energies,* he was "clairvoyantly anticipating a central premise of modern science." [15] But that really will not do at all. Clairvoyance does not enter into it. The mind of Coleridge was present in the whole intellectual ferment that eventually brought about the transition from classical to modern physics. He was, to say the least, not only aware of it but in it.

Toward the end of Chapter 3* we quoted at length the passage from the *Friend* in which he contrasts the history of magnetism with the history of electricity and predicts important results from a methodical rapprochement between the two. This was almost certainly written between 1812 and 1818, and probably towards the end of that period.[16] In 1819–20 H. C. Oersted (with whose work Coleridge was acquainted), by observing a hitherto unnoticed relation between the two, discovered the electro-magnetic field. But we must look farther back. Coleridge's relation to Sir Humphry Davy has already been referred to, and Davy was the portal through which Michael Faraday entered the arena, and with whom he remained in close contact throughout his formative years. We do not know if Coleridge ever met Faraday, though he was acquainted with his work; and we can only speculate on the precise nature of the intellectual exchange that went on, in the first place between Coleridge and Davy and in the second between Davy and Faraday, who, with Clerk Maxwell, was a key figure in the transition from mechanical theory to field theory, and from a physics of matter to a physics of energy. But the question that awaits determination, and which may perhaps be determined some day if further material becomes available, is not whether Coleridge's probing concern with the idea of forces in polarity was influential in the transition, but how far it was initiative.[17] A full semantic history of the *words* "pole" and "polarity" in the eighteenth and nineteenth centuries, if it could ever be written, would probably be of assistance here. Magnetism, as long as it remained alone, could be dealt with in terms of attraction and repulsion (which can still be conceived mechanically), but upon its fusion with electricity a new verbal-psychological matrix became indispensable; and that matrix appears to have been polarity, as the term is

---

* Pp. 38–39, above.

used, or the notion conceived and half-imagined, in the current science of electricity and magnetism, and, through that, of physics.[18]

That is probably as far at present as speculation on Coleridge's historical relation to modern science can be carried. And when it has all been said, it remains that the polarity that is indispensable to field and atomic theory, and in electronics, is of course not taken by that theory to be the universal law, applicable to "every power in nature and in spirit," which Coleridge himself intended by the term. It is perhaps nearer to it than anything that had gone before; but the most we can really say is that, upon observing the relation between electricity and magnetism, physical enquiry was pitchforked into a sort of notion of polarity that is limited and askew from Coleridge's universal law— but not unconnected with it—somewhat as the magnetic poles of the earth itself are askew from its geographical poles—but not unconnected with them.[19]

Nevertheless the resulting developments, including the "discovery" * that in certain experiments the act of observing is part of the object observed—which are sometimes together referred to as "the crisis" in modern physics—must be especially interesting to anyone who takes Coleridge at all seriously. For the question these developments have raised is surely this: can a "field" physics, a physics of energies, achieve any further radical advance without facing and determining precisely the issue on which Coleridge's logical relation to science as a whole depends? Can an interpretation of nature, in which some notion of polarity is basic, continue retaining the presupposition of "outness"— and confining itself to the methodology, which that presupposition prescribes? Or is there something in the idea of polarity that is repugnant to the presupposition itself? We have shown that the realisation of that idea was, in Coleridge's view, impossible without praying in aid imagination, and have added—since this appears to follow from the whole of his thought—that it is itself the basic act of imagination. On the other hand we have seen that it is possible for a physical idea —and even an "initiative" one—to be exploited by the understanding without any such realisation. This has been the case with the law, or let us say with the idea, of gravitation. And it would seem that the effort has been made, not up to now without success, to reduce and

---

* Compare Chapter 10, p. 125, above.

exploit the idea of polarity after the same fashion; and with the same result, namely that it ceases to *be* an idea.[20]

The question however that may now be arising is the question whether polarity, assuming that it *is* a universal law, is not one of a rather different order. Coleridge himself distinguished on one occasion between what is *representable* and what is *comprehended* in time and space: "Whatever is representable in the forms of Time and Space, is Nature. But whatever is comprehended in Time and Space, is included in the Mechanism of Cause and Effect." [21] Are we entitled to say that, whereas both polarity and gravity are representable, only gravity is *comprehended* in them—and that, in imagining polarity, the mind is already participating in *natura naturans;* whereas imagining gravity may still leave us within *natura naturata?* Because, in a sense, it *is* *natura naturata?* [22] The difference could be stated in another way. The relation between subject and natural object—between mind or spirit and nature—is such that every law is, potentially, also an idea. Such is the case with, inter alia, the law of gravitation. But the idea of polarity, the law of "separative projection"—being a universal law of nature and of spirit—is of a different quality; inasmuch as it is at the same time the idea of the *relation* between nature and spirit, the very law that governs that relation. That is why its proper realisation demands, not just the substitution of a new theory for an old but a mental *saltus*—a definite step forward in the long, slow process of human consciousness, more comparable in abruptness with the wholesale abandonment of Aristotelianism, which took place at the threshold of technology, than with the recent transition from classical to modern physics. Any radical further advance may well depend on a similar abandonment of the whole inveterate fancy of a world external to, *because absolutely other than,* mind and a candid acceptance of the fact that natural science is self-knowledge. It can hardly be otherwise if Coleridge was right in divining that the new physical category of polarity is no longer only the way, but also an inchoate *assertion* or half-revelation of the way, in which reason itself appears in the moulds of the understanding.[23]

Let us take one more look at it. In terms of logic the principle of polarity is, quite brazenly, an excluded middle between contradictories. In terms of nature, for any mechanically determined notion of causality, it is beautiful nonsense. Yet it is there. That is its significance. It is there, as a sort of hedgehog in the garden of the "epoch of the understanding and the senses." We have already noticed in Chapter 3 how carefully even Coleridge scholarship itself has refrained from touching it.

Meanwhile the epoch is still very much with us. It continues; and with it that head-on collision between nature and the mind of man, which is alone dignified with the name of 'science,' and which Coleridge nevertheless called "a science of delusion." [24] There is much the same head-on collision between what Coleridge thought on the one hand and 'science' on the other. We have, it is true, suggested that that collision is rather less violent in the sphere of physics than elsewhere, but we have no desire to exaggerate the difference at the time of writing. Here too it is not of much use to handpick Coleridge's many particular hints and suggestions and pat him indulgently on the back for an occasional bullseye or something like it, though it may be tempting to do so. Take for example the following from a MS note:

> . . . all Power . . . either tends to draw *out* and to *distinguish;* or to draw *back* and to bring into one mass without distinction of parts. Let us call the latter the Agglomerative Power; the former the Distinctive Power: or (to avoid repeating such long-tailed words) A. and D.
>
> A. tends *inward* and *to* the centre, and is therefore *intro*-active or what is called *centripetal.*
>
> D. tends *outward* from the centre; or to the periphery (i.e. circumference). D. is therefore extroitive, or what is called *centrifugal* . . .
>
> Well then, I say that all Powers may be reduced, in the first instance, into
>
> Light & Gravity.
>
> But each of these beget two other powers. Under Gravity we place Attraction and Repulsion: and under Light the Powers of Contraction and Dilation . . .[25]

Though no doubt remote, it sounds a good deal less remote from textbook physics than the passage cited on pages 135–136 did from textbook biology. In both cases alike however, if Coleridge was not right in his central contention, then his particular speculations, hints and suggestions can be of little significance. If he *was* right, on the other hand, they are still, it is conceived, not outstandingly significant. What, in that case, does matter—and it matters much—is his whole critique of method, with its insistence that an ultimately viable one cannot be based on the absolute outness of phenomena, but on the contrary must proceed by reducing their *experienced* outness. Thus, we cannot begin to determine Coleridge's relation to science without first proceeding to the somewhat unacademic extreme of making up our minds whether or not we must agree with something he said.

Should we find that we *must* agree,[26] then the inorganic realm is at the moment the more *interesting,* because it is only there that the nature of Nature itself is on the agenda, only there that the compelled participation of man in nature, even in his would-be 'detached' activity as an observer, has become an issue, and only there accordingly that the soil shows any signs of having been loosened about the roots of the Cartesian fiction.[27] But it is not necessarily the more *important.* Man's participation in the processes of the organic realm, not as observer but as actor, and more particularly as depredator, is being made more and more obvious by the damage it is doing and the problems it is raising. We are being forced into such concepts as that of the 'biosphere,' and to begin talking about an 'environmental science.' If physics is in the van, the younger discipline of ecology may have to bear the brunt of the engagement with destiny. And if so, how important that it should start off on the right foot—that it should not be hamstrung from the outset by exclusive adherence to the very method that brought about the menace it will be seeking to avert, the method that can only "torture" nature's secrets from her, the method that has ended in confounding technology with knowledge. If polarity is in truth a universal law of nature and of spirit, and is at the same time the basic law of the relation *between* nature and spirit, then it may well need to be recognised, perhaps more than anywhere else, as the "initiative idea" of ecology.

All this is well beyond the province of a mere exponent of Coleridge, but a few concluding observations on the development of method in science may not be out of place. Coleridge records Plato and Bacon as both agreeing in the conviction that there could be "no hope of any fruitful and secure method, while forms, merely *subjective,* were presumed as the true and proper moulds of *objective* truth." [28] When Bacon advocated the abandonment of Aristotelianism, he did not advocate any such presumption. But that is exactly what the 'model' in scientific description does presume—namely, that forms, merely subjective, are the true and proper moulds of objective truth. The substitution of models for the literal descriptions in which nineteenth century physics believed itself to be engaged—and in which, outside of physics, most twentieth century science still assumes itself to be engaged—, marks, it is true, an incipient liberation from the "despotism of the eye." Yet the concept of the model is itself a product of that bastard realism, which Coleridge distinguished so carefully from "true and original realism," * and which is philosophical rather than scientific in origin; namely, the realism (or now the 'common sense') that fancifully interposes an "object as experienced" between the mind and some supposedly "actual" object or objects.[29] Physics currently employs two different languages, the one embodying the "metaphysical ideas" of pure mathematics and the other (to which it is obliged occasionally to return in order to maintain the connection with physical reality) the language of description. But the description is in terms of models and both languages are therefore subjective only. Linguistically regarded, the model is neither an idea nor a symbol; it is a simile or metaphor.[30] Method however, as Coleridge saw it, must in future involve accepting that an "object as experienced" is, in plain terms, the object itself; and that there is no other, and somehow still more objective, object lurking coyly behind it. But that in its turn must surely involve our learning—and no doubt learning very painfully—to substitute for models, or perhaps to develop out of them, something that both Coleridge and Goethe had perceived to be necessary before models were yet heard of. In many different realms Coleridge had been concerned with it throughout most of his life. But in the realm of natural science in the end it was Goethe, rather than Coleridge, who best succeeded in setting forth clearly and systematically[31] what that something is, namely, imaginations that are both subjective and objective—and wherein idea and operative law become one in human being.

---

* Chapter 5, pp. 64–65, above.

Man and God

THE preceding chapters have been predominantly concerned with what Coleridge thought about man in nature. We began with that and have allotted most of the book to it, and it is in that connection that we have sought to expound his views, not only on imagination, but also on such topics as understanding, method, reason and ideas. If however we have allotted the greater part of the book to Coleridge on man in nature, it is not because Coleridge himself regarded this as the most important of all philosophical enquiries; but rather because this is the one which, in the prevailing climate of opinion, best brings out and most sharply emphasises the divergence of his premises from the opposite ones which have produced that climate. Unless we have first fully realised how subversive his basic argument is of the most cherished assumptions in which our present civilisation and culture are rooted—the angry no less than the complacent part of it; the scepticism and alienation no less than what remains of the faith and confidence—we shall never grasp more than superficially his teaching on problems other than that of man in nature; problems which can perhaps best be classed under the two headings of man in society and man in God. In the former of these Coleridge was hardly less deeply interested than he was in the problem of man in nature; in the latter much *more* deeply.

This brings us to his theology, an aspect of his thought which has often been carefully examined in the past. Our task is to approach it, not as critical theologians, but specifically in the light of the preceding chapters. From the former point of view we shall no doubt be seriously over-simplifying. From the latter it is hoped that, though they must be insufficient to enable us to comprehend it in all its length, breadth and depth, those chapters, together with the present one, may at least assist us to avoid hopelessly *mis*understanding both the theology itself and its place in Coleridge's system and his life.

One way of characterising the idea of polarity would be to say that it encourages, if indeed it does not compel, a deeper sense than is usual of the possible meaning of the preposition *in*. That is evident for instance in the peculiar, and non-spatial, relation between whole and part which we have seen it entails. Man in nature is, for one thing, a spatial object among other spatial objects, and an organism among other organisms. We all know that well enough. But Coleridge's argument is that we are thinking and speaking ignorantly as long as we fail to realise that man in nature *is at the same time* nature in man; since "man is a nature humanized." Interpenetration is quite other than position.

It is the same with man in society, to which we shall come later; and it is the same with man in God—or rather, since here the prevailing wind of doctrine blows the other way, let us say with God in man. Among those who are prepared to use the word *God* at all, there are plenty today who can conceive of God in man, but very few to whom it means anything to speak of man in God. Yet Coleridge held that the one is correlative to the other; and that, unless we realise that, it is simply not meaningful to speak of "God" in man at all.[1]

As it is the nature of reason to be universal as well as particular, so it is the nature of God to be superindividual as well as individual. Indeed the two propositions are the same for Coleridge, who frequently implies, and in the *Prometheus* expressly affirms, that "God is reason." [2] If the nature of reason cannot be understood without imagining polarity (the process whereby one becomes two, while yet remaining one), neither can the nature of God. But another name for the principle of polarity is triunity: the two poles, with their originating unity as the relation between them.[3] The operations of the understanding are always, whether knowingly or unknowingly, based on a bare principle of identity. Coleridge's subversiveness consisted in his perpetually drawing attention to this and to the disastrous limitation it entails alike for the practice of cognition and for human consciousness as a whole. Psychologically and theologically the point he makes over and over again, now in one formulation and now in another, is that apprehension of the bare principle of identity can give us no more than the bare *fact* of personal identity. The *content* of self-consciousness on the other hand is always tri-une, or three "in" one and one "in" three, and it is only in realising tri-unity that we can be said to realise our actual selves.[4]

To show, then, as we have been endeavouring to do, that polarity is at the root of what Coleridge thought is to show that the principle of

tri-unity is at the root of it. We have already had occasion to remark*
that the difficulty for a would-be exponent is, not to combine the different aspects and applications of that thought, but rather to keep them
sufficiently separate for the purposes of orderly exegesis. It is a difficulty
to which Coleridge himself was no stranger. At all events it is with the
idea of preserving some such order that we have reserved any discussion
of his trinitarian theology to this late stage. Coleridge was a trinitarian,
and could not have been anything else, because for him tri-unity (that is,
in theological terms the doctrine of the Trinity) was the *"Idea Idearum,
the one substrative truth which is the form and involvent of all truths."* [5]
This did not prevent him from holding that the doctrine transcends the
understanding, for, as we have seen, he held that reason itself transcends
the understanding. But that in its turn did not involve that it is altogether beyond the scope of the human mind. If it transcends the understanding, it does so because reason, and with it the principle of tri-unity,
is itself the source and existential condition of the understanding. It
cannot itself therefore be "understood," but only *experienced* by the understanding as self-evident.

If we take the trouble to read Coleridge's notes on theological writers
we shall find this borne out. His comments show him following with
sympathy and interest the arguments of those of them—Sherlock and
Waterland for instance—who attempt to deal with the Trinity. But they
also show his clear conviction that all such attempts were doomed to
failure, because the understanding alone is itself doomed to failure. In
the last resort, after all the logic-chopping, the understanding is bound
to judge inexorably: '*either* one God *or* more than one (three, for instance); you can't have it both ways.' The trinity which is reason cannot
appear in the understanding except in the form of contradictories—in
this case the contradiction between tri-theism on the one hand and uni-
tarianism on the other. Contradictories cannot be reconciled, but by that
very token they can point the mind back to the source from which they
spring. They can point it back to

> the simple doctrine of the Trinity, plain and evident *simplici intuitu,* and
> rendered obscure only by diverting the mental vision by terms drawn

---

* Chapter 9, pp. 112–113, above.

from matter and multitude. In the Trinity all the Hows? may and should be answered by *Look!* [6]

In other words it is because God is reason that reason transcends the bare principle of identity. It is because the divine act is the act of "separative projection," or God's projection of his own "alterity." [7] "Reason is from God, and God is reason, *mens ipsissima.*" [8] To apprehend "productive Unity" may therefore also be to apprehend the relation between the Father God and the Son God; to speak of method as the principle of "Unity with Progression" is to say that the Son is the Word proceeding from the Father; and at the same time to say that the Father is the Son; for the unity remains throughout the progression. [9]

But reason is not only divine; it is also human. The Son, who created mankind, remains, in each individual man, the representative of humanity as a whole; and it is in that sense that man is entitled to regard himself also as "creative." "The Trinity is the Idea; the Incarnation, which implies the Fall, is the Fact." [10]

For this reason it can also be said that God and man stand to each other in the relation of polarity; [11] and it is *as* that polarity that we best adumbrate the meaning of Spirit. If it is to the understanding that man owes his separateness, as an individual soul, it is to reason as the energy within that soul that he owes its actuality. ". . . the Spirit is an Energy not a Soul." [12]

In another approach the imagination may choose to lean on geometrical imagery. Coleridge enquires, as philosopher or scientist:

What are the conditions under which a Unit having a centre in the distance can manifest its own centrality, i.e. be the centre of a system and (as, in dynamics, the power of the centre acts in every point of the area contained in the circumference), be the centre and the *copula* (*principium unitatis in unoquoque Toto*) of a System? [13]

It is the problem of the atom, or elementary particle over again—the problem, that is, of simultaneous particularity and ubiquity. If however we are in any doubt that this was also, for him, the problem of the relation between God and man, we need only turn to a pencil note in the margin of Schelling's *Philosophische Schriften,* where the problem of a containment *by,* which is also an identity *with,* reappears as the religious awe of the creature before his Creator.

Is it; yet *comprehends* it

Quere—At once to *be* the ignorant human *Heart* (dreadful Abyss!) and yet to *comprehend* it = Man + God = Θεανθρωπος [Theanthrōpos]. The mystery of the Incarnation truly μυστηρι[ον] [mystērion]. We close the lips *naturally*, when we intensely meditate inward.[14]

The problem of the one and the many was not, for him, a mere philosophical conundrum; it was the practical and moral problem of how to be a human being.

If we look once more at the "Order of the Mental Powers" referred to in Chapters 9 and 10, and recall that it can only be intelligibly construed in the mode of polarity, it is perhaps not a criminal over-simplification to say that, in Coleridge's system, the Holy Spirit is that polarity and "the spirit" its realisation in human life.

It must never be forgotten that for him nature and the human soul were not two separate entities. Not only was their creation not two consecutive processes; it was not even two simultaneous ones; it was one and the same—nature being "in" man no less than man is "in" nature. The Word continues active in the word. Thus, what he has to say about, for instance, the genetic function of the verb and the noun in human speech is intended neither as mere philosophy nor as mere psychology.[15] It must be equally relevant to natural history. But behind all that, and as it were underpinning it stands the divine Tri-unity. The *origin* of species cannot fruitfully be considered apart from the origin of *all* "distinctities" in the proceeding Word. Nor this in turn except in connection with the formula of creation propounded in the opening verse of St. John's Gospel: that the Word was in the beginning, that the Word was "with" God and that the Word was God. "Our translators, unfortunately as I think, render the clause πρὸς τὸν θέον [pros ton theon] *with* God; that would be right if the Greek were σὺν τῷ θεῷ [syn tō theō]. By the preposition πρὸς in this place, is meant the utmost possible *proximity* without confusion; likeness, without sameness."[16] Once again, he insists, it is distinction without division; it is what *we* experience, as the ground of our own human being, in the fact, and in the nature, of reason.

It is this "begetting" of the Son by the Father that enables the creation of man)(nature by the Son. πάντα δι' αὐτοῦ ἐγένετο [panta di' autou egeneto]—all things came into being through him,[17] that is through the Second Person of the Trinity, through the Word. The Father God, as the Will underlying creation or, if it is preferred, as the will aspect of reason,[18] is super-natural in a sense that the Son is not.[19] Indeed the Son is, or is potentially, one both with nature and with man:

> might not Christ be the World as revealed to human knowledge—a kind of common sensorium, the total Idea that modifies all thoughts? And might not numerical difference be an exclusive property of phenomena so that he who puts on the likeness of Christ becomes Christ? [20]

This could bring us to the question which has often been debated both during Coleridge's life and since his death: whether his system ought, or ought not, to be classified as pantheism. But it is a question into which we do not propose to enter—beyond affirming that it could, and perhaps ought, to be so classified *if* his frequent and careful distinction between Father God and Son God is sedulously ignored; though even then it is difficult to know how a pantheist could say of himself that he teaches "the real existence of a Spiritual World without a material." [21] Some years ago a certain type of humorous story was much in vogue, in which the hearer was first presented, as though it were a matter of course, with a camel of incredibility, and then it was solemnly pretended that the real point of the story lay in the question whether or not a consequential gnat could also be swallowed. It was sometimes called a "shaggy dog" story. In Coleridge's time pantheism was a very live issue for a very large number of people. But it is felt that, at this juncture in the "epoch of the understanding and the senses," the really tough morsel for most people is, firstly, to realise the idea of tri-unity *at all,* secondly to grasp that it is the underlying principle of all nature and all experience, and thirdly to accept that, that being so, it is nevertheless also a moral and theological principle. To take all this for granted and expend many pages discussing whether or no it ought to be called pantheism strikes us as out of proportion, and we have preferred to expend those pages on the business of *not* taking it for granted. That is of course not to say that the question whether Coleridge's system is pantheistic or not is of no importance. In its appropriate context it is of the utmost importance. But it is a question which cannot be adequately determined until the system itself is really comprehended; and it is mainly this preliminary step which we are endeavouring to take.[22]

Meanwhile, pantheism or not, one thing is clear, though it was rarely stated by Coleridge in so many words, since he had not acquired the modern habit of flinging the name *Christ* about with easy abandon. And that is, that the idea, or picture, of the Word as the "common sensorium" was constant at the back of his mind. It was this (and we have seen from the *Theory of Life* that "koenaesthesis," as we have learnt to call it, was for him no static and unchanging relation) that induced him to add the words "and the Evolver" as a synonym for Logos,* and this that enabled him to propound, in the *Biographia Literaria,* that primary IMAGINATION is "the prime *Agent* of all human perception"; since perception itself is an activity, but yet an activity of *l'homme général* and not of *l'homme particulier*.[23] It is as the "high-priest and representative of the Creator" that man exerts primary Imagination in the act of perceiving.[24]

There remains the issue of the identification of the Second Person of the Trinity, or God the Son, or the Logos, with the historical figure of Jesus Christ. And here it must be said that the validity of his system, as we have hitherto sought to expound it (that is, as it concerns man in nature), is not dependent on that identity, though it certainly is dependent on the Word having become "incarnate" in humanity. For it does assume that, at a certain stage of his evolution, the human being acquired, or was given, a relation to reason, and therefore to God, that differed from the relation of life as a whole in being a *direct* relation. Reason, in its aspect of will—and thus the *life* of nature, and of man with it—had given birth to understanding both in the higher animals and in man; but now, in man, reason, as *light,* is also directly *present* to the understanding.[25] It is however only when we come to man in history and man in society that the relation of this development with the events narrated in the Gospels is disclosed as an integral part of his system.

The disclosure is connected with, or perhaps even depends on the

---

* Chapter 9, note 45, above (the words 'and the Evolver' were added at a later date).

difference between *faith* and *belief,* and on the proper relation between the two, as he saw it. He frequently protested against the fatal insistence of his contemporaries on confounding the two, pointing out that, whereas belief is a matter of rational judgment based on evidence, faith is something very different. It is not another name for belief, but a possible foundation for it; and, in the case of belief in the "supernatural," the only really sound foundation. Faith does not judge the evidence, but makes the evidence available, on which belief may or may not thereafter be settled.

Unlike belief (which, if it really *is* belief is compelled), faith is an act of the will. It is "a state and disposition of the will, or rather of the whole man, the I, or finite will, self-affirmed." [26] And that state may also be called "fidelity." But fidelity to what? The brief *Essay on Faith* begins with the definition:

> Faith may be defined as fidelity to our own being—so far as such being is not and cannot become an object of the senses.

But this entails, and the definition continues:

> and hence, by clear inference or implication, to being generally, as far as the same is not the object of the senses;[27]

"So far as such being is not and cannot become an object of the senses. . ." We may recall that line 'between understanding and understanding' in the Order of the Mental Powers. Human will lurks between the two Janus heads, with which the understanding faces both inward to reason and outward to sense; and faith is its initial and innermost revolt under the despotism of the eye. We have seen that the nature of reason is such, that we cannot acknowledge our individual being without at the same time acknowledging that which transcends individuality.

> Faith . . . is fidelity—the fealty of the finite will and understanding to the reason, *the light that lighteth every man that cometh into the world,* as one with, and representative of, the absolute will, and to the ideas or truths of the pure reason.[28]

We are free however to *refrain* from acknowledging it; the understanding can reject the light of reason and, when it does so, a man is refusing fidelity to his own humanity—and may even end by denying it, as indeed he is doing all round us in this day and age. Acknowledgment of our human being and fidelity to it are matters respectively of conscience and of will, and the relation between the two lies very deep—at the foundation in fact of *human* consciousness as such. We have seen that "fidelity to our own being" entails fidelity to our thinking nature, in defiance, when necessary (and it is here that both science and theology are failing at once themselves and *our* selves), of our unthinking nature and and its laws.[29] But at the moment we are only concerned with the relation between faith and belief.

The ideas or truths of the pure reason cannot then be realised without an initial fidelity to our own being; but once they have been so realised, they become part of the evidence which belief or unbelief must take into account. And it was Coleridge's conviction, because it was his experience, that if we approach the Bible in particular—the Old Testament no less than the New—not with the understanding alone, but with an understanding irradiated by reason, certain judgmental consequences can hardly fail to follow. It is in that sense that "reason and religion are their own evidence." [30]

It is noteworthy that the *Statesman's Manual,* which deals primarily with the importance of the Bible as a study for educated men, is also one of the richest, if not the richest, source in all Coleridge's prose for his teaching on the subject of reason and understanding and on the nature of ideas. It is the source from which we ourselves have been moved to quote most frequently, when dealing with those topics in the three preceding chapters (we refer to the *Manual* itself together with its long Appendix B, which is in point of fact annexed to the sentence just quoted). The main topic of the *Manual* however, and indeed all this (man and God) side of his system, was so fully elaborated by Coleridge himself that it is hardly necessary to go into it at length. Besides the *Manual* there are the *Aids to Reflection,* the *Notes on the English Divines,* much of the *Friend* and many shorter and very carefully couched utterances such as the *Essay on Faith* and the *Formula of the Trinity,* which are relatively systematic and consecutive—provided that the reader is clear to begin with on those fundamentals, which Coleridge expounded so much less consecutively and less systematically, though in sum hardly less fully; that is, understanding, reason and ideas. Briefly, the argument of the *Statesman's Manual* is as follows:

The importance of the Old Testament as a study for educated men is twofold. It lies, first, in the fact that, provided it is approached with an understanding unshuttered from reason, it reveals itself as the book which beyond all other books is both the product of ideas and their embodiment. It is for that reason, and in that sense, that it is "revelation." [31] But it is also for that reason that it is required reading for the student of political science; since the ideas it embodies are the ideas constituent of human nature itself. And it is upon those ideas that we must look if we would penetrate to "the true *origin* of human events."

Moreover it is only such a penetration that will serve to illumine the future. Without that, the statistics and analyses, in which the 'planning' expert delights, are like those lights in the stern of a vessel that illumine only the path that has been past over.[32] Coleridge urges his educated readers:

> to apply their powers and attainments to an especial study of the Old Testament as teaching the elements of political science . . . in the same sense as the terms are employed when we refer to Euclid for the elements of the science of geometry, only with one difference arising from the diversity of the subject. With one difference only; but that how momentous! All other sciences are confined to abstractions, unless when the term science is used in an improper and flattering sense.—Thus we may speak without boast of natural history; but we have not yet attained to a science of nature. The Bible alone contains a science of realities: and therefore each of its elements is at the same time a living germ, in which the present involves the future, and in the finite the infinite exists potentially. That hidden mystery in even the minutest form of existence, which contemplated under the relations of time presents itself to the understanding retrospectively, as an infinite ascent of causes, and prospectively as an interminable progression of effects;—that which contemplated in space is beholden intuitively as a law of action and reaction, continuous and extending beyond all bound;—this same mystery freed from the *phaenomena* of time and space, and seen as the depth of real being, reveals itself to the pure reason as the actual immanence or inbeing of all in each.[33]

He offers some examples of this "science of realities," and challenges his opponents to search the works of the wisest secular historians, and then "to point out any one important truth, any one efficient practical direction or warning, which did not pre-exist (and for the most part in a sounder, more intelligible, and more comprehensive form) in the Bible." [34]

Faith then—or its product, a reason-illuminated understanding—will begin by apprehending the Bible as wisdom. But, for judgment and belief, there is also the other aspect of the Bible—as history. And here we have again to call to mind the sharp divergence between Coleridge's whole idea of evolution, together with its final stage, history, and the received nineteenth-twentieth century view. Both the Bible itself, as an historical phenomenon, and the content of the Bible as history, are to be seen, if we would see them through Coleridge's eyes, as "parts" of the whole polarity between God and man, of which evolution is the process in time. The "life" relation between part and whole applies to parts in time as well as to parts in space.

Now this relation entails, as we have seen,* that the part may be a symbol of the whole; and, for the purpose of history, that signifies that an actual event may also be a symbol; so that, in dealing with an event recorded in an historical narrative, we are not necessarily bound to choose between "taking it literally" and taking it metaphorically. It may be both; because the event itself was both. "It is among the miseries of the present age that it recognises no *medium* between literal and metaphorical." Therefore it "confounds symbols with allegories"; and indeed it must continue to do so, as long as its fails to apprehend "the stream of time continuous as life and a symbol of eternity, inasmuch as the past and the future are virtually contained in the present." [35]

This stream is presented more clearly than anywhere else in the Old Testament, where "The truths and the symbols that represent them move in conjunction and form the living chariot that bears up (for us) the throne of the Divine Humanity." [36]

In the same way the Bible itself, together with the life-history of the Hebrew nation from which it sprang, is "part" of the whole process of evolution, inasmuch as it is part of the Logos in its "light" aspect—the aspect which Coleridge also termed "the communicative intelligence in nature and in man." [37] For it will be recalled that, for Coleridge, evolution is not *only* a 'life-force.' "The productive power, which in nature acts as nature, is essentially one (that is, of one kind) with the intelligence, which is in the human mind above nature";[38] or the Word is not only the life; it is also the light of men.[39]

It is a measure of the tenacious unity underlying the whole broad extent of Coleridge's thought that the relations between the Creator and

---

* Chapter 9, note 38, above.

his human creatures, between Reason and the partakers in Reason, should prove to be most viably exponible in terms of the leading definition of "life" in the *Theory of Life: "the tendency at once to individuate and to connect, to detach, but so as either to retain or to reproduce attachment."* Either to "retain" or to "reproduce": There may be a measure of detachment of a part from its whole, with retention of the original attachment; but beyond a certain point, the totality of *natura naturans,* which is life itself, must find and establish a fresh centre in the detached "part," from which to begin, as it were, over again.[40] The *Theory of Life* attempts to display this process as it is manifested in the forms of space. But when it is the act of *consciousness* that is in question—so that the "part" that is becoming detached from its source is a separate *self*-consciousness, that is, a separate individual will (a "finite will")—the proper name for "detachment" can only be "apostasy." That is, in Christian terminology, original sin.[41] It was Coleridge's contention that pre-Christian history as a whole will reveal itself to "faith" as having marked the growth and increase of apostasy with, in its later stages, an increasing awareness of it as such. "In the assertion of original sin the Greek Mythology rose and set." [42] But the Bible reveals far more clearly that the Hebrew nation was far more clearly aware than any other of the human will's apostasy from the will of God.

Now the alternative to *retention* of attachment is its *reproduction.* But reproduction of attachment to the original source of life, following on the loss of it, is, for a created individuality, regeneration by redemption. If there is to be that fresh beginning, which the reproduction of attachment alone enables (for *final* detachment from *any* originating centre of life can only be followed by death), the totality of the original source must penetrate the detached (and therefore individual) soul and establish a fresh centre within it. There must be an "incarnation" of the divine ground of all being within the human being. "Man fell as a soul to rise as a spirit. The first Adam was a living soul; the last a life-making spirit." [43] So much is evident to faith—which is fidelity to "one's own being," where the roots of conscience and of consciousness itself are intertwined.[44] It does not follow from this alone that the central moment of redemption was the historical birth and death of Jesus Christ. But the congruence of the Gospels, and particularly the Gospel of St. John, and of the New Testament as a whole—its essential fitness as an account of such a moment—is solid ground for judging that it was so. Nor is that the only consideration. Faith will divine, in the New

Testament, "revelation" in the same sense, only in an enhanced degree, as in the Old, and in the same sense as it does in other inspired utterances of human genius; and it is this divination that will become the keystone in the arch of belief.[45]

It was thus from the same point of view as that in which he beheld the Old Testament that Coleridge also saw both the New Testament itself and the relation between the Old and the New. Since we are not aiming at completeness—which would require, if it could be achieved, a book three or four times the length of this one—we shall not extract from Coleridge's scattered observations on the subject of prophecy. They may be said to follow from his concept of revelation and are not limited to the prophetic books of the Old Testament.[46] Prophecy is however a major link, for Christians, between the Old Testament and the New and it was so for Coleridge. But neither the prophecies of the Old nor the miracles of the New were to be treated as *evidential* for belief. Miracle may, in that respect, be compared with experiment. It is only significant when it is, and is seen to be, "idea realised." [47] And then it may be very significant indeed. But without faith (as already defined) as the light by which the mind looks *through* it, it is either irrelevant or worse. Miracles are not for looking *at;* they are for seeing *with.*[48]

The New Testament is read with faith, when it is read with a full understanding of what it signifies to say that the major events it records are "symbols." And we have seen that precisely what that does *not* mean is, to say that they are not also history:

> . . . the crucifixion, resurrection, and ascension of Christ himself in the flesh, were the epiphanies, the sacramental acts and *phaenomena* of the *Deus Patiens,* the visible words of the invisible Word that was in the beginning, symbols in time and historic fact of the redemptive functions, passions, and procedures of the Lamb crucified from the foundation of the world; the incarnation, cross, and passion,—in short, the whole Life of Christ in the flesh, dwelling a man among men, being essential and substantive parts of the process, the total of which they represented; and on this account proper symbols of the acts and passions of the Christ dwelling in man, as the Spirit of truth, and for as many as in faith have received him, in Seth and Abraham no less effectually than in John and Paul! For this is the true definition of a symbol, as distinguished from the thing, on the one hand, and from a mere metaphor, or conventional exponent of a thing, on the other.[49]

For the understanding, the fancy and the senses alone either Christ was, metaphorically speaking, crucified from the foundation of the world, or Jesus was crucified on Golgotha. You cannot have it both ways. But for reason, and therefore for faith, you both can and do:

> Alas! how many Protestants make a mental idol of the Cross, scarcely less injurious to the true faith in the Son of God than the wooden crosses and crucifixes of the Romanists!—and this, because they have not been taught that Jesus was both the Christ and the great symbol of Christ. Strange, that we can explain spiritually, what to take up the cross of Christ, to be crucified with Christ, means; yet never ask what the Crucifixion itself signifies, but rest satisfied in the historic image. That one declaration of the Apostles, that by wilful sin we *crucify the Son of God afresh,* might have roused us to nobler thoughts.[50]

We cannot comprehend nature without first having grasped that the whole may be "in" each part, besides being composed *of* all its parts. We cannot comprehend imagination, or revelation, in literature without first having grasped that that very fact provides the distinction between a symbol and a metaphor. We cannot understand the Old Testament, for we cannot comprehend *any* significant historical record, without first having grasped the fact that particular events, or particular stretches of history, may themselves be symbols of the whole. And we cannot comprehend the New Testament, unless we have also understood that we are confronted with the paradigm of all symbol both in space and in time, when not merely *natura naturans* becomes manifest to the understanding and the senses as *natura naturata*—which was and is happening all the time and everywhere—but also the one voluntary origin of *natura naturans* itself became manifest as *natura naturata* in the body of a single human being. Or, putting it another way, we cannot comprehend Coleridge unless we have first divined how all this was what he thought and felt from the bottom of his soul.

⤐ 13 ⤏

Man in History and in Society

COLERIDGE, as we saw in Chapter 4, extended the term *life* to include all that "really *is*." But this did not mean he used it merely as a synonym for "everything." For he was also prepared to define life as "the *power* which discloses itself from within as a principle of *unity* in the *many*" and again, more briefly, as "the principle of individuation." [1] He affirmed moreover that the *form* taken by the process of individuation is "unceasing polarity." The tendency to progressive individuation by the means of polarity is thus the central idea of his cosmology, applying as it does not only to the whole of the phenomenal world, but to the noumenal also. If it is most graphically revealed in the 'organic' sector of the line of evolution; if it is in the vegetable kingdom that we first see "totality dawning into individuation," [2] with effect that the vegetable creation "becomes the record and chronicle of [nature's] ministerial acts, and enchases the vast unfolded volume of the earth with the hieroglyphics of her history," [3] nevertheless the same principle and process are at work in the prior and inorganic sector, and before that, in the pre-phenomenal forces out of which matter itself has emerged. And we have seen in the preceding chapter that the same principle and unceasing process continue to apply in the *post*-organic sector; that is to say, after the principle of individuation has reached a certain culmination in the human being; for they apply also to the inner life of man so individualised. They apply also to the individual human spirit.

It follows, if he is right, that in the long run neither evolution nor history will ever be fruitfully discerned unless they are contemplated as substantially one and the same process.

> My system, if I may venture to give it so fine a name, is the only attempt I know ever made to reduce all knowledges into harmony. It opposes no other system, but shows what was true in each; and how that which was

true in the particular, in each of them became error, *because* it was only half the truth . . . I wish, in short, to connect by a moral *copula* natural history with political history; or, in other words, to make history scientific, and science historical—to take from history its accidentality, and from science its fatalism.[4]

The late R. G. Collingwood, who based his philosophy of history on the proposition that "all real history is history of thought," sought to establish this proposition by making an absolute distinction between man and nature. Human actions, he said, have an "inside," and that inside is thought. They are totally different from natural events, because "nature has no inside." And on that maxim he based his main contention that history is no part of science, but a different discipline altogether.[5] Coleridge made it his principal business to demonstrate that nature, and indeed matter itself, *has* an "inside." Thus, while Collingwood and some other recent historicists have felt the need for liberating history from the bondage of science, Coleridge, on the contrary, aimed at making "history scientific."

But he did not mean by this: treating history as a 'science,' in the way the nineteenth century was already beginning to advocate. He did not mean the application to history of a method founded on an initial presumption of the fixed "outness" of the phenomenal world. We have seen enough of what both science and method meant to him to make it hardly necessary to point this out. His very concept of "method" rules out that inveterate presumption from the proper study of either nature *or* history. For method demands of us a prior realisation, first, that natural phenomena have an inside that is not itself phenomenal and, secondly, that that "inside" is, not any apparatus of objectively occult qualities or forces, but the human self in polar counterpoint to the natural world.

The principle of individuation, ascending the ladder of increasing consciousness, eventuates in that counterpoint, but does not stop there. Or rather it *should* not stop there. For it has merely provided the necessary platform for continuing internally the same unceasing process of polarity. The human self does not cease to be modifiable because it is focussed in the least modifiable of natural organisms. On the contrary:

Internal or mental energy and external or corporeal modifiability are in inverse proportions. In man, internal energy is greater than in any other animal; and you will see that he is less changed by climate than any animal. For the highest and lowest specimens of man are not one half as much apart from each other as the different kinds even of dogs, animals of great internal energy themselves.[6]

But it follows from the very nature of selfhood that, from that point on, the modification will depend increasingly on the self's own activity, directed by its own choice.

—whatever of good and intellectual our nature worketh in us, it is our appointed task to render gradually our own work.[7]

And it is a sound guiding principle, no less for the study of history than for the study of nature, that

all things that surround us, and all things that happen unto us, have (each doubtless its own providential purpose, but) all one common final cause: namely, the increase of consciousness in such wise that whatever part of the *terra incognita* of our nature the increased consciousness discovers, our will may conquer and bring into subjection to itself under the sovereignty of reason.[7]

Until it is brought under that sovereignty, nature is the *terra incognita* of human nature; except where it is being perceived, it is our unconscious.

The human self in fact "can have no notion of desirable Progression (i.e. desirable for the Progressor, as well as for all others) but what supposes a growth of consciousness . . ."[8] But what is meant by self, or selfhood, in such contexts? Not, clearly, the self that is identified with the individual understanding. It is the selfhood, not of *l'homme particulier,* but of *l'homme général*—that "I representative," out of which it was claimed that Shakespeare evolved his individual characters. But then—as the allusion to the Shakespeare lectures[9] may have served to remind us—it is just this universal self of humanity that is also, in each individual, his most individual self. As reason is reason, so man is man, by being universal and particular in one and the same moment. Man is "that class of Being . . . in which the Individual is capable of being itself contemplated as a Species of itself";[10] and if we want a true universal for him, we must think, not of a single species of the genus *animal,* but of a genus *anthropos,* in which "each Soul is a Species in itself."[11]

We have already, in the previous chapter, tried to look at this relation of identity between individual human being and Being, in its teleological aspect. From that point of view it is something to which, looking ahead as far as we can, we may hope to approach nearer but hardly to attain. For this is "that incommunicable attribute of self-comprehension, to which all creatures make approaches such as the Geometricians figure to us in the demonstration of the Asymptote." [12] But (and this is the basis of Coleridge's whole mental picture both of evolution and of history) there is, besides this Omega aspect, the Alpha one in which we must contemplate selfhood as potential. It is, once more, the difference between an original "totality" and the final "unity," which is a unity in multeity. [13] The "Order of the Mental Powers" displayed between the extremes of sense and reason, has thus an evolutionary as well as a psychological and epistemological significance, as is indeed apparent from the *Theory of Life*: the transformation of sense and fancy, through instinctive intelligence, into understanding, and of understanding itself into the light of reason, is also an historical ascent.

It is fairly clear that, for Coleridge, as for Collingwood, all real history was history of thought. At least this was so as far as his main interest was concerned. "I have read," he remarked towards the end of his life, "all the famous histories, and, I believe, some history of every country and nation that is, or ever existed; but I never did so for the story itself as a story. The only thing interesting to me was the principles to be evolved from, and illustrated by, the facts." [14] The story he was interested in was the whole story of the development of the human mind. Most of the historical matter that occurs in the *Friend* and in his other prose writings glances, directly or obliquely, in that direction; but the nearest approach he made to telling the whole story consecutively is to be found in the *Philosophical Lectures*. Or rather let us say the later chapters of the whole story. The avowed object of this course was to "consider Philosophy historically, as an essential part of the history of man, and as if it were the striving of a single mind . . ." [15] or, as he put it when referring to the lectures later, "as the gradual Evolution of the Mind of the World, contemplated as a single Mind in the different stages of its development." [16]

This evolution, like the biological evolution that preceded and by imperceptible gradations led into it, was in the direction of increasing self-consciousness; and it was in that light that he saw the diverse contributions of different past cultures and civilisations, notably those of the Hebrews, the Greeks and the Romans.[17] The essay on the *Prometheus of Aeschylus* should be consulted here, along with the *Philosophical Lectures,* but it is characteristic of the whole corpus of Coleridge's published prose and literary remains that, rather than having a large canvas provided for our survey, we ourselves must first paint the picture on the back of our minds, in order then to keep coming upon it focussed in some tiny detail—such, for example, as the want of adverbs in the *Iliad*:

> The want of adverbs in the Iliad is very characteristic. With more adverbs there would have been some subjectivity, or subjectivity would have made them.
>   The Greeks were just then on the verge of the bursting forth of individuality.[18]

In order to contemplate, with Coleridge, "the mind of the world as a single mind," we must first have received, at least hypothetically, the philosophy and the psychology that informed his contemplation. We must, in particular, have raised in our own minds the iron curtain of presupposition and fancy that sunders mind from nature, since it is the same iron curtain that sunders mind from mind.[19]

The process of evolution from totality to unity is one single process, which in its later stage is properly called history. But before proceeding to the brief observations we shall allow ourselves on Coleridge's treatment of history, a word must be said on the transitional phase—perhaps best thought of as "pre-history"—where evolution is gradually *becoming* history, or where nature is becoming humanized. This intermediate phase between unconscious (= nature) and conscious energy is one on which Coleridge never appears to have expatiated, at least not in those of his writings that are at present at all easily accessible. It is however obvious that it was a transformation rather than a succession, that we must first put out of our minds anything in the way of an abrupt and extraneous addition. There is no question, for him, of inanimate matter appearing from nowhere, "going on by itself," and eventually giving birth to mind; because there is no question of inanimate matter at all. Matter, so conceived, is not a reality, but the factitious product of our own "disanimation" of nature. But we can go a good deal further than this. From the *Theory of Life,* taken together with scattered observations on such topics as Language,[20] Instinct, Understanding in

Being . . . and hence to Being generally," we both realise the first polarity and, as conscience, experience its already straining to generate the second. It is this that is reflected in the history of mankind as a whole.

Historically therefore man becomes man through society, as well as by counterpointing nature. Philosophically contemplated, "fidelity to our own Being so far as such Being is not and cannot become an object of the senses" is reason.[26] It is reason as reason, while conscience is reason in its aspect of will; and these are the two principles that underlie Coleridge's interpretation of history, whether as a whole or in almost any particular event to which he is giving his attention. We have seen something in Chapter 12 of the importance he attached to Hebrew history. But he also saw them in indispensable relation to the history of Greece; and it was in the polarity between the two cultures that progress—that is, the evolution of the individual—above all resided; in the polarity and in the varying predominances by which polarity is characterized. Thus, in point of the man)(God relation, experience of the will aspect of reason was predominant in the Hebrew mind; experience of the reason aspect in the Greek.

> —in all that makes Greece Greece to us, we find it the great light of the world, the beating pulse, that power which was predetermined by Almighty Providence to gradually evolve all that could be evolved out of corrupt nature by its own reason; while on the opposite ground there was a nation bred up by inspiration in a childlike form, in obedience and in the exercise of the will.[27]

While, in point of the man)(nature relation, with the Hebrews it was the subjective pole, with the Greeks it was the objective that predominated. If it is systematizing rather glibly, it may nevertheless help to evoke the underlying structure of Coleridge's thinking, not only on history but on all or most matters, to say that, for him, the Hebrew culture stood to the Greek in substantially the same relation as Milton did to Shakespeare or, as we have ourselves suggested, as Coleridge himself to Wordsworth.*

The organic processes leading from plant to fruit go on whether or no the fruit will ultimately "set" and become the germ of a new plant, by receiving the totality of the organism into itself as a fresh centre—

---

* Chapter 7, pp. 90–91.

whether or no the seed, when it later becomes "detached," will therefore be able to "reproduce attachment."

> Had the Christians failed, a kind of Christianity would and must have prevailed. Compare Julian with even the Antonines—much more with Scipio or Augustus; Plotinus and Porphyry with Cicero or with Plato himself. Metaphysics ceased to be a science of speculation: it had already become an art of life, a discipline, a religion . . .[28]

Already, before the actual event, Christianity was historico-philosophically present. It was present as what Kathleen Coburn, expounding in her Introduction to the *Philosophical Lectures,* has called "the supreme example of the principle of trichotomy, the reconciliation of opposites in a new dynamic force." Or, as Coleridge himself puts it:

> —at length the two great component parts of our nature, in the unity of which all its excellency and all its hopes depend, namely that of the will in the one, as the higher and more especially God-like, and the reason in the other, as the compeer but yet second to that will, were to unite and to prepare the world for the reception of its Redeemer.[29]

It would perhaps be difficult to overstate the contrast between this picture and the picture often presented in modern theology of the Gospels themselves, and still more the "Kerygma," as the principal, if not the ultimate, source of Christianity. Coleridge held uncompromisingly that a long-prepared cosmic reception did in fact take place—and, more particularly, that it took place in Judea in the reign of Tiberius Caesar,

> just at the time when the traditions of history and the oracles of the Jews had combined with the philosophy of the Grecians, and prepared the Jews themselves for understanding their own scriptures in a more spiritual light, and the Greeks to give to their speculations, that were but the shadows of thought before, a reality, in that which alone is properly real.[29]

The point here being made is that, when Coleridge discusses, in *The Constitution of the Church and State* and elsewhere, the "Church of Christ," distinguishing it from the National and other Churches on the one hand and from "Christianity" on the other,[30] we imbibe a very gritty sediment—almost a caricature—of his meaning, unless we are prepared (at least while actually reading him) to see Christianity itself, as he did, in the whole context of the evolution and history of mankind.

As a part of life, human society at any given moment is a cross-section of its process, and can only be intelligently grasped as such. The link between the study of politics and the study of history is thus an extremely intimate one. The conduct of political affairs demands "prudence"; but prudence is blind without wisdom, and indeed it is the wisdom-content in it that makes it *really* prudence—a human quality, distinct from that adaptation of means to immediate ends by which animals maintain themselves. Just as the understanding should be aware of, and direct itself by, the reason from which it depends, so prudence should direct itself by wisdom. If the *maxims of prudence* are all of high value,

> Yet there is one among them worth all the rest, which in the fullest and primary sense of the word is, indeed, the *Maxim,* (i.e. the Maximum) of human Prudence; and of which History itself in all that makes it most worth studying, is one continued comment and exemplification. It is this: that there is a Wisdom higher than Prudence, to which Prudence stands in the same relation as the Mason and Carpenter to the genial and scientific Architect; and from the habits of thinking and feeling, that in this Wisdom had their first formation, our Nelsons and Wellingtons inherit that glorious hardihood, which completes the undertaking, ere the contemptuous calculator (who has left nothing omitted in his scheme of probabilities except the might of the human mind) has finished his pretended proof of its impossibility.[31]

Like any other process, society is ultimately governed by constitutive principles which, approached from one direction, are ideas, and, approached from the other, are laws. We have seen that it was on this basis that Coleridge recommended the study of the Old Testament as an indispensable discipline for the education of public men in the conduct of affairs.

For "moral ideas" Coleridge more often uses the term *principles.* Long before he had worked out his concept of method and of the relation between idea and law, indeed from the time of his first public utterances as a political speaker and journalist, he was already insisting that political reform must be derived from principles before expediency; and it was with a view to demonstrating this that, in one of the later numbers of the *Friend*, he re-printed without alteration an Address delivered at Bristol in 1795.[32] But we are concerned here with his developed philosophy, according to which history and politics alike are 'sciences,' in the proper sense of the word, because they are ultimately dependent on *method;* that is, on the illumination of the understanding by the mind's participating in the constitutive ideas of reason. Thus, in the eight *Essays on Method,* his main emphasis is on method in natural science, which he illustrates by his parallel between Bacon and Plato; but we find, in the two culminating essays (X and XI of Section 2), that the stress is laid neither on *physical,* nor on *metaphysical* ideas, but on that third category of *moral* ideas, which is relevant to history and politics. Essay XI for instance, which seeks to draw together the threads of the whole treatise on method, opens with a brief discourse on Trade and Literature and a statement of the polarity between the two, whereon the existence of a progressive society depends:

> As is the rank assigned to each in the theory and practice of the governing classes, and, according to its prevalence in forming the foundation of their public habits and opinions, so will be the outward and inward life of the people at large: such will the nation be. In tracing the epochs, and alternations of their relative sovereignty or subjection, consists the PHILOSOPHY of History. In the power of distinguishing and appreciating their several results consists the historic SENSE. And that under the ascendency of the mental and moral character the *commercial* relations may thrive to the utmost *desirable* point, while the reverse is ruinous to both, and sooner or later effectuates the fall or debasement of the country itself—this is the richest truth obtained for mankind by historic RESEARCH: though unhappily it is the truth, to which a rich and commercial nation listens with most reluctance and receives with least faith.[33]

As with his theology, it is not our purpose to expound Coleridge's various writings on history and on sociological and political theory, but rather to assist by focussing on the writings themselves the light of those general principles of his, in which we conceive they must be read if they are to be properly appreciated. Particular applications therefore are referred to, not with any suggestion that they will together give a complete, or even a partially adequate, picture but by way of illustration.

The full title of the short work on the Church and the State is *The Constitution of the Church and State according to the Idea of Each.* And there are three things it is important not to forget: firstly, that it is *always* the *idea,* of which Coleridge is primarily thinking when he speaks of either of them; secondly, that the idea is, for him, not less real nor less really constitutive because it happens to be imperfectly realised.[34] All ideas are, by definition, teleological as well as constitutive. But of moral ideas (in an as yet largely immoral world) it is naturally the teleological aspect that is most easily apparent: hence the current meaning of the word *ideal,* especially when used as a noun. The third thing to be remembered is, that it is *frequently* the *idea,* of which he is primarily thinking, even when he is referring to phenomena other than those of Church and State themselves. Obviously, in addition to this we must pay attention to the particular, and usually *extended* meanings he explicitly, and with caveats, attaches to many of the terms he employs. "Church" itself for example, as correlative to "State," signifies neither the established Church nor even "the Churches" in general:

> —religion may be an indispensable ally, but is not the essential constitutive end, of that national institute, which is unfortunately, at least improperly, styled the Church; a name which in its best sense is exclusively appropriate to the Church of Christ.[35]

The national Church, as he would use the expression (with history of course in mind), means approximately all those vocations to which the visible institution was formerly, in Europe, the only avenue of approach. Its personnel (whom he wished to designate "the Clerisy") would include, in addition to the Clergy, all the learned and most of the professional element in the population.[36] But in the same way the terms *trade* and *literature* are given a very wide extension, the former signifying all within the State that has for its origin, as well as for its object, "the wants of the body, real or artificial, the desires for which are for the greater part . . . excited from without"; while the latter "has for its origin, as well as for its object, the wants of the mind, the gratification of which is a natural and necessary condition of *its* growth and sanity."[37] *Trade* therefore includes industry, and *literature* includes education.

But it is still not enough simply to keep these extended meanings in mind; it is not enough to remember that, whatever else Coleridge at any time means by "Church," in these contexts, he also means "the national Clerisy" as a whole, or that whatever else he elsewhere means by "literature," he here means intellectual and spiritual activity in general. If we really want to grasp what he is talking about, we must also be seeing Church as something that bears a similar relation to State, and Literature as something that bears a similar relation to Trade, as *natura naturans* does to *natura naturata*. It is not in nature alone that *forma formans* is one with, and yet distinguishable from, *forma formata;* nor there alone that the parts of which it is comprised are to be seen, not as parts combined by an ingenious mechanic, but as dynamic forces in momentary arrest. We must also feel the "due proportion of the potential, that is, latent or dormant power to the actual power"—and that "The balance is produced by the polarization of the actual process, that is, the opposition of the actual power organized to the actual power free and permeating the organs." [38] This is so within "the State in the larger sense of the word, or the nation dynamically considered (ἐν δυνάμει κατὰ πνεῦμα [en dynamei kata pneuma],* that is, as an ideal, but not the less actual and abiding, unity)." [39]

We may well be obstructed, in doing so, by the same unavoidably ambiguous reference of the words *state* and *nation* as of the word nature. Just as the word *nature* is sometimes used to cover both the *naturans* and the *naturata* aspect, and sometimes confined to *natura naturata* alone, so the words *state* and *nation* must sometimes mean the nation "dynamically considered," and thus including the Church; while at other times it is necessary to contrast the two and to use either term in such a way as to signify the state excluding the Church.[40] Moreover, just as natural science has been characterised by its growing inability, or refusal, to conceive of nature except as = *natura naturata,* so political science has grown increasingly impotent to conceive of the State otherwise than in its secondary and narrower meaning that excludes the Church from its ambience. "The epoch of the understanding and the senses" from which reason is excluded, is in statecraft the epoch of prudence from which wisdom is excluded.

Wisdom, if it were allowed to grow, would apprehend the nation as an organism having that relation between whole and parts, which is characteristic of life in general and of organisms in particular. Beneath the conflicting interests of party and party, and of class and class, it would divine the dynamic opposition between Permanence and Progression, on which life itself depends. Unity with Progression (the tendency to retain attachment with the tendency to detach) is Life's *method*

---

* In it's spiritual potentiality.

of producing the new out of the old. It must therefore be our method of apprehending and consciously participating in the process.

But the institutions, the classes, the historical adventures of a nation as a whole are not the only parts of which that whole consists. The nation is a whole consisting of individual citizens, who also are its "parts." They are its most detached and individualised parts; and it is here that the other principle, which distinguishes organic from mechanical form, becomes important—the *totus in omni parte*—the whole in every part. The sharper the detachment, the further individualisation has already advanced, the greater is the possibility of "reproducing" attachment by virtue of that principle. Politically Coleridge found this reflected in Rousseau's formulation of the problem of "a perfect constitution of government":[41] "Trouver une forme d'Association—par laquelle chacun s'unissant à tous, n'obéisse pourtant qu'à lui meme, et reste aussi libre qu'auparavant." * Rousseau's "social contract" is the idle fancy of a social structure based on mechanical form, which never existed historically. But "the idea of an ever-originating social contract" [42] is the reverse of nonsense; and so, properly understood, is Rousseau's own distinction between the *Volonté Générale* and the *Volonté de Tous;* only, he failed to realise that the *collective* will—

> that sovereign will, to which the right of universal legislation appertains, applies to no one Human Being, to no society or assemblage of Human Beings, and least of all to the mixed multitude that makes up the PEO-PLE: but entirely and exclusively to REASON itself; which, it is true, dwells in every man *potentially,* but actually and in perfect purity is found in no man and in no body of men.[43]

Mere prudence, like the mere understanding, knows nothing of "potential," and holds that only the actual is real. For it, "nothing is left obscure, nothing suffered to remain in the idea, unevolved and only acknowledged as an existing, yet indeterminable right." [44] Failing to acknowledge that the individual is himself potentially and spiritually the whole (because he has the same "principle of unity within himself" as the constitution also has) it must end by treating him not as a *person* but as a *thing*.[45] From such a state, while there may still be "civilisation," "cultivation" will have disappeared.

---

* To find a form of association—by which each uniting himself to all nevertheless obeys only himself and remains as free as before.

We may return to history for a moment, since this very danger has recently been advanced as an argument against "historicism," that is to say, against any conception of history as an intelligible evolutionary process. The argument is that historicism implies determinism and determinism entails justifying, as Oswald Spengler did and Marxism does, totalitarianism. If the state, on the basis of history as process, claims any "ideal" reality at all, it will end by becoming absolute and the doctrine will be accepted that the individual exists for the state and not the state for the individual. It is better therefore to hold that it has no such ideal reality, indeed that the whole notion of ideal reality is a politically motivated fantasy,[46] and that history has been a series of more or less blind accidents.

Now Coleridge, as we have seen, was resolved to "take from history its accidentality," and it is not surprising that his insistence on the idea as reality *in potentia,* and on the potential identity of each part with the whole, should be relevant, not only to the issue of "historicism" in general, but also to the related "means-or-end" issue between the individual and the State. On the latter he could even observe:

> Without the slightest reference to Kings or their right divine, who are themselves like all other parts of the State, not *the State,* I hold that the former Position (to wit that *the* Men were made for, i.e. have their final cause in, the State, *rather* than the State for *the* Men) is capable of being maintained in a weighty and even sublime sense. I say *rather,* because both may be true. Not only is the Whole greater than a Part; but where it is a Whole, and not a mere All or Aggregate, it makes each part that which it is.[47]

We are perhaps led back again to the little word *in,* and to the not so simple meaning it may acquire in a dynamic philosophy that has repudiated fixed outness, and has therefore added to the concept of juxtaposition that of real interpenetration. We may fearlessly acknowledge that there is a sense in which the individual in a state exists for the State, only when we have also acknowledged that the State is in each individual. Or rather, when we shall have not merely acknowledged it, but *embodied the idea in the constitution.*[48] And this is what Coleridge wished to do, with his concept of the "Church" as a distinct (not "separate") third Estate of the realm. Not separate, because every citizen is a member of it, as well as of the State, although only some find their vocation in it, but distinct, because autonomous as a property-owning organisation. In his view the constitution must be a tri-unity, because the individual human being is himself a tri-unity. Only in such a commonwealth therefore can the whole man participate. The constitution is to be an evolving tri-unity, in which the "unceasing polarity" of life is reflected and embodied in the political opposition between its Permanent and its Progressive elements; and the "law of its direction" (that is, the tendency to individuation) is reflected and embodied in the intellectual and spiritual permeation of the whole by the third estate—education, science, art, religion—for which the national Clerisy is primarily responsible. It is sometimes forgotten that if the word *progress* is to mean anything at all, other than just "change," it must mean change in one direction rather than another.

It is complex—but then so is life—and it would be a mistake to find any inconsistency between this latter picture and the picture of a polarity between the Church as a whole and the State as a whole; the latter being analogous to the polarity between mind as a whole and nature as a whole.

The concern of the Clerisy should be solely with the citizen as an individual (and progressive) human spirit. And precisely with this the State, in its narrower sense—the political administration—should *not* concern itself. Its limited function is to provide and preserve a social structure, within which the individual can happen. Thus, the political State is concerned, not with individuals as such but with "interests"—institutions and parties—and in particular with the Permanent and the Progressive interest. Of course individuals do come to feel themselves identified from time to time predominantly with one or the other, and then the conflicting interests create conflicting "classes." In his own time Coleridge found the ideas of Permanence and Progression paramountly, though very imperfectly, embodied in the Landed interest and the Personal interest respectively, and these were, for him, the other two estates of the realm or commonwealth, the unity of the political "State" depending on their equipoise and interdependence.[49] They were also socially distinct classes, though with considerable fluidity of interchange between the individuals comprising them. In Victoria's time "every boy and every girl that's born into this world alive" was, it was pointed out by W. S. Gilbert, "either a little Liberal or else a little Conservative." The Permanent and the Progressive may be sharply divided from one another, but they are divided in order to be united as the stuff of life; and it is the task of political wisdom to discern how at this moment they are already unconsciously working, where beneficially and where imperfectly or injuriously, and to provide, as far as possible, for their un- hampered interinanimation. For human beings, as such, are not really to be distinguished on those lines at all. On the contrary each one of them has the polarity between Permanence and Progression within himself, as well as the tendency to individuation, which is the law of its direction. Each one of them therefore should be able to say, and in a well-knit constitution *would* be able to say: *l'état c'est moi!* We might perhaps ask ourselves whether, in the continued absence of *some* such underlying idea, any further social "progress" is possible, if by that word we mean changes in the direction of neither anarchy followed by chaos in the one alternative nor the technologically contrived unity of an ant-heap in the other.

*   *   *

We have attempted, in this chapter and throughout, to present the body of Coleridge's thought as a complete and coherent structure, using as materials verbatim extracts from his writings and from his lectures and conversation as reported. Numerous as they are, these quotations have been selected from a very much larger number that could have been used for the same purpose, and indeed the choice has often been difficult for that very reason. It remains true of course that they are selected. Many of them are brief and taken, necessarily, out of their context. It is not suggested that Coleridge never said or wrote anything inconsistent with that structure as we have presented it; and there are certainly others which, taken out of context in the same way, are out of harmony with it. He was not the only philosopher who, on one or more particular occasions, has seemed to deny his own principles almost to the point of perversity. How many thinking people are there at whom we have never exclaimed, or felt like exclaiming: *You* of all people to say that! Yet it is not the incoherent or the inconsistent (for they may be expected to say anything) at whom we exclaim but their oppo- sites.

As an example, we have sometimes imagined ourselves expostulating with Coleridge over the two pages he expended in the *Biographia Literaria* (Chapter XXII) on castigating Wordsworth for addressing a child in the famous Ode as "Thou best philosopher!" . . . after first of course assembling a whole array of his own remarks on such matters as the unconscious but potentially conscious mind, the difference between instinct in human beings and in animals, the development of intellect out of life in the growing child etc. and capping the whole with his remark, in the closing paragraph of *On Poesy or Art,* on "the seeming identity of body and mind in infants, and thence the loveliness of the former." One may like it or dislike it oneself; but if ever there was a reader who might be relied on to rejoice in that particular metaphor, finding it (like Milton's "blind mouths") as apt as it is bold, one would have expected that reader to be Samuel Taylor Coleridge. But no. He prefers to expatiate on various reasons why, as a literal statement of fact, it is incorrect.

But there are other and, at least on the face of them, more serious discrepancies. Thus it is disconcerting, after following closely his careful build-up in the Treatise, and the eight Essays, on Method, of an epistemology, and even a scientific method, based on elevating the mind from the level of understanding to that of reason, to come in the last paragraph of the last Essay* upon the sentence: "But let it not be supposed that it is a sort of *knowledge.*" True, he immediately adds: "No! It is a form of BEING, or indeed it is the only knowledge that truly *is,* and all other science is real only as far as it is symbolical of this." But surely, in the light of all that had gone before, this hurried qualification required some expanding!

It may be well to pursue this very discrepancy a little farther, raising as it does the not swiftly answerable question of what Coleridge really meant by "knowledge." Coleridge's philosophy of nature is that of an evolution from unconscious, or un-self-conscious, mind to self-conscious mind. His philosophy of history presents that as a continuation of the same process. Thus the history of philosophy, which we find embedded in the *Philosophical Lectures,* is conceived as the history of a single mind. Or rather (and the distinction is important) it is the history of "the *striving* of a single mind"—which is how he himself described the Lectures in his Prospectus. Thus it aims, if obscurely, at being an account of the evolution of unconscious, as well as of the history of conscious, mind—an evolution in which "the foetal throb" † of philosophic genius in Greece heralded "the bursting forth of individuality." ‡

Moreover by unconscious mind ("that which lies *on the other side* of

---

* Essay XI, Section 2. See Chapter 10, above.
† See n. 13, p. 256.
‡ P. 162, above.

our natural consciousness")* he did not of course mean any reflection from physical events or processes. He meant a "world of spirit" that is "correspondent" to our spiritual organs, as the sense world is to our sense organs;† a world which may be called "subjective," inasmuch as it cannot become an object of the senses, but which is "objective" (more so in fact than the sense-world itself) inasmuch as it is *other* than what any man habitually calls "himself." This "world" is nevertheless "the *terra incognita* of our nature" ‡ and, as such, is what actually constitutes our true selves. Each true self is (*totus in omni parte*) a distinctive unity of that multeity. Another name for it is Reason. But Reason is Being, and Ideas, as the "distinctities" § within Reason, are clearly Beings. The Ideas of Reason are moreover hierarchically related to one another.‖

Commenting, not as it happens on this part of Coleridge's thought but on a passage from the *Theory of Life,** R. H. Fogle has well remarked that ". . . the inferences of his method are irresistible . . . The phrase "a new series" strongly suggests a further orderly ascent from man to angels and archangels, thrones, principalities and powers as in the imagined hierarchies of *The Ancient Mariner*." [50] And if this is the inference from his method, the inference from his *methodology,* in the *Treatise on Method* and the eight *Essays,* would appear to be equally irresistible: namely, that this world of noetic hierarchy is not only actual but also, in theory, knowable—though only by a knowing which is at the same time a being. Coleridge seems further committed to the view that such qualitative knowledge could be *communicable,* not it is true directly, in terms of an understanding working only with quantities, but by that "symbolic use of the understanding," † which is the function of imagination.

Yet he not only never, as far as we know, expressly considered any such inferences, but sometimes went out of his way to deny them. In his *Notes* on Isaac Taylor's *History of Enthusiasm*[51] he ridicules "all this Pelion upon Ossa of imaginary hierarchies," and there is more than one

---

* BL I, 168.
† BL I, 167.
‡ P. 160, above.
§ Chapter 10, p. 115, above.
‖ Chapter 10, p. 120, above.
* Stauffer 577.
† Chapter 3, note 29, above.

passage in the *Aids to Reflection* where he insists with emphasis on the unknowableness of Spirit.*

The question arises: Do such discrepancies betoken any fundamental confusion in Coleridge's thought? We believe not. Generally speaking, we believe closer inspection will reveal that what he is repudiating is the possibility of knowledge and communication, not absolutely but in the limited sense in which those terms are ordinarily understood; that is to say, knowledge and communication by a method which he himself regularly criticised as inadequate. In informally expounding a position radical enough to affect the accepted meanings of many common words (*knowledge* for instance), there is always the difficulty that one must sometimes use the words *with* their accepted meanings, if one is to speak at all. He was, in intention at all events, denying any claim to knowledge of the supersensuous, as knowledge was understood by the empiricists, and to its communication by any *non*-symbolic use of the understanding—any "*semi*-Cartesian" jumble, in short, such as he detected in the works of Henry More.[52] He would not, at any cost, have sensuous experience *masquerading* as noumenal; and it was the detection of this, where it had hitherto lain undetected, that he especially valued in Kant.

It is not suggested that such an elucidation frees Coleridge from the charge of verbal self-contradiction at all points in all the written expressions of his thought that have any epistemological bearings. On one occasion he himself candidly admitted the "heavy difficulties that weigh on the doctrine of Ideas or Knowledges that are supersensuous and yet truly objective." [53] Heavy they unquestionably are; and it is perhaps on those difficulties that we should reflect when we pounce on him for apparently unsaying here what he has said there. The true question is: Does his system as a whole, and fully comprehended, succeed in meeting them?

Instead of answering the question we shall conclude by asking another. Would he perhaps have found those difficulties less heavy, if he had succeeded more conclusively in marrying his epistemology to his philosophy of evolution and history? Like Hegel, he was moving on from the notion of a history of thought ('history of ideas' as it is commonly called) towards that of an evolution of consciousness. But neither of them reached clearly the conclusion, which for example Rudolf

---

* Page 42, for instance.

Steiner had reached before writing his own history of philosophy[54] and developing his own epistemology of the supersensuous: that the Scientific Revolution, the "disanimation of nature" and the whole "epoch of the understanding and the senses" has itself been the culmination of that evolving polarity between man and nature, on which self-consciousness is based; and that it is important mainly for that reason. It is only as a self that being can begin to become knowing, and a pre-condition of selfness is exclusion from the being that is nevertheless its ground. Mental participation in *animated* nature remained more live because it remained less conscious. Coleridge has it that the medieval Nominalists "lost the Dynameis, or denied their existence." [55] It would seem to be an inference from his philosophy of nature and history that they denied their existence because they had lost the live instinctive intelligence that could still experience the Dynameis as nature—though admittedly "hidden and overlaid by Idolism." [55] Was his own mind still too much involved with the epoch of the understanding and the senses, too near to its recent origin, to be able to stand right outside it, so as to see it in historical perspective; and thus to accept that very "losing" of the Dynameis as the pre-condition of their being found again by a Coleridge—but in a new way now and identified, as his two forces, with the act of consciousness itself? The question and its answer are beyond the purview of the present work, the purpose of which has been to display, if possible, what Coleridge can be shown to have thought, not to speculate on what he might have thought if he had been born a little later, or even perhaps if he had gone on living a little longer.

Appendix

POLAR LOGIC

We had studied in the same school; been disciplined by the same
preparatory philosophy, namely the writings of Kant; we had both
equal obligations to the polar logic and dynamic philosophy of Giordano Bruno . . .

So Coleridge wrote in that part of Chapter IX of the *Biographia
Literaria* where he is describing the relation, as he sees it, of Schelling's
philosophical development to his own; leaving us to draw these two
conclusions: firstly, that there is such a thing as "polar logic," and
secondly that it is to be found in the writings of Giordano Bruno. The
attempt now being made is to examine both these conclusions, beginning with the second and more easily containable one.

Whereabouts in Bruno's voluminous writings, not all of which he
had read,[1] did Coleridge lay his finger on this that he calls polar logic?
In one of his marginal notes on Baxter's *Life of Himself* he tells us:
"I have not indeed any distinct memory of Giordano Bruno's *Logice
Venatrix Veritatis*; but doubtless the principle of Trichotomy is necessarily involved in the Polar Logic . . ."[2] This title is incorrectly quoted
from memory, but there can be no real doubt that it refers to two Latin
treatises by Bruno, of which the first (a very short one) is entitled *De
Progressu Logicae Venationis* and the second and longer one *De Lampade Venatoria Logicorum*. The two were generally, perhaps always,
printed together and were commonly referred to under the single title:
De Progressu et Lampade Venatoria Logicorum. Under that name they
are included in a list of Bruno titles (no doubt for future reading)
which Coleridge jotted down while he was in Malta (1804-5). That

he succeeded in obtaining them, read them with interest—and left them behind in Malta—is suggested by a later note (c. 1810) in which he records a wish to see again the *Logica Venatrix* of Bruno, a wish strong enough to have made him consider sending out to Malta for them.[3]

Did he do so? At all events it seems unlikely that he ever got them. He was, as we have seen, already hazy about the title in 1810. Moreover, in 1818 or thereabouts, when he was reading Tennemann's *Geschichte der Philosophie* to help him with his own *Philosophical Lectures,* he complained in a marginal note:

> —the article of Giordano Bruno especially heartless and superficial—a mere skim from one or two only of Bruno's writings—while his interesting attempts in Logic and Mnemonic are passed over altogether—tho' they would have thrown a light on his whole philosophy.[4]

He himself, it must be added, makes no reference either to mnemonic or to logic in his brief account of Bruno in Lecture XI.

Tennemann was not alone in his indifference to Bruno's logic. There is little or nothing, in any other attempt we have come across to expound Bruno's philosophy, either about logic in general or about the *De Progressu et Lampade Venatoria Logicorum,* which appears to be the only place where it is to be found. We turn therefore to the *De Progressu* itself, as we will call the two treatises together; and here our difficulties begin in earnest. It is, *at least* on a first reading, almost entirely unintelligible. We soon find that one major reason for this, though not, alas, the only one, is that Bruno's exposition assumes in his readers a thorough previous acquaintance with the logic, and indeed with the whole metaphysical system, of Ramon Lull. Even today the works of Bruno are not very easy to come by. In Coleridge's time they were still less accessible. He is most likely to have read them in a volume in which the *De Progressu* is bound up with a collection consisting mainly of various works by Lull, the only other contribution from Bruno being a little work called *De Lampade Combinatoria Lulliana.* This, which precedes the two treatises constituting the *De Progressu,* is in substance a brief exegesis of the "ars," or method, developed by Ramon Lull and applied by him throughout his life to a wide variety of topics. A reader would be expected to have mastered it before going on to the *De Progressu.* Lull's *Ars Brevis* and *Ars Magna,* in which the "art" found its final expression, are both printed in the same volume.[5]

We ourselves found it impossible to make anything at all of the *De Progressu* without first perusing the *De Lampade Combinatoria Lulliana*; and equally impossible to make anything of the *De Lampade* without first acquiring a more direct acquaintance with Lull's *Ars Brevis* and *Ars Magna* themselves. It must be added that, even after going to these (not unrewarding) lengths, we have still found it impossible to extract from Bruno's *De Progressu* anything that could with confidence be described as "polar logic." For this reason, after taking into account all Coleridge's explicit references to polar logic that are known to us, and subject to what we shall say of the *De Progressu* a little later on, we have reached the following tentative conclusions.

In the first place Polar Logic could stand in his mind, generally, for his own metaphysic based on the universal law of polarity, in contrast with the metaphysic of abstractions developed by exclusive reliance on the understanding and the senses. We know that he associated the universal law of polarity, as he understood it, especially with Bruno. He hoped to write a life of Bruno. Bruno had written a treatise on logic. Irrespective of what Coleridge actually found in the treatise, the label could have darted into his mind and remained in his memory saturated there with the excitement of a moment of special insight obtained while reading not only Bruno's *De Progressu*, but also Bruno on the art of Lull and something of Lull's own exposition of his "art" and of the whole philosophical background from which it sprang.[6]

Such an interpretation is supported by the account of polar logic given in what appears to be part of a draft letter to Hartley Coleridge in the British Museum:

> Yester morning, my dear Hartley! you appeared to agree with me on the truth of the universal principle of the Polar Logic, as far as it is Logic, i.e. confined to Objects of the Sense and the Understanding, or (what is the same) to the Finite, the Creaturely. You agreed with me, that *One* could not manifest itself or be wittingly distinguished as One, but by the co-existence of an Other: or that A could not be affirmed to be A but by the perception that it is *not* B; and that this again implies the perception that B *is* as well as A. We can become *conscious* of Being only by means of Existence, tho' having thus become conscious thereof, we are in the same moment conscious, that Being must be prior (in thought) to Existence; as without seeing, we should never *know* (i.e. know our-

selves to have known) that we had Eyes; but having learnt this, we know that Eyes must be anterior to the act of seeing. With equal evidence we understand that Existence supposes *relation*—for it is, Sisto me *ad extra,* and therefore distinguished from Being. . . .[7]

Anyone who turns to the *De Progressu* expecting to find something like this is going to be somewhat disappointed. Polar logic, as Coleridge here expounds it, is little different from the "Transcendental Logic" of the following passage on Kant and Baxter in the *Treatise on Logic*:

> The singular circumstance of this three-fold division or Trichotomy obtaining throughout the analysis of the mind, and which the founder of the Critical Philosophy contents himself with noticing as being singular and worthy of notice, and which he supposes himself to have noticed first, may be found in a much earlier writer, our own celebrated Richard Baxter. Any attempt to explain it would be out of place in the present disquisition. It is a primary datum of the understanding, the *way in which* we reflect, proved to us by our pure products of reflection . . . ; but not to be explained by them. Its purpose is *to account for* the results of reflection and it would be preposterous to expect that these should account for it. Briefly, in common Logic the fact has no interest; in Transcendental Logic it is a necessary element, but its explanation belongs to neither as transcending the faculty of which the one gives the results and the other the Analysis.[8]

Polar Logic, Transcendental Logic and the Principle of Trichotomy appear, at most, slightly different aspects of the same idea. Witness the following very similar note on Baxter's *Life of Himself* (from which we briefly extracted above). Baxter had written: "I have been twenty-six years convinced that dichotomizing will not do it, but that the divine Trinity in Unity hath expressed itself in the whole frame of nature and morality." On which Coleridge comments:

> Among Baxter's philosophical merits, we ought not to overlook, that the substitution of Trichotomy for the old and still general plan of Dichotomy in the method and disposition of Logic, which forms so prominent and substantial an excellence in Kant's Critique of the Pure Reason, of the Judgement, and the rest of his works, belongs originally to Richard Baxter, a century before Kant;—and this not as a hint, but as a fully evolved and systematically applied principle. Nay, more than this;— Baxter grounded it on an absolute idea presupposed in all intelligential

acts: whereas Kant takes it only as a fact in which he seems to anticipate or suspect some deeper truth latent, and hereafter to be discovered.

On recollection, however, I am disposed to consider *this* alone as Baxter's peculiar claim. I have not indeed any distinct memory of Giordano Bruno's *Logice Venatrix Veritatis*; but doubtless the principle of Trichotomy is necessarily involved in the Polar Logic, which again is the same with the Pythagorean *Tetractys,* that is, the eternal fountain or source of nature; and this being sacred to contemplations of identity, and prior in order of thought to all division, is so far from interfering with Trichotomy as the universal form of division (more correctly of distinctive distribution in logic) that it implies it. *Prothesis* being by the very term anterior to *Thesis,* can be no part of it. Thus in

Prothesis

Thesis   *Antithesis*

Synthesis

we have the Tetrad indeed in the intellectual and intuitive contemplation, but a Triad in discursive arrangement, and a Tri-unity in result.

The three passages, taken together, suggest that we should take polar—or transcendental—logic as signifying discursive thought in general, but with an added awareness, so to speak, of how it comes about.[9] In the fact of logical predication we have the mere *product* of *reflection;* explanation can make us aware of the mental *act* of predicating, from which the product originated. Logic is then experienced in its true nature, as the Logos itself, in its aspect of "communicative intelligence."

We have referred already to the close bond between Bruno's treatise on logic and the "art" of Ramon Lull. If this were a full-length book on historical sources and not merely an Appendix, it would be appropriate at this point to give some account of Lull's meticulously developed pre-Cartesian system, with its interpenetrating Triads and its psychology of intellectual "descent" and "ascent" to and from the divine "Dignities" of the spirit, which are constitutive of nature and the mind of man. We should be drawing attention, for instance, to his sharp distinction between the Absolute and the Relative principles (corresponding to Coleridge's between reason and understanding) and perhaps in particular to the Triad: *Differentia, Concordantia* and *Contrarietas,* mediating descent from the absolute to the relative.[10] And we should no doubt be showing how this points us back to the whole long line of "Christian Neo-platonism" . . . Pythagoras, Plato,

Plotinus, Proclus and Porphyry, pseudo-Dionysius, Augustine, Scotus Erigena, the Florentine Academy and a host of others. It is a line with which Coleridge was, from an early age, well acquainted.[11] But here we are limited to investigating the special importance he attached to Bruno.

For it seems to have been especially in Bruno that he located the link between all that line and modern thought. Modern thought, that is to say, not as it is, but as it might and should be. Modern thought, as it has in fact developed, and particularly scientific thought, presupposes a "metaphysics of quantity" by contrast with the "metaphysics of quality," which the whole line presupposes and presents.[12] Moreover this metaphysic is inseparably bound up with a critique of logic. Aristotelian logic and all developments from it, being grounded on the understanding and the senses, inevitably end in admitting only quantities as "real." But, since it is a matter of immediate experience that the world consists of qualities as well as quantities, modern thought will remain exiled from knowledge, unless it develops its own metaphysic of qualities to supplement the other, which it has. And a metaphysic of qualities will be one which *starts* from qualities as the basic and constitutive principles of the universe, instead of from the mechanical and ultimately quantitative process, to which the understanding and the senses have succeeded in 'reducing' it.

It seems that what Coleridge valued so highly in Bruno was his vigorous and versatile effort to develop the metaphysic of quality into a method of *knowledge;* for Coleridge himself prophesied, as we have seen, not only a metaphysic but a *science* of qualities.[13] Such an effort towards a science of qualities was indeed part of the general climate of Renaissance thought and it may be seen as what distinguishes the Renaissance end of the "line" from its beginning in a remote Pythagorean past. Moreover Bruno may not unreasonably be claimed as its paramount representative. Bruno valued Lull as an "inventor," and it is significant that Lull himself always referred to his system as an "art," or as we should say, *method*. He was firmly convinced of its usefulness for "discovery" in the sublunary world, as well as for a Bonaventurian ascent to the contemplation of divinity. The "artist" must first be well-grounded in both logic and the natural sciences, Lull tells us, but he seems to have distinguished Aristotelian logic as being expository only and not "inventive," and he contrasts the logician who draws a conclusion from two premises with the "artista huius artis" who draws it from "the mixture of principles and rules."

The word *mixture* (*mixtio*) is important. It is not possible here to expound the principles of the *ars Lulliana;* but the concept of total interpenetration underlies the whole of it. The divine "Dignities" (qualities) which are constitutive of the universe interpenetrate both each other and the phenomenal plane at all levels. And this assumption is as basic to the texture of Bruno's thought as it is to that of Lull, whence it was largely developed.

It may be questioned whether it was not this concept of the reciprocal interpenetration of principles or "ideas," which Coleridge really had in mind when he fathered on Bruno his own "universal law of polarity." That, and the essentially qualitative principles of *Beginning, Middle* and *End* (themselves interpenetrating), which are equally fundamental, not only to Bruno and Lull, but to the whole historical line of thought to which we have referred. Both of them might be felt to suggest polarity, as Coleridge expounds it. "To detach, but so as either to retain or to reproduce attachment . . ." or Lull's *Differentia, Contrarietas, Concordantia,* as a triad interpenetrating with the other triad *Principium, Medium, Finis:* either way it is a process of "separative projection" that is being envisaged.

We have been pointing out that it is difficult to find in Bruno anything that could comfortably be described as "polar logic." We fear we must now add that it is almost as difficult to find polarity *simpliciter;* that is to say, "the law of polarity" as it is presented by Coleridge himself. That Coleridge judged otherwise is clear from a number of references. There is the footnote reference in the *Friend,* which we quoted in Chapter 3, to

> the universal law of polarity or essential dualism, first promulgated by Heraclitus, 2000 years afterwards re-published, and made the foundation both of logic, of physics, and of metaphysics by Giordano Bruno.[14]

Still more specific is the relative clause we have italicized in the following MS note:

> Bruno adopted, corrected and extended the Astronomical System of his great Contemporary, Copernicus—and was himself the first who asserted the infinity or immensity of the universe against Aristotle. He contended

that the Fixed Stars were Suns, each the centre of a centro-peripheric Process, a primary Law of Matter: *which he elsewhere calls the Law of Polarity,* in this as in many other instances anticipating the Ideas and discoveries generally attributed to far later Philosophies, even those of the present age.[15]

Two questions arise: first, did Bruno in fact ever use the expression, "Law of Polarity"? and secondly, apart from labels, is there in fact to be found in Bruno anything that is fairly recognisable as the law of polarity as Coleridge propounded it? The first and less important question must almost certainly be answered in the negative.[16] We suggest, though with slightly less confidence, that the second must be answered in the same way.[17] But this raises the whole issue of the difference between Coleridge's law of polarity and the so-called "coincidence of opposites."

If, once again, this were a book about historical sources and not merely an Appendix, we should be obliged at this point to say a good deal about another eminent figure in the history of Western thought; one that stands very definitely between Lull and Bruno, namely Cardinal Nicolas of Cusa.[18] Cusa had been a careful student of Lull; and Bruno was sufficiently indebted to Cusa to have been described by at least one commentator as his "disciple." Cusa is generally acknowledged as the main source (not of course the ultimate one) of the doctrine of "Coincidentia oppositorum." But how much has this to do with polarity? One of Lull's nine constitutive "Dignities" (which were *absolute* principles) was *Magnitudo.* The third of the three interlacing triads of *relative* principles, to which we have referred, consisted of *Majoritas, Aequalitas* and *Minoritas.* It is clear from Cusa's *De Docta Ignorantia* that his primary approach to the coincidence of opposites was mathematical. And it would seem that, for him, the "essential dualism" underlying the universe was conceived as analogous to the essential duality between the geometrically finite and the infinite, such as we see displayed in the asymptotic curve.[19] Of course the mathematical duality was put forward as an analogy only—a "vehicle," we might say, of which the "tenor" was the relation between Creator and creature— but it remains true that the "feel" of Cusa's coincidence of opposites is that of a static relation between finity and infinity rather than of any energising relation between infinitely expanding and infinitely contracting "forces."

Bruno appears in one respect to have resembled Coleridge. His enthusiasm for other thinkers never prevented him from substantially modifying their thought in the process of adapting it to his own. And this seems to have applied to that passion for infinity which was no doubt fed and inflamed by what he found in Cusa. Nevertheless Bruno altered the direction of its emphasis. That which Cusa and his predecessors attributed to God, Bruno began attributing to the universe.[20] Can it be said, and did Coleridge sense, that, with his attention fixed more upon the working out of the creative process below than on its source from above, Bruno was feeling his way towards a more "dynamic" coincidence of opposites than Cusa had succeeded in portraying? The question must be left for answer by some learned Brunonian scholar. The meteorically rapid development of his thought, its terrifically wide range, and the time required to acquaint oneself with the considerable bulk of his writings are obstacles too formidable for us to surmount.

We are still inclined to suggest that Bruno's "essential dualism" was much more Cusan than it was Coleridgean. Indeed in the *Cena de le Ceneri* there is a sense in which he, as it were, out-Cusa's Cusa. The emphasis there is *all* on the infinite/finite duality, and he lapses more than once into that "everything-is-everything-else" type of rhapsodical paradox, from which Lull was saved by the methodical rigour of his "art" and Cusa himself by the severity of his mathematical approach.

A logical contradiction is mere negation; contemplated as "paradox" it becomes, in a sense, affirmative and positive; but it is still static. But the essence of polarity is a *dynamic* conflict between coinciding opposites. Coleridge, as we have seen, cites Heraclitus as the first promulgator of the law of polarity; and the element of conflict, the quality of psychic oppugnancy,* between opposites is evident there in a way it hardly is in Bruno. Heraclitus lived and thought before Aristotle; that is, long before that first great step forward in the "disanimation" of nature, which culminated philosophically in Cartesianism. In the later age this quality of oppugnancy, considered as the fundamental energy in the life of nature, is far more express in Böhme than in Bruno; it is Böhme who succeeds in making us *feel* the *presence* of a *natura geminata, quae fit et facit, et creat et creatur,*[21] and, until someone convinces us to the contrary, we shall maintain that, as far as the

---

* Compare Chapter 7, p. 89, above.

law of polarity is concerned, Coleridge actually *received* a good deal more from the shoemaker of Görlitz than he ever did from the philosopher of Nola.[22] We have already noticed that a number of his observations on physical science occur as marginal notes to Böhme's *Aurora*. No Bruno marginalia have come to light.

Why then, in his memory, did he connect the law of polarity so very specifically with Bruno? We must remember that, above all in dealing with Coleridge, the primary assumption on which a vast body of academic research is based is itself in issue; the presupposition namely that, whenever a thought or body of thought in B's mind is also found in A's, it must (if B comes later) have been copied by B from A. Early philosophical source-hunting always tacitly assumes that we are dealing not with reality itself manifest in human thinking, but with certain animistic fancies, invented at some time within some head or other. To the extent that we refuse, with Coleridge himself, to accept this limitation of thinking to the operation of the understanding and the senses, we shall be disposed to accept what he says of himself and Plato as true, and to wonder whether it may not also apply to the relation between himself and Bruno:

> [Plato] leads you to see that propositions involving in themselves a contradiction in terms are nevertheless true; and which, therefore, must belong to a higher logic—that of ideas. They are self-contradictory only in the Aristotelian logic, which is the instrument of the understanding. I have read most of the works of Plato several times with profound attention, but not all his writings. In fact, I soon found that I had read Plato by anticipation.[23]

"A Shakespeare, a Milton, a Bruno," he had written much earlier, "exist in the mind as pure *action,* defecated of all that is material and passive." [24] Did he perhaps find in Bruno not only the thoughts that are there, but also some that are only potentially there? The scholarship of "interacting" thoughts, if and when it is developed, will have plenty of use for—but it will be rather different from—the valuable scholarship of historical sources in the accepted sense.

What have we done up to this point? Seeking to investigate Coleridge's reference to a little-known work of Bruno, we have been led back, by the nature of the quest, to two other thinkers in particular: Ramon Lull and Nicolas of Cusa. And in the sense of the preceding paragraph (the sense in which Bruno himself might have said: "A Lull, a Cusa exist in the mind as pure *action* . . .") we are tentatively disposed to detect the following predominant historical correspondences with different aspects of the thought of Coleridge as we have tried to present it. With Lull (the absolute and the relative Principles), the relation between understanding and reason; with Cusa, that relation between the whole and the part, by virtue of which the whole is present in each part, and ultimately the infinite is present in the finite (this is really the sense of Cusa's *coincidentia oppositorum*); with Bruno himself, the individual creative imagination[25] and, together with that, a more dynamic, "centro-peripheric" coincidence of opposites, which it remained for Coleridge himself to interpret or develop as a polarity of forces.

We could let it go at that; and we could please ourselves with supposing some one particular moment of particularly deep insight which happened to come while Coleridge was dipping into the *De Progressu et Lampade Logicorum,* and which remained ever afterwards more or less accidentally associated with it in his memory. But we are reluctant to do so, because we remain a little fascinated by the fact that he did select for express reference that one treatise of Bruno's, a lucubration so technical and so "minor" that we doubt if more than one Bruno scholar has ever gone beyond including it (without reference to its content) in a footnote.[26] *Did* he find in that treatise—or might he have eventually found there, if he had succeeded in getting it back from Malta—something of particular value for "polar logic" in a narrower sense?

Its wider sense derives, as already observed, from the fact that the Aristotelian logic of the understanding and the senses, and all developments from it, lead inevitably, and exclusively, to a "metaphysics of quantity." If we are right in what we have said in the text about the essential relation between polarity and imagination, it can even be felt as a two-word epitome at once of Coleridge's epistemology and of his psychology. But what is the narrower sense?

We have seen him drawing attention to the significance of contradiction for revealing the relation between understanding and reason. The narrower sense of "polar logic" would appear to be that relation focussed, as it were, into the actual moment of logical contradiction, or—which is the same thing in obverse—into the moment of predication. The moment of predication is the moment in which the presence of reason in the understanding is manifested in its effect, but only *as* effect. To meditate faithfully on the principle of contradiction, upon which predication and syllogism are based, is to have one's attention drawn, on the one hand, to the fact that predication is an *act* of mind and, on the other, to the effective reality of Reason as a universal and constitutive principle.

Now the *De Progressu* is certainly meaningless, except against a background of Lull and Cusa. Even so we have had to admit that we found it largely unintelligible. One reason for that may be that much of it is rather hideously condensed. The connection between its various parts is so obscure to a modern reader that we cannot offer to summarise or describe it as a whole. Nevertheless, simply because it would be cowardly to leave it altogether alone, we have struggled with it up to a point; and, in doing so, we have thought we detected one or two passages that may have seemed to Coleridge especially relevant. We shall conclude by referring to these and giving a brief and no doubt much oversimplified account of what we conceive that relevance to be.

Bruno's thinking was aggressively anti-Aristotelian—and predominantly spatial. One of his philosophical adventures was an endeavour to set up, in the infinitesimal, a distinction between "minimum" and "limit" (*terminus*), the *minimum* being that which is arrived at by progressive division and sub-division, whereas the *limit* is a kind of Cusan "absolute," or infinite, minimum.[27] (It remains an acknowledged scientific principle, we believe, that the limit to which any system increasingly approximates cannot itself form part of that system.) Neither absolute Maximum nor absolute Minimum is any part of the finite world. They are infinite—or they are infinity.

If, for example, we bisect a line, so as to divide it into two lines meeting each other:

the inmost minimal point of each line that we reach by dividing and sub-dividing it will remain separate from the corresponding inmost minimal point of the other line. We progress towards a limit, but in the finite world we only succeed in reaching a minimum, and a minimum that belongs exclusively to the line along which we have been progressing.

If we contrast the two "minima" (one to each line) with the "limit" in Bruno's sense, we could say of it what Coleridge says of the unity which is "the essence of all opposites": that "it is neither because it is the essence of both." [28] The limit, though it belongs relatively to neither line, belongs absolutely to both; and in it the two lines coincide and are one line. This is taken to illustrate a universal principle; namely, that the infinite is present, or involved, in the simplest relation between finites.[29] And, in logic, it may be taken as illustrating the problem of the excluded middle—which has also somehow to be both only one of two and not only one.

In the composite volume to which we have referred, Lull's *Dialectica seu Logica Nova* is followed by a brief excursus entitled *Tractatus de Venatione Medii inter Subjectivum et Praedicatum: De Medio Naturali et Logico*. It will be recalled that one of Lull's primary triads is *Principium, Medium, Finis;* and it must now be added that each of these three is itself a triad, *Medium* being compounded of the triad *Medium Conjunctionis, Medium Mensurationis* and *Medium Extremitatum*. Bruno, in his *De Lampade Combinatoria Lulliana* (which, as we have said, is virtually one with the two treatises that constitute the *De Progressu*) comments on the third member of this sub-triad: "Est tertio medium extremitatum, in quod quomodolibet aliter seposita concurrunt. Unde actio medium esse intelligitur inter agentem et patientem . . ." [30]

Notice the concept of action as the *medium,* or middle, between agent and patient. But the problem of the excluded middle may be seen as also the problem of the univocal term. In the old stock sample of a syllogism:

> All men are mortal
> Socrates is a man
> Therefore Socrates is mortal

its *validity* depends on a relation of identity between a genus, "man," and a particular species of it, "Socrates." But, on the other hand, its *meaningfulness* depends on the relation being other or *more* than that of identity. It depends in fact on there being a distinctity within the identity. If, as more modern logic has preferred to do, we abandon the the old-fashioned terms "genus" and "species" and substitute "class" and "member of a class," we are soon reduced to tautology:

> Every man is a member of a class of units called "mortals"
> Socrates is a member of that class
> Therefore—he is member of that class.

Or, to put it another way, the only meaningful statement that has been made is that mortality is part of the definition of the word *man;* and that was already announced in the major premise. But it is not only the syllogism. The bare understanding demands of a *proposition* itself, that the subject and predicate be univocal with each other. If not, the proposition must be untrue. But if so, the proposition is reversible and so is no more than a tautology. We cannot however even *define* without predicating; so definition (on which any meaning there may have been in a syllogism depends) is itself impossible; and syllogism not only ends in tautology, but also starts from one. The logic that has developed since Coleridge's day has spent a good deal of time and a good deal of ingenuity in scratching at this mortal wound.

The fact is, at all events for Coleridge, that genus and species *will* mean no more than class and member of a class, *if* we decline to accept the metaphysics of "descent" and "ascent" with which Lull and Cusa and Bruno and their predecessors worked—though we may have to learn to phrase it differently. Coleridge did not often use the *word* "tautology." His way of putting it (not his only way) was rather to point out that, in using the word "is" *exclusively* as a connective or copula, the mind affirms nothing about the world; it merely "bears witness to its own unity." [31]

That witness was the ultimate achievement of the older logic, that of exposition—which merely discriminates and displays more precisely such meaning as was already implicit in the terms it employs. That function having been performed, the older logic has, as a vehicle of cognition, nothing more to offer. In the logic or discourse, of *discovery,* on the other hand, the terms themselves must have a potential of expansion. Which entails that, from the point of view of the old logic, they will have been used equivocally. But the negation, which self-contradiction entails, though it is pure zero for the understanding alone, may (whether we say, for imagination, or for an understanding to which reason is *present*) be the growing-point of meaning and truth. What is only potential is not on that account unreal.[32]

It only remains to suggest that, if we look in particular at two sections near the end of the *De Progressu,* entitled respectively *Angulus Differentiae* and *Angulus Identitatis,* it is possible to feel, if somewhat obscurely, that the above is the type of problem with which Bruno is here attempting to deal in his own way. Both "angles" are included in the *Ager Definitionis* or "field of Definition"; and the second section begins:

> Hunc etiam spectare videtur ut ex opposita veluti quadam ratione locos identitatis, differentiae locis adjacentes intueamur. Sic enim an definitio definito congruat descriptioque descripto secundum generalem rationem judicare licet. Consideretur ergo primo in conjugatis si illa sint idem, ut destruas, vel confirmes positorum identitatem: idem enim fortitudo erit atque justicia, si nullam inter justum fortemque invenias differentiam, itidem in oppositis concomitantibus, potentia activa, passivaque agere ipso atque pati.

Agere and *pati*—the all-pervasive Heraclitan *to poiein* and *to paschein* of Plato's *Theaetetus* and Aristotle's *De Anima*—would be allusions for Coleridge to the two forces on which his whole system was based.* A few such passages, together with the fact that Bruno's treatise as a whole is saturated with the structural principles of Lullism, could well have made him suspect that in the *De Progressu et Lampade Venatoria Logicorum* he had hit on what might prove an important attempt to develop a formal logic of trichotomy, by analysing what Coleridge himself called the "Trichotomy in all *real* definitions." [33] Whether he was right or wrong we shall not attempt to decide. We prefer to adopt Coleridge's own principle and presume ourselves ignorant of Bruno's understanding until (if ever) we can claim to have understood his ignorance. What finally matters of course is, not the question whether Coleridge interpreted Bruno (or Kant or any other predecessor) correctly or incorrectly; but whether there is indeed a sense in which it is proper to characterise as a nuclear—or polar—logic the exactness of the understanding, not blurred or cancelled, but pierced to its empty heart at each moment, by the energy of imagination[34] as the bearer of related qualities.

---

* Compare Chapter 7, note 3, above.

Notes

KEY TO ABBREVIATIONS

Books etc. by S. T. Coleridge:

AP   *Anima Poetae*. Ed. E. H. Coleridge (from the Notebooks). Heinemann. 1895.

AR   *Aids to Reflection*. Ed. H. N. Coleridge. Pickering. 1839.

BL   *Biographia Literaria*. Ed. J. Shawcross in 2 vols. Reprinted (with corrections) 1962.

CIS   *Confessions of an Inquiring Spirit*. Ed. H. N. Coleridge. Pickering, 1849.

CL   *Collected Letters*. Vols. I to IV. Ed. E. L. Griggs. Clarendon Press. 1956–59.

CS   *On the Constitution of the Church and State*. Ed. H. N. Coleridge. London. 1839.

Egerton   Collection of numbered MSS in the British Museum.

F   *The Friend*. Ed. Barbara E. Rooke in 2 vols. Routledge and Princeton University Press. 1969.

IS   *Inquiring Spirit* (Anthology). Ed. Kathleen Coburn. Routledge. 1951. (Numbers refer to items, not pages.)

LR   *Literary Remains*. Ed. H. N. Coleridge in 4 vols. Pickering. 1836–39.

N   *The Notebooks of Samuel Taylor Coleridge*. Double vols. (Text and Notes) I and II. Ed. Kathleen Coburn. New York. Bollingen Foundation, Inc. 1957 and 1961.

P   *On the Prometheus of Aeschylus* (Vol. 4 of LR, pp. 344–365).

PL   *The Philosophical Lectures of Samuel Taylor Coleridge*. Ed. Kathleen Coburn. London. The Pilot Press Ltd. 1949.

the mind is *active* when it thinks, which was at the back of Coleridge's response while he was reading Newton's *Optics;* and which led to his well-known comment: *"Mind* in his [Newton's] system is always passive—a lazy Looker-on on an external world." (Letter to Thomas Poole, March 1801—CL II, 388.) Moreover it was in rectifying just this fallacy by commencing his *Wissenschaftslehre* "with an *act,* instead of a *thing* or *substance"* that Fichte "laid the first stone of the *dynamic* philosophy." (BL I, 101 and 246.)

18. The story of Coleridge's early enthusiasm for the psychology of Hartley, after whom he named his first-born child, and of his subsequent reversal of opinion is well enough known. The reader should consult (and not for that purpose only) J. Shawcross's long and admirable Introduction to his two-volume edition of the *Biographia Literaria.* Other sources are J. H. Muirhead's *Coleridge as Philosopher* and J. A. Appleyard's *Coleridge's Philosophy of Literature.* Professor Appleyard contends interestingly that, *in the whole history of psychology,* the theory of association of ideas played a positive as well as (through Coleridge) a negative part in developing the romantic doctrine of imagination. Of the integral part played by his refutation of Hartley in arriving at his own conclusions, Coleridge himself has given us a full account in Chapters V to VII of the *Biographia Literaria.*

19. BL II, 8.

20. AR 17 (from Introductory Aphorism XXVI).

21. TT Oct. 27, 1831.

22. F I, 177n; and IS 108.

23. BL I, 74.

24. PL 379.

25. PL 361.

26. PL 352.

27. From a note written on a flyleaf of Coleridge's copy of the *De Divisione Naturae* of John Scotus Erigena (see PL 434). The preceding quotations are of course merely a representative selection of numberless observations to the same effect. It was this inability, or refusal, to distinguish unless it is possible to visualize separates or separables, which had led, he held, to the atomic or, as he more often called it, the 'corpuscularian' philosophy. That he considered it also responsible for the arch presupposition underlying and limiting the methods of orthodox scientific investigation, according to which effective research always involves physical separation into minimal units, is clear from his *Hints Towards a More Comprehensive Theory of Life.* This is of course the "still worse" (page 19) practice of *distinguishing in order to divide:*

> demanding for every mode of existence real or possible visibility, it knows only of distance and nearness, composition (or rather compaction) and decomposition, in short, the relations of unproductive particles to each other; so that in every instance the result is the exact sum of the component qualities, as in arithmetical addition. [TL 586–87.]

Interesting also, in regard to the 'despotism of the eye,' is the note on Kant's use of the word *intuition* to be found on page 190 of Vol. I of the *Biographia Literaria.*

Here, after quoting Kant in *support* of the impropriety of taking the words *irrepresentable* and *impossible* "in one and the same meaning," Coleridge goes on to show that the German philosopher's own use of the word *intuition* is open to the like objection. "I take this occasion," he adds:

> to observe that here and elsewhere Kant uses the term intuition and the verb active (Intueri, *Germanice* Anschauen) for which we have unfortunately no correspondent word,* exclusively for that which can be represented in space and time. He therefore consistently and rightly denies the possibility of intellectual intuitions. But as I see no adequate reason for this exclusive sense of the term, I have reverted to its wider signification, authorized by our elder theologians and metaphysicians, according to whom the term comprehends all truths known to us without a medium.

See also, on the word *intuition,* Coleridge's MS notes on his copy of Thomas Taylor's *Proclus* (N I [*Notes*], Appendix B, p. 456).

28. *Treatise on Logic* II, 403–4. Snyder 126–27. Compare Chapter 8, p. 100.

29. See for instance *Treatise on Logic* II, 39 (original not italicised):

> . . . what I say are conceptions or thoughts? Wherein does the discursive act of the mind consist? In other words what is that act or effort which declares or manifests itself in any conception and on which the possibility of conception itself as a species of Knowing rests? What is *the act that must be presupposed in* the conception as *the product of that act* in order for it to become intelligible to us?

2. Naturata and Naturans

1. London: Routledge and Kegan Paul, 1957.

2. AR 185.

3. *Ib; natura* is the future participle of the Latin verb *nasci* (to be born).

4. F I, 500.

5. Chapter 1, above, note 27.

6. But not as yet very much, since Coleridge's observations on particulate theory applies also to field theory, so far as the field is conceived and treated as phenomenal. His point is that "the final solution of phenomena cannot itself be a phenomenon." (PL 145.) See Chapter 11, below.

7. In PL (p. 329) Jakob Böhme is praised for his "constant sense of the truth that all nature is in a perpetual evolution." Compare CS 196n: "Nature is a line in constant and continuous evolution." And see TL generally.

8. AR 185n.

9. PL 370. *Forma formans* and *forma formata* are of course united and disdistinguishable in the same way:

---

* The verb *to intuit* had evidently not yet come into use among philosophers. It is surprising that Coleridge did not coin it himself.

The word Nature has been used in two senses, actively and passively; energetic (= *forma formans*), and material (= *forma formata*). In the first (the sense in which the word is used in the text) it signifies the inward principle of what-ever is requisite for the reality of a thing, as existent . . . In the second or material sense of the word Nature, we mean by it the sum total of all things, as far as they are objects of our senses, and consequently of possible experience —the aggregate of phaenomena, whether existing for our outward senses, or for our inner sense. The doctrine concerning material nature would therefore (the word physiology being both ambiguous in itself and already otherwise appropriated) be more properly entitled Phaenomenology distinguished into its two grand divisions, Somatology and Psychology. [F I, 467n.]

And compare with the above the following passage from the essay *On Poesy or Art,* reminding us (if we needed reminding) that, unlike Aristotle, Coleridge emphatically does *not* place the artist in "antithesis to nature":

If the artist copies the mere nature, the *natura naturata,* what idle rivalry! If he proceeds only from a given form, which is supposed to answer to the no-tion of beauty, what an emptiness, what an unreality there always is in his productions, as in Cipriani's pictures! Believe me, you must master the es-sence, the *natura naturans,* which presupposes a bond between nature in the higher sense and the soul of man. [BL II, 257.]

The necessity, and perhaps the difficulty, of positively grasping this distinction is well illustrated in conflicting generalisations about Coleridge as a philosopher. Thus, R. Wellek in the rather patronising third chapter of his *Kant in England* (Princeton: 1931) stigmatizes Coleridge's "fatal dualism" and deplores it as an illegitimate departure from Kant and his idealist successors. Compare Alice Snyder in *The Critical Principle of the Reconciliation of Opposites:* "Distinction he would allow, but never, as a fundamental philosophical fact, division" (Michigan: Ann Arbor, 1918).

   10. P 354.
   11. Shedd I, 450.
   12. CL IV, 917.
   13. For instance:

By . . . the understanding or abstracting powers, a class of phenomena was in the first place abstracted and fixed in some general term: of course this term could designate only the impressions made by the outward objects, and so far therefore the effects of those objects, but having been thus generalised in a term they were then made to occupy the place of their own causes, under the name of occult qualities. Thus the properties peculiar to gold were ab-stracted from those it possessed in common with other bodies, and then generalised in the term Aureity . . . [PL 340.]

In the first place, therefore, I distinctly disclaim all intention of explaining life into an occult quality; and retort the charge on those who can satisfy

themselves with defining it as the peculiar power by which death is resisted. [TL 567.]

14. Quoted PL 434.

3. Two Forces of One Power

1. On Coleridge's own authority (see Shawcross's note, BL I, 271). The
harassing circumstances under which he composed this literary autobiography
(originally intended and begun as the Preface to a volume of his own poems) and
saw it through the press sufficiently appear from his correspondence in the years
1815–17. The references will be found assembled in the Index to CL IV, under the
heading COLERIDGE, SAMUEL TAYLOR, sub-heading *Biographia Literaria*.

2. Occasionally in his other prose writings and frequently in his letters. References in the Letters are assembled in the Index to CL IV, under COLERIDGE,
SAMUEL TAYLOR, SPECIAL TOPICS, MAGNUM OPUS. For instance: "Whether I shall
live long enough to finish the Work, to which all my past labours have been
preparatory, is most uncertain: and even if it were finished, it is not probable that
any publisher would undertake to print it" (Nov. 24, 1818, to C. A. Tulk); "And
lecturing is the only means by which I can make myself to go on at all with the
great philosohical work to which the best and most genial hours of the last twenty
years of my life have been devoted." He sometimes referred to the projected work
as his *Logosophia*.

3. The purpose of this book is to expound Coleridge's philosophy, not to
demonstrate its 'originality' or to insist that it is exclusive to Coleridge. The question of the reading he had done, the opinions he had formed before he learned
German, and the precise nature of his debt to Kant and Schelling in particular
among the German philosophers, has been frequently and extensively discussed
and is well considered in Shawcross's Introduction to the *Biographia Literaria*.

4. I. A. Richards, for instance, in his *Coleridge on Imagination*, makes no
mention of them at all. Shawcross in his Introduction to BL quotes a brief reference to them at the end of BL Chapter XII, which however he leaves without
comment. J. A. Appleyard devotes eight or nine lines to them in his *Coleridge's
Philosophy of Literature* (pp. 197, 198). And these are three of the best books I
have come across on Coleridge's thought! By contrast Donald Stauffer, in his brief
Introduction to *The Selected Poetry and Prose of Samuel Taylor Coleridge*, and
R. H. Fogle, in *The Idea of Coleridge's Criticism*, bestow on them a degree of
attention more in accord with Coleridge's own sense of proportion in the matter.

5. The wording of Coleridge's "letter" to himself in BL Chapter XIII evinces
how painfully well aware he was of the universal prevalence, and the unconscious
depth, of the presuppositions that were likely to render his arguments unacceptable and even unintelligible. On one occasion, he analysed them as follows:

> The obstinacy of opinions that have always been taken for granted, opinions
> unassailable even by the remembrance of a doubt, the silent accrescence of
> belief from the unwatched depositions of a general, never-contradicted, hear-

say; the concurring suffrage of modern books, all pre-supposing or re-asserting the same principles with the same confidence, and with the same contempt for all prior systems;—and among these, works of highest authority, appealed to in our Legislature, and lectured on at our Universities; the very books, perhaps, that called forth our own first efforts in thinking; the solutions and confutations in which must therefore have appeared tenfold more satisfactory from their having given us our first information of the difficulties to be solved, of the opinions to be confuted. [Appendix E to the *Statesman's Manual* in Shedd I, 481.]

Compare Chapter 11, note 9, below.

6. BL I, 197.

7. BL II, 235. The distinction between "opposite" and "contrary" made in a footnote to *Church and State* (CS 24n) may, I think, be ignored. In common use both terms are taken to connote mutual exclusion. Coleridge was there apparently attempting to "desynonymise" them by appropriating this connotation to one of them ("contrary") only. The distinction however is not one that he maintained. While, in the footnote, "contrary" is made virtually equivalent to "contradictory," elsewhere it is not infrequently synonymous with "opposite."

8. Coleridge normally uses the word *power* to signify the unitary source from which the two 'forces' are generated. The "opposite" here spoken of as being "evolved" would thus be one of the two "forces"; and the generating power would constitute the other "force," while still remaining the power that generates both forces. Or that is as near as it is possible to come to distinguishing the terms by abstract definition. In Coleridge's use the two terms *power* and *force* sometimes overlap, or coincide, as their referents do; and, if his attention is concentrated on the dual manifestation, apart from its unitary origin, he will sometimes employ the word *power,* where we should (strictly) expect *force.* A comment of his own may make this clearer:

> Thus + and − or Positive and Negative Electricity are the twin *Forces* of the Electric Power; Attraction and Repulsion the constituent Forces of the Power of Magnetism. Thus too the Polarity of a Power *implies* its Forces: and its Poles *are* its Forces. To this sense I would appropriate and confine the term, Force and Forces—Where, however, the sense is determined by the context, or when in any other way, all ambiguity is precluded, the *amphoteric* character of the word itself is of small practical importance. [Egerton 2801, f. 139 (verso)]

9. F I, 94n.

10. One of Coleridge's many coinages: from the Greek *psilos*—"mean" or "trifling." Thus by contrast with *philosophy* (love of wisdom or learning) *psilosophy* signifies "learning brought to bear on the trifling."

11. F I, 94n. Compare with this Michael Faraday's "final brooding impression"

> that particles are only centres of force; that the force or forces constitute the matter; that therefore there is no space between the particles distinct from the

particles of matter; that they touch each other just as much in gases as in liquids or solids; and that they are materially penetrable, probably even to their very centres. That, for instance, water is not two particles of oxygen side by side, but two spheres of power mutually penetrated, and the centres even coinciding. [Notes for a Lecture, 1844, in *Life and Letters of Michael Faraday,* by Bence Jones (Longmans, Green, 1870), II, 174–75.]

And see Chapter 11, below.

12. *Egerton* 2801, f. 143. See also note 8, above.

13. Herbert Read, *The True Voice of Feeling* (London: Faber & Faber, 1953), at p. 21. The chapters on Coleridge in this book are probing, original and sympathetic, but this only emphasises the point made in the text. Sir Herbert (or Herbert Read, as he was then) is one of the few critics who have actually quoted from the first part of BL Chapter XIII; and, immediately after doing so, he records it as his contention that Coleridge's literary criticism "derives its penetrative power from the use of the systematic method he had established by his philosophical speculation" (p. 175). Unfortunately this does not prevent him from lapsing, a few pages later, into conventional Coleridge hearsay: "Coleridge at an early age had made his standpoint the Christian revelation. He had a horror of any kind of self-consistent system . . ." It has required some self-restraint to refrain from italicizing the last ten words—and even pointing them with the rather offensive dunce's cap of an exclamation mark; but the rest of the book is much too good to permit of it.

14. "—all that is *outside* is comprized in length and surface—what remains, must therefore be *inside*—but again, the sole definition of matter is that which fills space—now it is with length, breadth, and length relative to Breadth that space is filled. In other words, Space has relation only to the *outside*. Depth therefore must be that *by* not *with* which Space is filled * . . . it must be that which causes it to be filled, and is therefore the true substance. Depth therefore cannot be an attribute of matter, which (i.e. Length + Breadth or Extension) is itself a mere abstraction, an ens rationis; but it must be a Power, the essence of which is *inwardness,* outwardness being its effect and mode of manifesting itself." [Egerton 2801, f. 150.]

15. CL IV, 775. And compare p. 760: ". . . in all pure phaenomena we behold only the copula, the balance or indifference of opposite energies."

16. Egerton 2801, f. 139.

17. P 356. Elsewhere Coleridge contrasts this view with the ordinary one, which considers "the powers of bodies to have been miraculously stuck into a prepared and pre-existing matter, as pins into a pin-cushion . . ." (TL 582.)

18. Egerton 2801, f. 139.

19. I am indebted for this formulation to Professor Craig W. Miller of the

---

* A distinction which perhaps requires a special measure of attention and reflection, to bring out its force.

Department of English, University of British Columbia, who very kindly presented me with a copy of his valuable doctoral dissertation: *An Examination of the Key Terms in Coleridge's Prose-Writings*. Professor Miller's article, "Coleridge's Concept of Nature," in the New York *Journal of the History of Ideas* (Jan.–March 1964) is a veritable oasis in the Sahara that confronts any traveller on the lookout for some real understanding in the twentieth century of what Coleridge thought and said on that subject in the nineteenth.

20. TM 18; F I, 479. The O.E.D. also gives him the first use of "polar" in physiology.

21. The expression is Richard Foster's, writing on R. P. Blackmur in his *The New Romantics* (Indiana University Press, 1962).

22. Shedd I, 471.

23. CS 38.

24. "Polarity is not a Composite Force, or *vis tertia* constituted by the moments of two counter-agents. It is 1 manifested in 2, not $1 + 1 = 2$ . . . The polar forces are the two forms, in which a one Power works in the same act and instant. Thus, it is not the *Power,* Attraction and the Power Repulsion at once tugging and tugging like two sturdy Wrestlers that compose the Magnet; but The Magnetic Power working at once positively and negatively. Attraction and Repulsion are the two Forces of the one magnetic Power." [Egerton 2801, f. 128.]

25. It may not be amiss, however, to quote the laudable attempt at definition made by Coleridge's disciple J. H. Green:

A One Power, which manifests itself in opposite and correlative forces, or in distinctive relations at once opposite and reciprocally complemented, and which therefore perpetuates itself in living reality and totality by *distinction in unity*. [*Spiritual Philosophy, founded on the Teaching of the Late S. T. Coleridge,* ed. J. Simon (London: 1865), I, 234.]

26. "Contrary to a very general impression, Coleridge was not just the inspired talker, a financial burden and practical problem to friends who supported the man Coleridge for the sake of the poet. It is perfectly clear to any reader of the letters that he entered into the lives and concerns of his acquaintances with a zestful mind interested in all manner of things and able to forget itself in its own energy. For example, take his relation to Thomas Poole and Humphry Davy. When he talked to Poole, a tanner and agriculturist, he asked him about the processes of tanning and the economics of agriculture. He stored up for him in his notebooks hints on how to plant trees and the sorts and uses of fertilizers. When Poole had a chemistry problem in his tanyard, it was Coleridge who asked questions of Davy, the solutions of which helped to further Davy's career. He also went to the Pneumatic Institution in Bristol and took part in some of the early experiments of Davy and Beddoes with nitrous oxide and other gases. Two or three years later when he was in Germany, in 1798–9, sugar was being experimentally produced from sugar beets, for the first time

on any scale. Coleridge visited the laboratory, talked to the Director and took notes on the whole process; and he may even have brought back some of the seeds to Davy. (He made a notebook memorandum to get some.) Davy was an adviser to the Board of Agriculture and would be interested. Sugar beets were not grown in England, so far as I can find out, till several decades later, but Coleridge, in the sugar shortage during the Napoleonic Wars and the blockade of the West Indies, may have been the first Englishman to think that the sugar ration might be supplemented by a crop at home." [IS 11–12.]

27. Somewhat surprisingly the Rev. Seth B. Watson, who in 1848 was enterprising enough to print the *Theory of Life* for the first time, falls into this very error in his Preface. Compare TL 564–68.

28. It follows therefore, that Body cannot be essentially *material*—but that Depth—i.e. a Power, manifesting itself in space, and contemplated in its *phaenomena*, Length and Breadth, is what we mean by Body. The term, matter, therefore, taken separately, should be confined to the Phaenomena—i.e. to Length and Breadth without Depth—now as in bodies the only universal Evidence of Depth is Weight, therefore matter but not body should be attributed to imponderable Phaenomena—Light, Heat, Magnetism, Electricity are material but not corporeal. [Egerton 2801 f. 151.]

29. That is, an understanding momently aware that the words and signs it makes use of are soft-focus' symbols rather than labels. For, once the "Idea" has been reached by a faculty, which is beyond the understanding, there can follow "Communication by the symbolic use of the Understanding, which is the function of Imagination." (From a note on the flyleaf of Tennemann's *Geschichte der Philosophie,* VII [2nd half].) Compare Appendix, below, n. 34, p. 267.

30. Coleridge is here using the word *imagery,* not as it is used in literary criticism, but to signify images reified—treated as things. He occasionally used the word *idols* in the same sense. He lived in an age when the scientist was a good deal more prone than he is today to take his 'models' literally and he advised his contemporaries to be aware "that the particular form, construction or model, that may be best fitted to render the idea intelligible is not necessarily the mode or form in which it actually arrives at realization." *

That not only our subjective models, but the phenomena themselves are "images"; that the function of the imagination is not only to create images but also to "dismiss" them; that it is only the imagination which can carry the mind to that which is "anterior to all image" †—all these are today fairly familiar notions in literary criticism and poetic theory, though not yet in the philosophy of science. Compare Chapter 11 below, pp. 142–143.

31. F I, 478–81; and IS 202 (where see also the Editor's Note at p. 431). See, further, Chapter 10, pp. 125–126, and Chapter 11, below. And compare F I, 50n.

---

* CS 21.

† *Treatise on Logic* II, 24 (on the sense in which he uses the word *idea,* contrasting Kant's concept of it as an *abstraction* from image).

4. Life

1. *Studies in Words* (Cambridge University Press, 1967).

2. F I, 500. It is interesting to note that one of the earliest opponents of Descartes raised the same objection. Giambattista Vico was not only a critic of the Cartesian dualism, but it was out of that critique that he developed his philosophy of history which, after long neglect, has recently begun to attract the attention it deserves.

In his *Autobiography** Vico points up the parallel with Epicurus, who "sets up in nature a principle falsely postulated: namely body already formed." Goethe put it another way, when, in his *Campagne in Frankreich,* he criticized "the rigid way of thinking—nothing can come into being except what already is." "With the Moderns," Coleridge himself wrote in a letter to Lord Liverpool (July 28, 1817): "nothing grows; all is made—Growth itself is but a disguised mode of being made by the superinduction of jam data upon a jam datum. This habit of thinking permeates the whole mass of our principles . . ." (CL IV, 757.) He also, of course, frequently pointed out that, because it is impossible that "a succession of different states should be the effect of the same agents in the same proportions of agency," † the system of materialism or mechanical causality ("the relation of unproductive particles to each other") is in fact only maintainable by the surreptitious smuggling in of unreduced "immaterial influences." This is usually done by impounding them semantically in some particular word or words. Democritus, and Epicurus, postulated not only atoms, but also the famous "swerve." Today the immaterial agent of change is more likely to be impounded in some such term as "tendency" or "pattern" or "mutation" (another way of saying "change") or "norm" or (in more up-to-date biology) "code," "message" or "information"—the whole change from e.g. a single cell to a complex living organism requiring no more than amino-acids and genes—*plus,* of course, an ability to code and decode, which last need not be unduly stressed. The trouble is, that particles *as such—"unproductive"* particles—cannot even arrange and rearrange themselves without more. Yet, if one credits them with immaterial "swerves" or "tendencies" and so forth, he has forgotten that those are the very things he was purporting to explain *by* them. He has overlooked

> the gross inconsistency of resorting to an immaterial influence in order to complete a system of materialism by the exclusion of all modes of existence which the theorist cannot in imagination, at least, *finger* and *peep* at! [TL 575.]

Of course the intellectual climate has altered since Coleridge's day and of course, with the transition from classical physics to "field" theory (in which his own thinking, through Humphry Davy and Michael Faraday, played a less than

---

* *The Autobiography of Giambattista Vico,* translated by Fisch and Bergin. Ithaca, New York, Great Seal Books. 1963.

† Unclassified MS in the possession of Victoria College, Toronto.

negligible part) * the advanced philosophy of science has altered, too. But, from Coleridge's point of view, as it would be, if he were alive today, it has not really altered very much (See Chapter 11, below).

The "forces" which are investigated are still conceived as exclusively physical forces. In Coleridge's terms, though they are not bodily, they are material. However it may be with the *philosophy* of science, *De non apparentibus et non existentibus eadem est ratio* remains built in, and as firmly as ever, to its *method*.

3. BL I, 90.

4. See, for instance, Chapter VIII of the *Biographia Literaria,* as well as the first paragraph of Chapter XIII already referred to. Its two opening sentences (italics not in original) are:

> To the best of my knowledge Descartes was the first philosopher, who introduced the absolute and essential heterogeneity of the soul as intelligence, and the body as matter. *The assumption, and the form of speaking have remained,* though the denial of all other properties to matter but that of extension, *on which denial the whole system of dualism is grounded,* has long been exploded. [BL 1, 88.]

Compare Chapter 3, above, p. 28.

5. BL I, 189.

6. (*Demosius and Mystes*) CS 196.

7. AR 44.

8. *Hints Towards a More Comprehensive Theory of Life.* This lengthy essay was out of print for very many years before Professor Donald Stauffer was enterprising enough to include it, in 1951, in his *Selected Poetry and Prose of Samuel Taylor Coleridge* (New York: Random House, The Modern Library). It was first published posthumously by the Rev. Seth B. Watson in 1848, and the date of composition is uncertain, though it can hardly have been earlier than 1816 or 1817. It was occasioned by Coleridge's participation in the scientific—and particularly medical—disputes of his day. He had numerous medical friends and, according to E. H. Coleridge, the essay was even intended to "form part" of an *Essay on Scrofula* to be written by James Gillman and read to the Royal College of Surgeons. Coleridge revered the memory of the great surgeon John Hunter, in whose mind, he tells us at the beginning of this Essay, "the true idea of Life existed." He also admired, and later became acquainted with John Abernethy, who propounded the theory that local diseases depend on general disorder of the system. He praises Abernethy in the Essay for the power and insight with which he asserted and vindicated the Hunterian theory of a vital principle independent of organisation or structure and prior to it. Elsewhere however he qualifies his praise with the criticism that Abernethy reified Hunter's vital principle in a way that Hunter himself never intended. Abernethy, he said, "clung to the phantom of a *supervenience,* instead of evolution, and of a supervenient *Fluid,* i.e. solved Phaenomena by

---

* See Chapter 11, below.

Phaenomena . . ." * There were in fact rival interpretations of Hunter's theory and five or six pages (584–89) of Coleridge's Essay are devoted to supporting the true interpretation by way of detailed replies to a recent attack on Abernethy by Sir William Lawrence. For a fuller account of the origin and background of the *Theory of Life* see Professor Snyder's *Coleridge on Logic and Learning* at pp. 16ff.

9. For the classical scholar this is impressively illustrated by the difficulty frequently experienced, of adequately rendering several Greek and Latin words such as *psyche, aiōn, bios, anima, vita,* all of which in some contexts merely connote, while in others they seem almost to denote *life (biological)*.

10. The corresponding earlier words were *inanimate* and *animate;* but *inanimate* signified, not merely "non-sentient" or "non-living," but *"no longer* sentient or living"; i.e. "having died." Whereas *inorganic,* and today usually *inanimate* also, denotes "not living," without any connotation of "having died." The concept of "life" in its modern sense is correlative to the equally modern concept of a lifelessness that is not the consequence of death.

11. As they saw it. But the rock on which religion was in danger of shipwreck was, in Coleridge's estimation, not the march of science itself, but mental indolence; and especially that of the clergy themselves. While he never tired of reiterating his respect for their cloth, he has made it abundantly clear that the triumph in England of the materialism he abhorred was being aided and abetted by the clergy, whose reasoning powers had fallen as much, or more, under "the despotism of the eye" as those of their opposite numbers in science and philosophy:

> But in the great majority of our gentry, and of our classically educated clergy, there is a fearful combination of the sensuous and the *unreal.* Whatever is *subjective,* the true and only proper *noumenon* or *intelligible,* is unintelligible to them. *But* all *substance ipso nomine* is necessarily *subjective,* and what these men call reality is object unsouled of all subject . . .†

It was the prevalence of this clerical and gentlemanly materialism that had impelled him to produce the *Friend* and to write *Aids to Reflection* and the *Statesman's Manual.*

12. A word of warning is called for here. The digression was historical rather than antiquarian. That is to say, it is still very relevant today. This needs stressing, because it is not uncommon, especially among those whose interests are psychological or biological, to see casual references to dualism as a fallacy that has long been "superseded." On closer examination however it appears that what is really being alluded to is simply the attempted elimination by Descartes of all *mental processes which can be linked with bodily functions.* This has of course long been rejected, and it is certainly important that modern psychology should tend to regard the whole human organism as "psychosomatic"; whereas for Descartes the only

---

* Letter to C. A. Tulk, Jan. 12, 1818—CL IV, 809.

† From a note written in Coleridge's copy of Southey's *Life of Wesley;* printed in *The Life of John Wesley* (Longmans, 1864), II, 49–51.

psychosomatic organ was the pineal gland. But its importance is severely circumscribed and, outside of the human organism, the dualism persists unchallenged. The "Cartesian dualism" which Coleridge was attacking would have been superseded only if, not only the individual's body, but also the world's body were today regarded as psychosomatic.

Philosophically of course it is another matter. But the fact that, for some decades now, "dualism" has been something like a dirty word in philosophy has not prevented its remaining the foundation on which the whole edifice of natural science is erected. See however Chapter 11, below.

> 13. "Their claim to this rank [i.e. the third gradation, represented by the greatest number of integral parts presupposed in the whole] I cannot here even attempt to support. It will be sufficient to explain my reason for having assigned it to them, by the avowal that I regard them in a twofold point of view: 1st, as the residue and product of animal life; 2nd, as manifesting the tendencies of the Life of Nature to vegetation or animalization. And this process I believe—in one instance by the peat morasses of the northern, and in the other instance by the coral banks of the southern hemisphere—to be still connected with the present order of vegetable and animal life, which constitutes the fourth and last step in these wide and comprehensive divisions." [TL 577.]

14. The distinction apparently drawn here between the two words *tendency* and *law* does not appear to be important. Indeed, later on the tendency is itself referred to as a law, when he speaks of "the unceasing *polarity of life, as the form of its process, and its tendency to progressive individuation as the law of its direction*" (589). This formulation, and the one just referred to in the text ("the tendency at once to individuate and to connect, to detach, but so as either to retain or to reproduce attachment") are perhaps the best epitomes and the most important to keep in mind. The key words are not *tendency* and *law*, but *polarity* and *individuation*.

15. In his striking article on *Coleridge's Concept of Nature*,* which has the high distinction of including the only attempt I have ever seen made to elucidate and expound the *Theory of Life* for the benefit of the ordinary reader, Professor Craig Miller writes:

> It would be idle to recapitulate what the *Theory of Life* says about the polypus, mollusca, coral, vermes, plants, fishes, birds and animals. Coleridge's comments on these, based mainly on mis-information, wild guesses and wishful thinking, make no contribution to modern biology. But once again, the method is more important than the details, the theory more important than the application, since it is the theory which is essential to an understanding of Coleridge's view of the human mind.

I find this rather surprising in the light of the rest of the article. It is no

---

* See Chapter 3, note 19, above.

doubt true that Coleridge's comments *have made* no contribution to modern biology; but that could hardly be otherwise in view of the fact that modern biology has up to now been based at all stages on cast-iron presuppositions which he himself vehemently rejected; and it must surely depend on the validity of those presuppositions (more often treated as established facts) whether the fault is mainly Coleridge's or mainly modern biology's.* Even in the matter of "mis-information" it would be safer to examine in each case how much of the "information" he missed is observed fact and how much of it a mixture of observed fact with unverifiable and equally unfalsifiable hypothesis.

I find it moreover difficult to see how a theory that is not in general borne out by its applications can be more important than the applications, or how a falsified theory of nature could contribute much, let alone be essential to an understanding of the human mind, which is not only Coleridge's but also (as I understand Professor Miller to have been suggesting) both luminous and veridical.

16. Perhaps only once, explicitly, in a parenthetical reference to "the primeval chemical epoch of the Wernerian School" (591). Elsewhere it is implicit only, as for instance in his contrast between geological residues and "the present order" of vegetable and animal life" (577, and quoted in n. 13, above).

17. On this dubious word and, much more importantly, on the dawn of historical consciousness in general, see a recent and original work: *Historical Consciousness or the Remembered Past,* by John Lukacs (New York: Harper & Row, 1968).

18. Compare Robert Preyer's undeservedly neglected contribution to Coleridge studies in *Bentham, Coleride and the Science of History,* and particularly Chapter 2, "Coleridge's Historical Thought" (Bochum-Langendreer: Verlag Heinrich Pöppinghaus OGH., 1958).

19. Compare Chalmers Mitchell's article on *"Evolution," Encyclopaedia Britannica* (13th ed.), X, 31.

20. However in *Aids to Reflection* Coleridge does on one occasion commit himself to the statement that "Nature is a line in constant and continuous evolution." (AR 196.)

21. The sort of *aporia* that results from terror of the argument from design plus inability to distinguish it from that teleological principle (goal-directedness) without which organism is simply unintelligible, was wittily expressed by Von Bruecke: "Teleology is a lady without whom no biologist can live; yet he is ashamed to show himself in public with her." Quoted in *The Art of Scientific Investigation,* by W. I. B. Beveridge, p. 62.

22. *Nature* is a word Coleridge used on many occasions and defined on several. I should not like to say there is no room for difference of opinion about his meaning, but what I have said here is said after careful consideration, not only of the *Theory of Life,* but also of (inter alia) the following contexts: AR 46n, 185 and 200; BL I, 174; F I, 467n, 470, 497–98 and 497 n. 2; PL 370.

23. F I, 467n.

---

* Compare Chapter 3, note 13; and see Chapter 11, below.

24. AR 200. Compare also AR 46n and the lengthy discussion of the word *origin* at AR 195 and 195n.

5. Outness

1. M. H. Abrams, *The Mirror and the Lamp* (New York: Norton, 1957), p. 168.

2. *Ib.* p. 186.

3. Taken out of context this would be an unpardonable overstatement. *The Mirror and the Lamp* (the quoted observation is on p. 169) is not a book that overlooks anything. Professor Abrams gives us, out of the rich store of his learning, every scrap of background we could ask for. It is all there, the historical link with Neoplatonism, Jakob Böhme, Herder, German *Naturphilosophie,* Goethe's biology and much more; so that an attentive reader should be left in no doubt that Coleridge's "organicism" was more than a metaphor to him. The complaint is only that this is ignored at important points in the exposition, and in such a way as to leave the unwary reader confused between Coleridge's organicism and what appears by implication to be the author's. It is, that the difference between the two could with advantage have been made clearer. If, for instance, at the point where he refers us to Kant's critique of *Teleological Judgment* (the effect of which is to deny cognitive validity to the goal-directed relation between whole and parts, which we cannot however help *assuming* in organic structures), Professor Abrams had added some such comment as: "and moreover Kant was right, and Coleridge and his friends were wrong; so that what they thought were literal descriptions were in fact metaphorical ones," all would be well. Obviously anyone is entitled to hold that Coleridge was deluded. But this is not what is said. Rather it is tacitly assumed that Coleridge himself cannot really have understood what he was saying, so that, in the very article and moment of exegesis, he must be accorded the indulgence of his exponent's corrective re-casting. Anyone who doubts that this has been the general practice in dealing with Coleridge's philosophy should keep a sharp look out for the point at which the word *hypostatized* is introduced. *The Mirror and the Lamp* is a book for which I have an almost unbounded admiration; it is a sort of paradigm for me of what such a book should be, and one which I have no hope of nearing myself. But that only adds to the importance of what I am saying. The point is, not that Professor Abrams falls short in this respect, but that *even* Professor Abrams does.

4. And compare *The Mirror and the Lamp,* p. 224.

5. AR 46n; IS 103.

6. F I, 497–98, as amended by Coleridge in a note dated June 23, 1829. (*The Friend,* Pickering, 1837, III, 178.) I have used this recension as being a little simpler in form than the similar one given in F I, 497 n. 2.

7. *Ib.* 498.

8. See, for instance, BL I, 167.

9. Yet Professor Jackson can describe the first paragraphs of Chapter XIII as "an opening bow to Descartes and Kant." (*Method and Imagination in Coleridge's Criticism.* (London: Routledge & Kegan Paul, 1969), at p. 71). This would be

rather odd even if there had been no Chapter VIII. In the light of that most explicit chapter it looks very odd indeed.

10. See Chapter 3, pp. 26–27.

11. BL I, 177. The English preposition *without*, which can signify both (*a*) exclusion and (*b*) independence, appears particularly apposite here.

12. "How can that be denied to be true, the contrary of which would destroy all meaning and intelligible purpose of that (the Subjective Understanding) by which the Truth is to be denied?" (Note on Tennemann's *Geschichte der Philosophie*, quoted PL 439.)

13. BL 178.

14. Shedd I, 430n (*Lay Sermon*).

15. BL 178. The reason why this sounds as startling as it does is that it is out of kilter with our inveterate conviction that perception is a process taking place inside the skin. For Coleridge the break betweeen inwardness and outness is not the skin or any organ it contains; it is the break between an act and its product, or between what is an act and what is not. Bergson, in his *Matter and Memory*, insisted that the real significance of the surface of the body is, that it is "the only portion of space which is both perceived and felt." We have to distinguish between perception itself and its directedness; or in the vocabulary that phenomenology has made more familiar to some contemporaries, between perception and the intentionality in perception. The very idea that "pure," or "impersonal" perception is not here within me, but out there among the objects, has however become such a stumbling-block, or scandal, that, even if it is entertained for a moment, it is quickly ignored. So, Bergson's *élan vital* is remembered with affection, and even respect, but his analysis of perception (with its conclusion: ". . . my perception is outside my body, and my affection within it . . . external objects are perceived by me where they are, in themselves and not in me") is rarely referred to.

Yet, ever since Kant's reduction of Cartesian "nature" to the status of appearances, the only alternative metaphysical stance is that concept of a psychic "projection" of nature as we know her upon a background consisting of something else; which has in fact been adopted both in the pursuit of science and by popular consent. Thus, the complex and ingenious historical interpretations of psychoanalytical theory have it for all their base; we owed to it, among much else, that advocacy of withdrawal into the splendid isolation of subjectivity, which characterised so much of the symbolist movement in art and literature; while the current spate of interest in metaphor, and in parabolic utterance in general, is always picking at it, and coming to the conclusion that the only thing we can really do about "reality" is to find new ways of saying that nothing can be said about it. Compare Chapter 7, below, note 3.

16. What is today most commonly acknowledged as real is not the familiar 'nature' of actual experience, but an inferred 'nature,' concluded from a mixture of experience, judgment and fancy. There are indeed, it is considered, "things without us"; the real object is independent of our consciousness. But between the one and the other, and dependent now on our forms of perception, there is interposed a something called "the object as experienced"; and a totality of these latter objects is wrapped round each perceiving subject like a kind of figured tapestry,

hiding the very objects themselves. Look a little closer however and you will find that, outside the higher échelons of non-descriptive physics, the "very objects themselves" turn out to be suspiciously like the "objects as experienced." And this is true both of scientific theory and of popular fancy. Indeed, "counterparts" would hardly be too strong a word. For instance, it must in theory be the former, the very 'objects themselves,' about which the story of a pre-human evolution is told to the children, though it is so often illustrated by colorful pictures of 'objects as experienced.' Moreover, for that greater part of the natural process, which even in the present is not being actually experienced, the imperceptible or unperceived goings on of these very 'objects themselves' are calculated, and when necessary described, in all respects as if they were objects as experienced. We find it technologically convenient to endow them with "modes of existence which the theorist can, in imagination at least, *finger* and *peep* at." (TL 575.)

For a lucid analysis of this sophisticated, or, as I have ventured to call it, bastard realism, couched in a modern, non-technical and non-philosophical idiom, compare Chapters 2 and 3 of *The Sciences and the Humanities,* by W. T. Jones (University of California Press, 1967).

17. BL I, 178–79. Both epithets are significant. "True" for the reasons elaborated in the quotation that follows; "original," because this kind of realism can in the end only co-exist with the conviction that the productive process which acts in nature "is essentially one (that is, of one kind) with the intelligence, which is in the human mind above nature" (pp. 60–61, above); and this belief was once universal. Now however it has become "disfigured . . . by accidental forms or accompaniments." (F I, 498.) The weaning of the Western mind from actual realism may be thought to have begun with popular acceptance of Copernicanism. What we see in the heavens is not at all like what is "really there." And that makes it easier to accept, from physics, neurology etc. that what we see on earth is not really there either. With the spread of literacy the sophisticated realism of a presumed gulf between appearance and reality has virtually taken the place of "naïve" realism as the form of common sense.

18. Marginal note in Kant's *Logik.* H. Nidecker, *Revue de Littérature Comparée* (1927), VII, 137. It may be observed here, though it is anticipating somewhat, that the determination to accept, and not thereafter to cease accepting, a conclusion of our judgment even though it contradicts a law of our nature, is, in Coleridge's view, an energy of the will. It constitutes that "fidelity" to reason, which was his definition of "faith." On that fidelity, among much else, the advance of science has depended; without it there could, for instance, have been no Copernican revolution, since it is a law of our nature to perceive the earth at rest and the sun and stars in motion round it. Compare Chapter 12, p. 151, below.

19. F I, 497.

20. *On Poesy or Art.* BL II, 259.

21. BL I, 182 (Chapter XII, Thesis V). Compare: "—the mind is distinguished from other things as a subject, that is its own object, an eye, as it were, that is its own mirror beholding and self-beheld." (*Treatise on Logic,* II, 54.) Compare PL 371.

22. Compare pp. 60–61, above.

23. ". . . the sum or I AM; which I shall hereafter indiscriminately express by the words spirit, self, and self-consciousness." (BL I, 183 [Chapter XII, Thesis VI].)

We know (*savoir*) by analysis and inference, that it must be so. We can only know (*connaître*) experientially that it *is* so, to the extent that we are aware, whether by native dower or from voluntary practice, of the act of thinking. Compare Chapter I (p. 13 ff.) and n. 29 (p. 198), above.

24. "I can conceive . . . Passivity . . . as a specific Grade of action; but by no effort can I conceive or imagine action as a mode of passivity, no act having been presupposed." (Marginal note in Jacobi's *Letters to Moses Mendelsohn on the Teaching of Spinoza*, p. 107 [BM].)

25. This second indispensable limb of Coleridge's argument in Chapter XII has been strangely overlooked. I. A. Richards for example ignores it altogether in his *Coleridge on Imagination* and is enabled by the omission to advance his ingenious claim that Coleridge's psychology of subject and object is equally susceptible of either an "idealist" or a behaviourist interpretation; while, in Professor Thomas McFarland's *Coleridge and the Pantheist Tradition,* the rival claims on our judgment of "it is" and "I am" (the actual crux, namely, on which Coleridge hung his refutation of Pantheism) are breezily disposed of in half a page out of 382 pages in all (Oxford: Clarendon Press, 1969, pp. 302–3). What is one to say— what *can* one say, unless perhaps *tantamne rem tam negligenter?*

It is otherwise with Professor J. A. Appleyard. He reproduces very fully the train of thought in this part of Chapter XII. Faithfully following in Coleridge's footsteps, he leads his readers up to its conclusion in that realism, which "believes and requires neither more nor less, than that the object which it beholds or presents to itself, is the real and very object." And then he comments as follows (p. 194):

> Coleridge's paradox is fascinating. He solves with apparent ease the central problem of several centuries of philosophy. Can his words be intelligibly interpreted, or is there here only more "metaphysical pathos"? There seems to be no way of answering.

And yet the writer has himself just finished giving us a perfectly intelligible interpretation and has drawn attention to no flaw in the analysis. Thus, he says, in effect: "I see how everything you say follows from everything else—but I feel there must be a catch in it." Poor Coleridge! Too subtle to be understood and, when at last he is understood, too obvious to be believed. The only possible reply to such a comment is, with deference, *ad hominem:* 'How I should hate to have you on the jury, my friend, if I were on trial for my life for a crime I hadn't committed!'

For a less reluctant exposition see "Coleridge's True and Original Realism," Nicholas Brooke, *Durham University Journal,* new series 22 (1961).

26. Egerton 2801 f. 47.

27. BL I, 183 (Chapter XII, Thesis VI).

28. "Born in the purple." That is, sovereign by right of birth. The whole passage, both its tone and its content, furnishes a striking commentary on Pro-

fessor Arthur O. Lovejoy's contention that the "unmistakable" main source of Coleridge's belief in free will was his emotional need to believe in original sin. Compare *Coleridge and Kant's Two Worlds* in *Essays in the History of Ideas* (Baltimore: Johns Hopkins Press, 1948), p. 244.

29. TL 601.

6. Imagination and Fancy (1)

1. BL I, 4. That is, "poetic thoughts" as distinct from "thoughts *translated* into the language of poetry." (*Ib.* p. 11.)

2. "I never judge system-wise of things," he wrote to Southey, "but fasten upon particulars." It is a pity that Lamb, who prided himself on keeping letters, somehow lost nearly all those from Coleridge to himself during this period, though we have several of his replies.

3. CL I, 406.

4. BL I, 13.

5. "I was in my twenty-fourth year, when I had the happiness of knowing Mr. Wordsworth personally, and while memory lasts, I shall hardly forget the sudden effect produced on my mind, by his recitation of a manuscript poem . . ." (BL I, 58.)

6. BL I, xxvii. Coleridge himself records how "even before my fifteenth year, I had bewildered myself in metaphysical, and theological controversy. Nothing else pleased me." (*Ib.* p. 9.)

7. "Christ's Hospital Five and Thirty Years ago" in *Essays of Elia.*

8. BL I, 94. Compare the following paragraph from the very long letter to C. A. Tulk, in which Coleridge has been expounding his views on life as polarity:

> Accept this very rude sketch of the very rudiments of '*Heraclitus redivivus*'— One little presumption of their truth is, that as Wordsworth, Southey, and indeed all my intelligent Friends well know & attest, I had formed it during the study of Plato, and the Scholars of Ammonius, and in later times of Scotus (Joan. Erigena), Giordano Bruno, Behmen, and the much calumniated Spinoza (whose System is to mine just what a Skeleton is to a Body, fearful because it is only the *Skeleton*) long before Schelling had published his first and imperfect view—. If I had met a friend & a Brother in the Desart of Arabia, I could scarcely have been more delighted than I was in finding a fellow-laborer and in the only Country in which a man dare exercise his *reason* without being thought to have lost his Wits, & be out of his senses. [September, 1817 —CL IV, 775.]

The "Scholars of Ammonius" were Plotinus and Origen.

9. And even before Cambridge. He had already, he says, "conjured over the *Aurora* at school." (Letter to Ludwig Tieck—CL IV, 750.) Years later he returned to Böhme and added further extensive annotations to his copy of William Law's translation in four volumes, which is now in the British Museum. These are of very great interest. Some of the comments are theological, and some are scientific

in their frame of reference, and bear closely on the *Theory of Life* (see Chapter 4, above). The following two extracts may serve to illustrate their nature and significance:

From the note on Para. 6 of Böhme's *Concerning the Threefold Life of Man* (Vol. II of Law's translation): ". . . that every life desireth its own Mother, (out of which the life is generated) for a food":

> This position is just, if only it be rightly interpreted. There is no union but of opposites, = the Law of Polarity—and the converse follows by the Law of Identity—viz. there are no opposites without a common principle—or the essence of all opposites, ex gr. the N. and S. Poles of a Magnet, is the unity, or that which is neither because it is the essence of both—even as all manifestation of unity is by opposition. Now that which each opposite seeks in the other as its own essence—in which seeking consists the tendency to union, Behmen entitles the Mother . . .

From the note (signed and dated 19th October 1818) on the front flyleaf to the same volume:

> Observe that during my earlier studies of these works I had entertained sundry convictions, which I have now outgrown—the πρωτον ψευδος (prōton pseudos) or root of my mistake being this—that in common with Newton, Kant, Schelling, Steffens, etc. I had assumed four primary forces, Attraction and Repulsion as the poles of Length, and − and + Electricity as the Poles of Breadth—and considered Gravitation as the *offspring* of the synthesis (not with Kant as the Synthesis itself) of Attraction and Repulsion. This schema leavens too many of my notes. At present I admit two *primary* forces only . . .

And see Chapter 11, below.

10. Compare: *The Platonic Renaissance in England*, E. Cassirer. (London: Thomas Nelson & Sons, 1953 [*Die platonische Renaissance in England und die Schule von Cambridge*, 1937, translated by J. P. Pettegrue]; *The Redemption of Thinking*, Rudolf Steiner (ed. Shepherd and Nicoll). (London: Hodder and Stoughton, 1956); and the author's *Romanticism Comes of Age* (essay entitled "Man, Thought and Nature") (London: Rudolf Steiner Press, 1966, and Middletown: Wesleyan University Press, 1967).

11. BL I, 56–58.

12. By Shawcross for instance, who however goes much too far when he says (Introduction, p. lxxvi): "the poetical criticism of the second part is based, not on the deductions of the metaphysician, but on the intuitive insight of the poet." M. H. Abrams on the contrary (and on this he is joined by I. A. Richards, Herbert Read, R. H. Fogle, J. A. Appleyard and no doubt many others) considers that Coleridge's "metaphysical premises, far from being alien to his critical practice, reappear as the chief critical principles which make possible his characteristic insights into the constitution and qualities of specific forms." (*The Mirror and the Lamp*, p. 115.) To this rule the most that can be said is that the Wordsworth criticism in the *Biographia Literaria* shows a few exceptions.

13. BL I, 58 and note 5, above. As to the identity of the poem see Shawcross's Note at BL I, 224. (In Wordsworth's *Collected Poems* "The Female Vagrant" occurs as stanzas 23-50 of the longer poem entitled *Guilt and Sorrow*.)

14. "They and they only can acquire the philosophic imagination, the sacred power of self-intuition, who within themselves can interpret and understand the symbol, that the wings of the air-sylph are forming within the skin of the caterpillar; those only, who feel in their own spirits the same instinct, which impels the chrysalis of the horned fly to leave room in the involucrum for antennae yet to come. They know and feel that the *potential* works *in* them, even as the *actual* works on them!" BL II, 167.

(Note: "The *same* instinct": i.e. not merely a similar or analogous one. The passage is one of many that reveal a wide difference between Coleridge's concept of "imagination" and Kant's "productive imagination." Philosophic imagination would appear to be primary imagination emerging from unconscious into conscious function. So also is secondary imagination—which however is predominantly poetic, while philosophic imagination is predominantly cognitive.)

Professor Appleyard, rather strangely, appears to equate the distinction between philosophic and poetic imagination with that between primary and secondary imagination, whose operation is attended to, whereas "in common usage we do not much attend to the mediating operation of the primary imagination." (*Coleridge's Philosophy of Literature,* 180n.) But surely it is just the being "attended to" that renders imagination philosophic! "They and they only can acquire the philosophic imagination . . ." Primary imagination not attended to is "common usage," because, even when not attended to, it is "the prime Agent of *all* human Perception." See page 74, below, and Chapter 7.

15. BL I, 86.

16. Appleyard 211.

17. As to his subsequent modification of this paragraph, see Chapter 12, note 24, below, (p. 253).

7. Imagination and Fancy (2)

1. BL I, 186 (Chapter XII, Thesis X).

2. Compare Chapter 1, above.

3. Compare Chapter 5, note 15, and Chapter 1, above. Coleridge was continually attempting, by a variety of routes, to approach and enter the very moment of perception and/or sensation. On one occasion,* for instance, he criticises Berkeley for assuming that all perception is reducible to sensation, all sensation is subjective, and therefore all perception is merely subjective. For him (Coleridge) perception is a more finely organised sensation, and sensation "a minimum, or lower degree of perception." But even sensation itself is *never merely subjective.*

"The whole difficulty lies," he comments, "in the co-existence of Agere et Pati [here perhaps best translated "being active" and "being passive"] as Predicates of the same subject." It could also be characterized as the difficulty (later

---

* Notes in Schelling's *System des transcendentalen Idealismus.* BM. Flyleaves at beginning and end of volume.

stressed by the phenomenologists) of distinguishing the element of directedness or intentionality in a sensation from the total event. One might even be tempted to "desynonymize" the words *sensation* (active) and *sense* (passive) for the purpose, the latter being reserved for sensation artificially considered apart from the intentionality in it. Only one would need to beware of surreptitiously taking *sense* as the "objective," and *sensation* as the "subjective" component of the total event— since to do so would be to revert to a fictitious basis in "outness." Thus (from the long footnote in Essay III, Section I, of the *Friend*): "Under the term SENSE, I comprise whatever is passive in our being . . ." (F I, 177.)

The difficulty is that which we have in conceiving an active principle or force that is forever giving rise to a passive one, or a passive one that is forever being generated by the active one and again being dissolved and dissipated by it. It is the difficulty of "pin-pointing" a concept that has nothing in common with the point of a pin. And the difficulty itself arises because the process is arrested for us by the despotism of the eye, which in its turn has arisen partly from the lethargy of custom and partly from the operation of active fancy. It is in fact a prison wall which, in the last resort, cannot be overleaped in discursive thought but only by an act of imagination. Or, as was propounded in Chapter 3, the apprehension of "separative projection," that is polarity, is *the* moment of imagination. For only imagination can grasp, and its essential function is to grasp, "that life-ebullient stream which breaks through every momentary embankment, again, indeed, and evermore to embank itself, but within no banks to stagnate and be imprisoned." (F I, 519.)

4. Compare Donald Stauffer's observation in his necessarily condensed but very penetrating Introduction to *The Selected Poetry and Prose of Samuel Taylor Coleridge* at page x: "What did he talk about? Everything. Yet essentially his one never-entirely-forgotten subject was relationship—"

5. "The imagination is the distinguishing characteristic of man as a progressive being . . ." (*Coleridge's Miscellaneous Criticism,* ed. T. M. Raysor [Constable, 1936], p. 193.)

6. "Could a rule be given from *without,* poetry would cease to be poetry, and sink into a mechanical art. It would be μόρφωσις [fashioning], not ποίησις [making]. The rules of the Imagination are themselves the very powers of growth and production." (BL II, 65.)

7. BL II, 167.

8. BL I, 85f.

9. F I, 475, 492.

10. "Much against my will I repeat this scholastic term, *multeity,* but I have sought in vain for an unequivocal word of a less repulsive character, that would convey the notion in a positive and not comparative sense in kind, as opposed to the *Unum et simplex,* not in degree, as contrasted with the *few.*" [TL 575n.]

"I felt that I could not substitute *multitude,* without more or less connecting with it the notion of 'a *great* many.'" [BL II, 230.]

11. TL 573.

12. *Lectures* (*1818*), quoted BL II, 270.

13. Raysor I, 224. Coleridge found, as others have found before and since, that Shakespeare himself had hintingly anticipated his deepest insight (Man is a nature humanized) two hundred years earlier. In his chapter on metre (XVIII) in the *Biographia Literaria*, he aptly quotes Polixenes' reply, in the *Winter's Tale*, to Perdita's objection against horticultural 'improvements' of nature:

> nature is made better by no mean
> But nature makes that mean . . .
>   This is an art
> Which does mend nature—change it rather: but
> The art itself is nature.

14. BL II, 253.

15. BL II, 10.

16. Lectures 1811–12. Raysor II, 66–67.

17. *On Poesy or Art.* BL II, 255.

18. TL 574. And compare Chapter 4, above, p. 50.

19. Culminating perhaps in I. A. Richard's *Coleridge on Imagination*, in which he begins by pouring something like scorn on the "complacency" of those, beginning with Pater, who would sweep the distinction away—and then proceeds to sweep it away himself with his projective theory of a purely *subjective* imagination that modifies experience or meaning by enabling its aggregate parts to "reciprocally stress" one another. Compare *Coleridge on Imagination*, 38ff. and 176.

20. CL II, 1034.

21. BL I, 59 and 60.

22. BL I, 64.

23. BL I, 108. And compare II, 64.

24. Richards, *op. cit.,* p. 154.

25. BL I, 64.

26. BL I, 188. And compare TL 572. In short, all so-called 'kinds' are to be seen as degrees of the one true *kind,* which is "Life and intelligence." What is needed, he wrote to Wordsworth in 1815, is

> a general revolution in the modes of developing and disciplining the human mind by the substitution of Life, and Intelligence (considered in its different powers from the Plant up to that state in which the difference of Degree becomes a new kind (man, self-consciousness) but yet not by essential opposition) for the philosophy of mechanism which in everything that is most worthy of the human Intellect strikes *Death,* and cheats itself by mistaking clear Images for distinct conceptions . . . [CL IV, 575.]

27. BL I, 194.

28. Marginal note to Baxter's *Life of Himself.* Shedd V, 326.

29. *Demosius and Mystes,* CS 194.

30. TT Aug. 20th, 1833. Compare BL I, 194:

I am disposed to conjecture that he [Wordsworth] has mistaken the co-presence of fancy with imagination for the operation of the latter singly. A man may work with two very different tools at the same moment; each has its share in the work, but the work effected by each is distinct and different.

31. The proper place and status of fancy are most explicitly indicated in one of Coleridge's Marginalia:

. . . The simplest yet practically sufficient order of the Mental Powers is, beginning from the

	lowest	*highest*
	Sense	Reason
Fancy and Imagination are	Fancy	Imagination
Oscillations, this connecting	Understanding	Understanding
Reason and Understanding; that	Understanding	Understanding
connecting Sense and Understanding	Imagination	Fancy
	Reason	Sense

[W. G. Tennemann, *Geschichte der Philosophie,* Vol. VIII (2nd half). Note on backboard.]

32. Compare note 3, above.

33. TT June 23rd, 1834.

34. BL I, 73.

35. BL I, 87.

36. BL II, 208.

37. It is the introduction of the concept of fancy at the end of Chapter IV that leads in to the three chapters (V, VI and VII) on the theory of association of ideas, with which the philosophical section opens.

38. BL II, 6.

39. BL I, 189. "I am in the habit of making marginal observations in the books I read—a habit indulged by the partiality of my friends. For the last 20 years there is scarce a book so be-penned or be-pencilled but some one or more instances will be found noticed by me of the power of the visual and its substitution for the conceptual." (IS 31.)

40. "This with all other similar attempts to render *that* an object of sight which has no relation to sight has been already sufficiently exposed . . . We are restless because invisible things are not the objects of vision; and metaphysical systems, for the most part, become popular, not for their truth, but in proportion as they attribute to causes a susceptibility of being *seen,* if only our visual organs were sufficiently powerful." [BL I, 74.]

The fixities and definites that are the product of passive fancy and primary imagination become "idols" when the active fancy wilfully treats them, first, as objective reality and finally as the *sole* objective reality—incapable therefore of being dissolved and dissipated (Compare F I, 518). Passive fancy results in the first place from "the despotism of the eye;" active fancy, by meekly accepting and *employing* it, enlarges and rivets the despotism. Compare TL 584: ". . . habitual slavery to the eye, or its reflex, the passive fancy, under the influences of the corpuscularian philosophy . . ."

41. Consider, for instance, the argument of Essays X and XI in Section II of the *Friend*: In the first place man is compelled "by an obscure sensation which he is unable to resist or to comprehend . . . to contemplate as without and independent of himself what yet he could not contemplate at all, were it not a modification of his own being." (I would equate this "obscure sensation" with the "passive" fancy, and the ensuing "law" with the "active" fancy). By "the law of his understanding and fancy" he is *impelled* "to abstract the changes and outward relations of matter and to arrange them under the form of causes and effects." Moreover "this was necessary, as the condition under which alone experience and intellectual growth are possible." But here Coleridge immediately adds that *"by the same law"* man is inevitably *"tempted"*

> to misinterpret a constant precedence into positive causation, and thus to break and scatter the one divine and invisible life of nature into countless idols of the sense; and falling prostrate before lifeless images, the creatures of his own abstraction, is himself sensualized, and becomes a slave to the things of which he was formed to be the conqueror and sovereign.*

Is it a *law,* or a *temptation,* that is being pointed to? Or is the temptation itself a law? It is, it appears, a "general" law which, unless it be tempered and counteracted by the intervention of "particular" laws, must actually "prevent or greatly endanger man's development and progression." Compare Chapter 8, note 42, below.

Coleridge perceives the intervention of these particular laws in the intermittent but progressive revelation of Reason through the Greek brotherhoods and Mysteries, the Hebrew prophets and ultimately the Christian revelation itself. Nevertheless this counterpoint between general laws and particular laws is in some sense itself a part of the total process of creation; for we find it at work in "all inferior things from the grass on the house top to the giant trees of the forest." By its subjection to universal laws each thing belongs to the whole, "as interpenetrated by the powers of the whole"; by the intervention of particular laws "the universal laws are suspended or tempered for the weal and sustenance of each particular class."

Finally this dichotomy between general and particular laws (involving the "intervention" of the latter in the former) may itself, for all Coleridge knows, be in the end resolvable. Possibly it "is, or with the increase of science will be, resolvable into the universal laws which they [the particular laws] had appeared to counterbalance." And this could be the case with the miracles, which were a part

---

* Recalling the closing paragraphs of the *Theory of Life*. See Chapter 5 above, p. 68.

(*not,* he elsewhere insists, a *proof*) of the Gospel revelation. If so, the only difference would be

> that what we now consider as miracles in opposition to ordinary experience, we should then reverence with a yet higher devotion as harmonious parts of one great complex whole, when the antithesis between experience and belief would itself be taken up into the unity of intuitive reason.

Possibly: but here Coleridge will not commit himself, since "wisdom forbids her children to antedate their knowledge, or to act or feel otherwise or further than they know."

42. BL I, 188.

43. "Polarity always supposes a contrariety in the Origins of its antagonist Forces—always pre-supposes a contradiction in its Grounds. For its end is to reconcile a contradiction, which yet must remain as long as Nature remains . . ." (Egerton 2801, f. 128). Compare Ramon Lull's definition of *Contrarietas* as *quorundam mutua resistentia propter diversos fines*—"mutual resistance on account of diverse ends." (See Appendix, p. 183, and n. 10, below.)

44. BL II, 12. I do not believe *magical* here is simply a glamour word. It is intended to be read with "synthetic," as showing that what is signified is the interinanimating synthesis of polarity and not the "synartesis," or joining together, from which it is to be carefully distinguished (cf. Chapter 3, above, p. 31).

45. BL II, 20. And see Shawcross's Note for similar observation elsewhere.

46. BL II, 6 (italics not in original).

47. BL II, 5.

8. Understanding

1. F I, 517 and 517 nn, 4–6 (Essay XI, Section II). The slight alterations made by Coleridge in various successive versions—fully recorded in the recent and admirable edition of the *Friend* (the first to be issued of the "Collected Coleridge")—suggest that he was particularly anxious here to say precisely what he thought and nothing else; and to say it as clearly as he knew how. For a brief summary of the argument in the Essay see Chapter 7, note 41, above.

2. F I, 158: "—every intellectual act, however you may distinguish it by name in respect of the originating faculty, is truly the act of the entire man." TT 29.7.1830. And see Shawcross's Introduction (BL I, lxxxvi–vii) for a full discussion of the point

3. F I, 177; and compare TT 29.7.1830.

4. Lectures 1811–12. Raysor II, 138.

5. BL I, 187–88.

6. F II, 76.

7. In the *Friend, Aids to Reflection,* and *Table Talk* passim, and in Appendix B to the *Statesman's Manual* (Shedd I, 456–71); F I, 177n; F I, 520–21; F II, 77; and F II, 217 (BL II, 159). See in particular, AR 157–72 (Stauffer, 536–48).

8. F II, 76 (with n. 5) and 77 (with n. 1). As to the alterations made in successive versions, compare note 1, above.

9. Compare Marginal note on Thomas Taylor's *Proclus*, N I (Notes), p. 456.

10. See for instance AR 157–72 (Stauffer 536–48) headed *On the Difference in Kind of Reason and the Understanding.*

11. It has already been noticed that Coleridge—perhaps unwisely—did not abjure the use of the *word* "faculty." He even occasionally employs it for reason, in one of its aspects (see e.g. F I, 158). It is clear that "faculty" was for him a term of very wide extension indeed. Thus, he could write, in the *Friend,* of ". . . a yet far higher Faculty (Self-consciousness for instance) . . ." Reason can safely be sometimes called a faculty—if even self-consciousness can.

12. *Treatise on Logic* II, 39.

13. Shedd I, 461.

14. Shedd V, 286.

15. AR 157.

16. BL I, 167.

17. BL I, 164.

18. BL I, 164. Cf. F I, 470 (IS 248).

19. F II, 75, n. 3.

20. F I, 402; and see 388 n. 1. This part of the Introduction to Vol. III (1818 edition) was contributed by Wordsworth, but the thought is clearly Coleridge's.

21. Shedd V, 286. The gamut also illuminates, I think, the following difficult passage from the *Treatise on Logic*:

> . . . provided we are aware of the unindividual and transcendent character of the Reason as a presence to the human mind not a particular faculty or component part of the mind . . . it is philosophically indifferent whether we take the term Understanding as a perfect synonyme of Mind and thus consider the Understanding in a twofold application, that is, now exercised discursively and now through the intuitive power, or whether we take the term of the mind exclusively as the common term or genus and the Understanding and the Sense as its two component faculties or species. [*Treatise on Logic* II, f. 34.]

22. "Perhaps the safer use of the term, understanding, for general purposes, is to take it as the mind, or rather as the man himself considered as a concipient as well as percipient being, and reason as a power supervening." [Shedd I, 46on.]

". . . the word, Understanding, may be used in two meanings, a wider and a narrower. In the first, it means the active power of the Soul, THOUGHT, as opposed to its passive or merely recipient property, the SENSE: (N.B. not the *Senses,* but that quality of the Soul which receives impressions from the Senses, even as the Senses receive impressions from objects out of us,). So defined it *includes* the Reason. In its narrower meaning the Understanding is used for the faculty, by which we form distinct *notions* of Things and *immediate,* positive judgments . . ."

"The few Readers, for whom this note [to the Friend] is intended" (as Coleridge puts it) will be well advised to read the whole passage at F II, 77.

23. P 350.

24. The faculty of course, not the *content,* of understanding. There is no idle speculation in Coleridge about "inherited memories." It is for the same reason that talent can be inherited, though genius cannot.

25. F 156.

26. AR 178. And compare AR 81: ". . . and most wonderfully, I say, doth the muscular life in the insect, and the musculo-arterial in the bird, imitate and typically rehearse, the adaptive understanding."

27. F I, 176.

28. AR 178.

29. *Treatise on Logic* II, 34; letter to Sir George Beaumont (CL III, 152); and elsewhere.

30. See, for instance, the footnote on the meaning of "instinct" in *Aids to Reflection* (Comment on No. IX of *Aphorisms on that which Is indeed Spiritual Religion*) and the ensuing excursus *On Instinct in Connexion with the Understanding.* AR 178–84; also P 357 and F II, 77.

The contrast is perhaps best exemplified in the distinctively human endowment of language; and here some of Coleridge's scattered observations on the subject of *grammar* become very relevant. We may talk loosely of a "language" of dolphins or other animals. But it is a language without grammar; which is to say that the meaning of the word *language* has first to be distorted beyond all candid recognition:

> If the power of conveying information by intelligible signs, visual or auditory, would constitute the possession of Language, Language is common to many and various animals; but if we use the word, Language in its only proper sense as the power of conveying not things only but the process and result of our reflection thereon, it is predicable of the Human Species alone. [Note in J. F. Blumenbach, *Über die natürlichen Verschiedenheiten.* BM. Front flyleaf (verso).]

In the case of humanity, it is not only understanding, but also reason *in* the understanding that is active. And it is reason, functioning as grammar, which "gradually raises into acts and objects of distinct consciousness what Nature and the alone true natural state of Man had previously called forth as Instinct." (*Treatise on Logic* I, 32, and pp. 99–100, below.)

31. CS 192ff. (*Demosius and Mystes*). The failure to conceive this is the unreflecting error of the multitude, both learned and unlearned, who suppose that understanding, whether in animals or man, is *reducible* to instinct.

32. TL 592. And see F I, 470 for a parallel exposition.

33. F I, 155.

34. For Coleridge on the word *abstract* and the concept of abstraction see F I, 520 n. 5.

35. AR 158.

36. AR 169.

37. *Ib.* Compare the passage on the importance of etymology from the *Treatise on Logic* quoted in Chapter 1, above (pp. 20–21). Under the "despotism of the

eye" the power of abstraction atrophies; and this is fatal for both imagination and reason. Imagination is the opposite of abstraction, but presupposes it; for without abstraction a manifold cannot be apprehended as "multeity in unity" but only as confusion. So too with reason: the mind must realise that there are "truths, which are distinctly *conceived,* which yet cannot be *per*ceived or imagined," before it can go on to realise "truths contemplable by Reason, but not *conceivable* by the Understanding." * The way to "ideal" reason lies through "conceptual" reason (see also Chapter 9, below).

38. *Treatise on Logic* I, 27–32. Cf. TM 6.

39. AR 169.

40. F I, 440.

41. F I, 518.

42. See Chapter 7, note 41, above. And compare, now the following passage from Appendix B to the *Statesman's Manual:*

> The reason first manifests itself in man by the tendency to the comprehension of all as one. We can neither rest in an infinite that is not at the same time a whole, nor in a whole that is not infinite. Hence the natural man is always in a state either of resistance or of captivity to the understanding and the fancy, which cannot represent totality without limit: and he either loses the one in the striving after the infinite, that is, atheism with or without polytheism, or he loses the infinite in the striving after the one, and then sinks into anthropomorphic monotheism. [Shedd I, 456.]

Temptation is in fact not single, but twofold. Man is seduced into allowing now one, now the other, of the two forces, whose polarity actually constitutes his humanity, to predominate unduly—instead of maintaining them *in* their polarity.

> 43. "Of the discursive understanding, which forms for itself general notions and terms of classification for the purpose of comparing and arranging *phaenomena,* the characteristic is clearness without depth. It contemplates the unity of things in their limits only, and is consequently a knowledge of superficies without substance. So much so indeed that it entangles itself in contradictions in the very effort of comprehending the idea of substance." [Shedd I, 460–61.]

> "Notions . . . have effected their utmost when they have added to the *distinctness* of our knowledge." [*Ib.* 433; italics not in original.]

44. Cf. *Theory of Life* (see Chapter 5, p. 68, above), and compare the following from the *Friend* (I 520–21):

> The ground-work, therefore, of all true philosophy is the full apprehension of the difference between the contemplation of reason, namely, that intuition of things which arises when we possess ourselves, as one with the whole, which is substantial knowledge, and that which presents itself when transferring

---

* MS addition by Coleridge to Gillman's copy of the *Statesman's Manual* (BM), p. xxxv.

reality to the negations of reality, to the ever-varying framework of the uniform life, we think of ourselves as separated beings, and place nature in antithesis to the mind, as object to subject, thing to thought, death to life. This is abstract knowledge, or the science of the mere understanding.

We have had to wait for the twentieth century for the philosophy of science itself to begin pointing out that its knowledge is not of reality but of the negation of reality; and that all its certainties are based, not on *verifications* but on falsifications.

45. F I, 439.
46. AR 162.
47. Shedd I, 459.
48. F I, 203n.
49. F I, 521.
50. F I, 447.
51. Shedd I, 466.

9. Reason

1. "Metaphysician or Mystic." In *Coleridge: Studies by Several Hands,* ed. E. Blunden & E. L. Griggs (London: Constable, 1934), 196–97.

2. F I, 156.

3. The following paragraph immediately precedes the paragraph containing the scale of mental powers, referred to in Chapters 7 and 8 (see Chapter 7, n. 31):

Gerson's and St. Victoire's Contemplation is in my System = Positive *Reason,* or R. in her own sphere as distinguished from the merely *formal* Negative Reason, R. in the lower sphere of the Understanding. The + R. = Lux: — R. = Lumen a luce. By the one the Mind contemplates Ideas: by the other it meditates on conceptions. Hence the distinction might be expressed by the names, Ideal Reason ※ Conceptual Reason.

The psychology of Hugh de St. Victoire (1078–1141) is likelier to have reached a twentieth-century student, if at all, through his devoted exponent St. Bonaventura.

4. See e.g. F I, 156 and 157. The following are a few of the many places where Coleridge has discussed reason and understanding: Appendix B to the *Statesman's Manual* (Shedd I, 456–72); *The Friend,* Essay V in the "First Landing-Place" (F I, 154); *Aids to Reflection:* "On the Difference in Kind of Reason and the Understanding" (AR 150–79).

5. Shedd V, 375.

6. *Notes on Asgill's Treatises.* Shedd V, 546.

7. See e.g. *Essay on Faith.* CIS 120 and 116.

8. CS 135, where however the reference is to the true Church.

9. AR 150ff. See pp. 108–109, below.

10. F I, 154.

11. Shedd I, 456ff.

226 WHAT COLERIDGE THOUGHT: *Notes* to pages 107–108

12. On the flyleaf of James Gillman's copy of the *Statesman's Manual* (1816), BM.

13. "In short, the human understanding possesses two distinct organs, the outward sense, and 'the mind's eye' which is reason: wherever we use that phrase (the mind's eye) in its proper sense, and not as a mere synonyme of the memory or the fancy." F I, 157.

The line in the scale of mental powers may thus be thought of as drawn between these two "distinct organs."

14. F I, 56.

15. These will be found discussed at some length in Appendix E to the *Statesman's Manual* (stylistically perhaps the worst piece of prose Coleridge ever produced). Shedd I, 478.

16.   There was a young lady of Niger
                    Who smiled as she rode on a tiger.
                      They came back from the ride
                        With the lady inside
                  And the smile on the face of the tiger.

17. Compare CL IV, 873 and 875, where he accuses Schelling of doing just that: "Who can believe on the strength of a mere assertion, that a position, the *contrary* of which is assumed by nine out of ten, and held and supported by such men as Des Cartes, Sir I. Newton &c &c, can be *self*-evident? . . . You open your mouth to ask a modest question: and he *spits clean into it* by way of answer."

18. "Let a young man separate I from Me as far as he possibly can, and remove Me till it is almost lost in the remote distance. 'I am me', is as bad a fault in intellectuals and morals as it is in grammar, whilst none but one—God—can say, 'I am I,' or 'That I am.'" (TT 1, 11, 1833.) On the equivocal reference of the terms "I" and "me," even in colloquial usage, compare BL I, 52n.

19. Compare:

This again is the mystery and the dignity of our human nature, that we cannot give up our reason, without giving up at the same time our individual personality. For that must appear to each man to be *his* reason which produces in him the highest sense of certainty; and yet it is *not* reason, except as far as it is of universal validity and obligatory on all mankind . . . He who asserts that truth is of no importance except in the signification of sincerity, confounds sense with madness . . . [F I, 97 (with n. 3).]

20. That is, "the identification of the universal reason with each man's individual understanding." (*Notes on Isaac Taylor's "Natural History of Enthusiasm."* Shedd VI, 133.)

21. Compare for instance C. G. Jung's concept of a "collective" (that is, aggregated from particulars) unconscious with the following passage from Coleridge's Shakespearian criticism:

Shakespeare shaped his characters out of the nature within; but we cannot so safely say, out of "his own" nature, as an 'individual person'. No! this latter is itself but a 'natura naturata', an effect, a product, not a 'power'. It was Shakespeare's prerogative to have the universal which is potentially in each 'particular', opened to him in the 'homo generalis', not as an abstraction of observation from a variety of men, but as a substance capable of endless modifications, of which his own personal existence was but one, and to use 'this one' as the eye that beheld the other, and as the tongue that could convey the discovery [T. M. Raysor, *Miscellaneous Criticism.* Quoted in Herbert Read, *The True Voice of Feeling* (London: Faber & Faber, 1953), p. 177.]

22. AR 150. The reader is of course informed of the alterations.

23. F I, 156.

24. F I, 159 (with n. 1). Coleridge sometimes names this mental act *seclusion,* one of the three on which syllogistic logic is based; the other two being *inclusion* and *conclusion.* See e.g. TT 23.9.1830. And compare Appendix, below.

25. See, for example, A. N. Whitehead's Lowell Lectures, 1925, printed as *Science and the Modern World* (New York: Macmillan, 1925; Cambridge University Press, 1926), etc.

26. *Treatise on Logic* II, 40.

27. "Without this latent presence of the 'I am', all modes of existence in the external world would flit before us as coloured shadows, with no greater depth, root, or fixture, than the image of a rock in a gliding stream or the rainbow on a fast-sailing rain-storm." (Shedd I, 465.) And see Chapter 5, above.

28. Logical judgment makes no distinction between existent and non-existent subject-matters. In the judgment "Cerberus is three-headed," just as in any other, it is

> the act by which the mind combines the three heads . . . with all the manifold which is again united in these into a one formed shape beheld in cne act, that is and must be real, and this reality it is, and not those so-called principles of identity and contradiction, which Logicians without exception have hitherto talked of as the foundations of logical evidence, which supplies us with the Archimedean standing-room from which we may apply the lever of all our other intelligent functions.

Thus, in a judgment "the mind affirms *firstly* its own reality, *secondly* that this reality is one unity, *thirdly* that it has the power of communicating this unity, and *lastly* that all reality for the mind is derived from its own reality . . ." (*Treatise on Logic* II, 63ff.)

29. See Chapter 5, above, pp. 60–61.

30. The effect of Descartes' formulation (on the repudiation of which, as was pointed out in Chapter 5, the validity of Coleridge's system depends) was of course to spread this *either:or* of the understanding over the natural world as a whole, so as to exclude intelligence from it. This result was refined, rather than superseded, when Kant reduced it to his own dichotomy between understanding and sense.

Relevant here is an emphatic MS note on "negation" in Tennemann's *Geschichte der Philosophie.*

. . . it is necessary to expose the fallacy of the Position, that all Circumscription is Negation. What can be more distinct than the Outline of a Leaf, or of one of Rafael's female figures, and a Line formed by my own arm while I am trying to stretch it as far as I can from above my head to my knee? Distinct, did I say? Is it not as diverse as Position and Negation themselves? Imagine the birth of a living circle. The circumference may be formed by the Radii all stopping there because they could go no farther = Negation; but it may likewise be formed because the Radii had pre-determined to go back again, both in order to form the circumference and *in order to be conscious of its having so done* = Position.

N.B. I can confidently acquit myself of vanity when, and tho', I say that the above is a *most important* Remark. S. T. Coleridge. [Vol. 7, front flyleaf 2 (the first italics are mine, the second Coleridge's own). See also Appendix, below.]

With which may not unprofitably be read the following MS note on Descartes:

This utter disanimation of Body and its *not* opposition but contrariety, *sicuti omnino heterogeneum,* to Soul, as the assumed Basis of Thought and Will; this substitution, I say, of a merely logical *negatio alterius omnino et singulo,* for a philosophic antithesis necessary to the manifestation of the identity of both — 2 = 1, as the only form in which the human understanding can represent to itself the 1 = 2; is the *peccatum originale* of the Cartesian system. [Marginal note to Article III of *De Passionibus,* Prima Pars, in Descartes' *Opera Philosophica,* printed in *The Philosophy of Descartes,* Series of Modern Philosophers (New York: Holt, 1892), and quoted in *Coleridge Marginalia in a Volume of Descartes,* Julian Lindsay, *P.M.L.A.,* XLIX (1934), 184.]

31. AR 171. And see Appendix, below.

32. Kant's πρωτόψευδος [prōtopseudos], or basic error, in Coleridge's view; and readers philosophically inclined would do well to study two long marginalia on the subject in Tennemann's *Geschichte*—wisely reproduced in full by Kathleen Coburn in her edition of the *Philosophical Lectures,* PL 425–28.

33. Let me by all the labours of my life have answered but one end, if I shall have only succeeded in establishing the diversity of Reason and Understanding, and the distinction between the *Light* of Reason in the Understanding, viz, the absolute Principle presumed in all Logic and the condition under which alone we draw universal and necessary Conclusions from contingent and particular facts, and the Reason itself, as the source and birthplace of *Ideas* . . . [Autograph Notebook—Snyder 135.]

Surprise has sometimes been expressed at the scant attention Coleridge appears to have paid to Hegel. On the other hand I have heard him accused of borrowing his all from Hegel without acknowledgment. From the sparse marginalia to Hegel's *Logic* and occasional references in the Letters it would appear that Coleridge considered Hegel as having mistakenly sought to deal with the *lumen a luce* as though it were itself the *lux intellectus.*

For a parallel statement of Coleridge's position, that contemplation of the cognitive limits of the understanding is the first step in superseding them, compare *The Case for Anthroposophy*, by Rudolf Steiner, together with the present author's Introduction thereto (London: Rudolf Steiner Press, 1970).

34. Shedd I, 464.

35. F I, 36.

36. This austerely numerical reduction of the mystery of communion and of creation is given poetic form by Shakespeare in *The Phoenix and the Turtle*. Coleridge also uses it to lead to a conception of the "first matter," or $\pi\rho\dot{\omega}\tau\eta$ $\ddot{\upsilon}\lambda\eta$ [prōtē hylē]: ". . . were it convenient to assume a first matter at all, it must be defined $1 = 2 + 2 = 1$: i.e. a one substance, that of necessity manifests itself in (and as) two opposites, that reciprocally suppose, each the other." [MS note on the end flyleaf of *Alazonomastix Philalethes*. BM.]

37. One place where Coleridge has made explicit his conception, frequently implied, of likeness as the polarity of sameness and difference is a section on the psychological basis of language in the *Treatise on Logic*. In the alphabet, he suggests, the *letters* give "the positive element of the Like = the Same," and their relative *positions* "the negative Element = the Different"; in accidence, the same is true of cases, tenses, moods on the one hand and the differing "roots" on the other. (*Treatise on Logic* I, 25–27.)

38. It is interesting to note that Coleridge, the major English critic of poetry, had comparatively little to say about metaphor and simile. On the one hand, as M. H. Abrams has pointed out (*The Mirror and the Lamp*, p. 292), almost all the examples of imagination in literature which he actually cites *are* examples of simile, metaphor and, occasionally, personification; on the other hand he gives us no theory of them. Moreover, although the type of simile which has since claimed most attention is the one that compares noetic or emotional experience with sensory objects or events, Coleridge's best known instance of imagination flashing forth in a simile, taken from Shakespeare's *Venus and Adonis*, is not of that type:

> Look! how a bright star shooteth from the sky,
> So glides he in the night from Venus' eye
> [BL II, 18]

compares two events, both of them occurring in the realm of the senses.

Whereas the type of simile which has since attracted most theoretic attention is the variety which establishes, or invents, a link (by way of comparison) between the two disshevered realms, of the senses on the one side and the mind on the other. Altogether detached, as it feels, from the natural world (T. S. Eliot's "dissociation of sensibility"), the mind seeks nevertheless for an "objective correlative" to itself in that world. Often the emphasis is on the severance rather than on the link, and the impulse behind the invention may be to increase the severance, in a kind of self-defence against the harsh and ugly world of 'reality' rather than to overcome it. A *symbol*, from this point of view, is a simile from which the element of comparison has largely dropped out of sight; and some have maintained that the ideal poetic symbol is the 'symbol without meaning,' when it has dropped out of sight altogether.

Coleridge, denying as he did that the severance between mind and world is a reality, had much to say about symbol, but little to say about simile. But by symbol he understood something quite different from a glorified simile in the above sense. In his vocabulary *symbol* depends for its existence on the organic relation between whole and part, according to which the part potentially contains the whole. It is characterised by a "translucence" of the symbolised, as whole, through the symbol, as part. "It always partakes of the reality which it renders intelligible and, while it enunciates the whole, abides itself as a living part in that unity of which it is the representative." (Shedd I, 437–38.) Compare AR 149; and see Chapter 12, below, pp. 154–155. On the mistaking of symbols for metaphors as "the occasion and support of the worst errors in Protestantism" see CS 130n.

39. (i) In the BM. (ii) Shedd I, 461.

40. *Essay on Faith*, CIS 113.

41. *Coleridge* (London: Weidenfeld & Nicolson, 1968). In Gillman's copy of the *Statesman's Manual* (n. 12, above), evidencing the degree of his attention and his anxiety to express his meaning as precisely as possible, he altered "product" to "artefacts," and "educts" to "produce"; adding, after the former alteration: "Or perhaps these μορφώματα [morphōmata] of the mechanic understanding as distinguished from the ποιησεῖς [poiēseis] of the imaginative Reason might be termed Products in antithesis to Produce—or Growths."

42. Shedd I, 436.

43. CL IV, 689.

44. Shedd I, 463n.

45. Shedd I, 470. It was in such or similar contexts that Coleridge was fond of quoting a passage from the Archangel's speech in Book V of *Paradise Lost*, beginning:

O Adam, One Almighty is, from whom
All things proceed . . .

and concluding:

So from the root
Springs lighter the green stalk, from thence the leaves
More airy: last the bright consummate flower
Spirits odorous breathes. Flowers and their fruit,
Man's nourishment, by gradual scale sublim'd,
To *vital* spirits aspire: to *animal:*
To *intellectual!*—give both life and sense,
Fancy and Understanding; whence the soul
REASON receives, and reason is her *being,*
Discursive or intuitive.

It is, for instance, one of the three quotations that head Chapter XIII of the *Biographia Literaria*. Reason is "discursive" in the understanding, where it is first "received"; "intuitive" as subsequently enlivening the understanding and transcending it. It is "That which we find within ourselves, which is more than ourselves." (AR 15n.)

Compare also the following concretion of the same principle:

In looking at objects of Nature while I am thinking, as at yonder moon dim-glimmering through the dewy window-pane, I seem rather to be seeking, as it were *asking* for, a symbolical language for something within me that already and for ever exists, than observing anything new. Even when that latter is the case, yet still I have always an obscure feeling as if that new phenomenon were the dim awakening of a forgotten or hidden truth of my inner nature. It is still interesting as a word—a symbol. It is Λόγος [Logos] the Creator, and the Evolver! [AP 136 and N II, 2546.]

46. Compare p. 108 and note 19, above.

47. *Galatians,* 2.20. And in general the mistake is easily made, in learning from Coleridge, of isolating such abstractions as:

In finite forms there is no real and absolute identity. God alone is identity. In the former, the prothesis is a bastard prothesis, a quasi identity only.

from such parallel concretions as:

Consider how many years I have been toiling thro' mist and twilight; but I have not a fuller conviction of my own Life than I have of the Truth of my present convictions. They have taught me the difference in *kind* between the *sense* of certainty and the *sensation* of positiveness. '*I Am,* in *that I am':* and St. Paul's Christ (as the Logos) the eternal *Yea* (Cor. 2.1. is the fontal Idea. [TT 29.4.32 and FII, 76 n. 4.]

48. *"Logic"* is ". . . the science appropriate to the Understanding (Logos) as one of the two faculties of the mind, the sense or intuitive faculty (mathēsis) being the other. The Reason (Nous) as the universal power presiding over both." It is: "A science which derives its name and character from the Logos or Understanding as distinguished from the intuitive faculty or the sense and from the Nous or Reason." (*Treatise on Logic* II, 38 and 39.)

49. Compare Shedd I, 46on.

50. *The Prometheus of Aeschylus*; a lecture delivered in 1825 to the Royal Society of Literature. LR II, 323 (at p. 336). See also Chapter 10, p. 122, below.

10. Ideas, Method, Laws

1. P 358. He defined it on a number of occasions. See, for instance, the conclusion of Appendix E to the *Statesman's Manual* (Shedd I, 484), where it is at once defined and distinguished from other terms such as *perception* and *conception*. For the history of the word *idea* and the contrast between the current usage and Coleridge's see BL I, 69n.

2. Shedd I, 460n.

3. *Treatise on Logic* II, 326–27: "Seeking a reason *for* all things, they take away Reason itself—and all the truths of Reason, for which no reason can without absurdity be required, because they *are* Reason. Logically speaking they *constitute* the Reason, but in the language of the Philosopher, the Reason affirms itself in them."

4. "Mathematician's Idea *of* a Triangle is falsely stated—it should be, his Idea, Triangle." (CL II, 691.)

5. F I, 523.

6. Occasionally in the *Lectures on Shakespeare*—and see BL II, 64. But, just as the practice of poetry demands "observant meditation," so the true practice of science demands "meditative observations." (F I, 471.) Compare note 27, below.

7. BL I, 100.

8. The whole of the sentence quoted from the *Biographia Literaria* (I, 100) runs as follows: "An IDEA, in the *highest* sense of that word, cannot be conveyed but by a *symbol;* and, except in geometry, all symbols of necessity involve a contradiction." The element of contradiction is most apparent in that particular form of symbolic utterance called a metaphor; but it is certainly (for the understanding) characteristic of figurative language as a whole. Primitive language is instinctively figurative. The further back we penetrate in the history of speech, the more symbolic, and therefore the less logical, it shows itself to have been. There are, for instance, Hebrew roots, whose semantic range is so wide that one end of their gamut of meanings appears to us to be positively the reverse of the other. Living opposites have not yet been reduced to contradictions. Freud had noticed the same self-contradictory element in dream symbolism, and he once compared the two in a brief review of a work by a contemporary author. See *On the Antithetical Sense of Primal Words,* reprinted in *Creativity and the Unconscious* (New York: Harper, 1958).

Coleridge asked himself as early as 1801 in a Notebook: "Whether or no the too great definiteness of Terms in any language may not consume too much of the vital and idea-creating force in distinct clear, full-made Images . . ." (N 1016.)

9. Notebook 52 (IS 178). Compare (N 2989): "I had a confused shadow, rather than an image, in my recollection, like that from a thin Cloud as if the Idea were descending, tho' still in some measureless Height."

10. Before Freud was born Coleridge had begun pointing to "a full sharp distinction of Mind from Consciousness—the Consciousness being the narrow *Neck* of the Bottle." (Notebook 44; IS 31.) The distinction was a fact for him, because it was a matter of immediate experience. But his interpretation of the fact differed sharply from Freud's; and we find something like a critique of the presuppositions underlying psycho-analytical theory in a marginal note on Socrates' "daimon," in Tennemann's *Geschichte der Philosophie*:

. . . the exceedingly contingent and accidental nature of the occasions, on which it was called forth, renders the solution of this Faculty from indistinct recollection of past minute, perhaps at the time unconscious, experiences very far from satisfactory. At all events the explanation can be regarded as sufficient only where such an extent and importance are given to the term, unconscious, in its combination with experiences, notices, and the like, as would amount to the assumption of an interior Man exercising higher powers than the self-conscious man or what each man calls *I*, is indued with. But if so, what is this less than a Daimonion (Divinum Quid) or θεος οἰκειος [theos oikeios], domestic God, or Divine Familiar—in short, what Socrates believed it to be? [Tennemann, Vol. II (front flyleaf 2).]

11. Compare Appleyard, 86ff. (the section headed *Indistinctness and the Subconscious*): and Jackson (*Method and Imagination in Coleridge's Criticisms*), Chapter 4.

12. "Horne Tooke was pre-eminently a ready-witted man. He had that clearness which is founded on shallowness." (TT 7.5.1830.)

13. CS 50n. And compare PL 91.

14. CL II, 961.

15. "Perhaps the safer use of the term, understanding, for general purposes, is to take it as the mind, or rather as the man himself considered as a concipient as well as percipient being, and reason as a power supervening." (Shedd I, 460n.)

16. Compare n. 9, above.

17. CL II, 814.

18. F Section II, Essays IV–XI. And compare Jackson, *op. cit.*, pp. 16–19 and 36–47, where there is a useful summary.

19. Shedd I, 427 (where it is in the past tense).

20. "A Maxim is a conclusion upon observation of matters of fact, and is merely retrospective: an Idea, or, if you like, a Principle, carries knowledge within itself, and is prospective. Polonius is a man of maxims. Whilst he is descanting on matters of past experience, as in that excellent speech to Laertes before he sets out on his travels, he is admirable; but when he comes to advise or project, he is a mere dotard. You see, Hamlet, as the man of ideas, despises him." [TT 24.61827 (IS 133).]

A leading significance of the figure of Prometheus in Coleridge's interpretation of the myth is the contrast it reveals between the *prophetic* power, which may avail to change the future, and the power of the "law," or "rule," which can only rivet the past. Compare also Shedd I, 445.

21. F I, 469.

22. F I, 466.

23. For the history of the *Encyclopaedia Metropolitana*, of Coleridge's Introduction thereto (subsequently issued independently as the *Treatise on Method*) and its mutilation by the editors of the Encyclopaedia, and for the text of the original *Treatise*, see *Coleridge's Treatise on Method*, edited by Alice D. Snyder (London: Constable, 1934). The substance of it is contained, and much of it was used *verbatim*, in the *Friend*, Section 2, Essays IV–XI. It appears to have been only when he came to incorporate it in the *Friend* that Coleridge revised the

work really carefully and at least one passage in the *Treatise* is more than misleading (compare e.g. p. 6 of the *Treatise* with F I, 460n, where the terms *idea* and *law* have been transposed).

24. TM 8; 22; and 63. F I, 466–67.

25. TM 9.

26. "From the first, or initiative Idea, as from a seed, successive Ideas germinate." (TM 7.)

27. F I, 453. Compare the similar remark on the Imagination in Chapter VII of the *Biographia Literaria* (BL I, 86 and Chapter 7, page 78, above). Method is the philosophic imagination 'in business,' the idea itself being "anterior to all image." (*Treatise on Logic* II, 24.) Thus, meditation is to imagination somewhat as philosophic imagination is to poetic: "*Meditatio* in Hugo de St. Victoire is the application of the truths of *Contemplatio* to inferior knowledges, i.e. in the evolution of the particulars contained in the unity of the Idea, or the bringing the facts of Natural History into the Light of the Ideas." (Marginal note to Tennemann, Vol. VIII, front flysheet 1.) Compare note 6, above, and Chapter 9, note 3.

28. P 357.

29. PL 357 and AR 129n.

30. CS 12–13. The first sentence is the result of very careful formulation. See F I, 497 and 497 note 2, containing Coleridge's own note on the text, beginning "Obscure from too great compression . . ." Finally (in the version here quoted) he sought to make it easier for the reader by twice substituting brackets for commas. *Natura Naturata* and *naturans* occur in the *Novum Organum,* but the last (Latin) sentence appears to be Coleridge's.

31. TM 10. In the *Friend* the terms *Metaphysical* and *Physical Ideas* are not used (compare F I, 459 and 467n.). Jackson comments on the distinction (in this instance misleadingly) as follows: "Coleridge discriminates similarly between *Metaphysical* and *Physical* Ideas, and appears to define them by their subject-matter." But, in Coleridge's diction, ideas do not have subject-matter; they *are* subject-matter.

32. Shedd I, 460n.

33. Where a law is in question, "the relation of the parts to each other and to the whole is predetermined by a truth originating in the *mind*"; where a hypothesis, that relation is "abstracted or generalized from observation of the parts." (F I, 459.)

34. P 358. And compare F I, 497: ". . . Idea and Law are the Subjective and Objective *Poles* of the same Magnet—i.e. of the same living and energizing Reason" and F I, 467. "Now a law and an idea are correlative Terms, and differ only as subject and object, as being and truth."

35. TM 12. Compare F I, 504. And see also, on Francis Bacon, PL 331–37.

36. F I, 504.

37. F I, 487. The point here is that Bacon lived and thought before that "utter disanimation of nature" in the general consciousness, which Coleridge pointed to in his note on Descartes (see Chapter 9, n. 30, above). To interpret the word *laws* in his writings as signifying what we mean today by "laws of nature"

is accordingly to miss the mark. In the *Novum Organum* it is almost always introduced in connection with, or as an alternative name for *ideas* (for which however Bacon normally used the term *forms*).

38. F I, 490. The words *natural or acquired* need to be particularly emphasised. Unlike the acquired idols, the natural (or, as Bacon calls them, "innate") ones, cannot be eliminated. They are built into the nature of the understanding itself: *At innata inhaerent naturae ipsius intellectus.* They are, as Coleridge put it elsewhere, "a law of our nature";* and all we can do is to be vigilantly aware of them. Coleridge once called himself an "idoloclast."

39. F I, 492. Compare TM 44: "Bacon establishes an unerring criterion between the Ideas and the Idols of the Mind; namely, that the latter are empty notions, but the former are the very seals and impresses of Nature." Compare also BL II, 39.

40. F I, 491. Experiment for Bacon meant "informing the senses from the mind, and not compounding a mind out of the senses." (TT 21.7.32.) It was to be "an organ of reason." (TL 565n.) When, but only when, *"an idea is an experiment proposed, an experiment is an idea realised"* (F I, 489) is experiment dignified into experience. (TL 565.) "This therefore is the true Baconic philosophy. It consists in this, in a profound meditation on those laws which the pure reason in man reveals to him, with the confident anticipation and faith that to this will be found to correspond certain laws in nature." (PL 333.)

See also, for the relation between *idea, law* and *experiment,* the many places where Coleridge discusses the relation between the idea of the perfect circle and the physically constructed *arch;* e.g. AR 127n; CL IV, 789, 875–76; CS 173; TT 17.3.33; F I, 176.

41. Coleridge's two essays leave us with an image of Bacon almost unrecognisably different from the more familiar one enshrined in political history and history of science—the Bacon who condemns those who value Knowledge as an end in itself; for whom Knowledge is not "a mistress for pleasure, but a spouse for fruit"; who sees the true end of science as "operation" and speaks of "torturing" nature's secrets out of her. In the first Essay (VIII) Coleridge certainly shows awareness of the less "amiable" aspects of the British Plato, emphasising his coldness of heart and his ruthless and ungenerous contempt for both his predecessors and his contemporaries. In particular his wholesale ridicule of classical and medieval thinkers ensured that those most ready to listen would be precisely those most likely to misunderstand him; for they would be the fundamentally brash, who thrive on the labour-saving and flattering conviction that ignorance of the past is the golden key to a future that will differ from it; and this, as we know, is the exact opposite of Coleridge's own conviction.

It is that misunderstanding which he pillories; and he certainly succeeds in showing that "fruit," and the *fructiferum experimentum,* were in Bacon's own mind something quite different from *mere* operational efficiency and the means

---

* Chapter 5, p. 65, above. And see *Novum Organum: Distributio Operis,* paras. 14 and 15.

to it, as we understand them. "Scientia et potentia in idem coincidunt";* but we are mistaken if we interpret that as the pragmatic doctrine that knowledge *is* power; or if we suppose the 'power' that coincides with knowledge was, for him, the power of technological manipulation. It was the power of mind participating directly in natural process—not manipulation but, in the strict sense of the word, magic. What we call 'natural science' was in fact sometimes called 'natural magic.'

It remains true that the whole drive and emotional emphasis in Bacon's mind appears to have been towards the power rather than the knowledge aspect of the two coincidents. If *law* and *idea* (or *form*) are synonymous in the *Novum Organum*—and they certainly are—the whole presentation weights the scales in favour of law and tends (in Coleridge's own language) to "desynonymize" them, with effect that the *idea* aspect, the "antecedent unity," can drop conveniently out of sight.† "Bacon names the laws of nature ideas," says Coleridge in the *Friend* (p. 124, below), but the converse is even truer, as he himself acknowledges by the way he puts it in *Aids to Reflection* (p. 44):

> —in the world we see everywhere evidences of a unity, which the component parts are so far from explaining, that they necessarily presuppose it as the cause and condition of their existing as those parts; or even of their existing at all. This antecedent unity or cause and principle of each union, it has since the time of Bacon and Kepler been customary to call a law.

Practical understanding (compare AR 314—Appendix) differs from practical reason in being the amoral adaptation of means to ends; and the concept of *law* is amenable to the understanding, as *idea* is not. All that is necessary is to eliminate, or forget, its other aspect as 'idea'; and, if this is what has since occurred, Bacon must surely bear a larger share of the responsibility for it, and for the consequent limitation of scientific method to the mere understanding and the senses, than the two essays suggest. In addition to coldness and contempt there was another ingredient in Lord Bacon's character to which Coleridge does not allude, namely the appetite for *personal* power and absolute control, if not for himself then for other Bacons yet unborn. This is a thread of motive that is seen over and over again to intertwine itself easily and surreptitiously with a genuine and compassionate desire to improve the human lot. The sincerity of occasional passages, such as the noble one in the Preface to *The Great Instauration* which expressly warns against the lust of power and insists that 'charity' must be the scientist's overriding motive, need not be doubted; but they must be weighed in the balance against the total impression, violent and enduring, left on the reader by such works as the *Advancement of Learning* and the *Novum Organum*—let alone the *Refutation of Philosophies,* to which Coleridge himself refers—which is, that a Wellsian dream of technological might coloured and biassed his whole presentation of scientific

---

* Shedd I, 433. *Novum Organum,* I, 3, and elsewhere.

† See, e.g. *Novum Organum* II, 17 ("Nos enim quum de formis loquimur, nil aliud intelligimus quam leges illas . . .") and compare II, 2.

method and the philosophy implied in it. And after all it is that dream which has come true.*

It need not be assumed that Coleridge was unaware of all this, or that in a different context he himself might not have expressed, only a good deal better, all that this note contains. In any case it does not affect one way or another the validity of the point he chose the *Novum Organum* to illustrate; effectively, because the thinking in the *Novum Organum* does not yet assume that "utter disanimation of nature" which is presupposed by the general consciousness, and by the scientific method and therefore the science, which have developed since Bacon's day. It does not affect the main contention of the group of essays on method; which is that only a method based not on the understanding alone, but also on the acknowledged superindividuality of reason, will ever bring itself to admit that a law is at the same time a 'power'—that the law of gravitation, for instance, is one and the same with the power of gravitation.

42. The εἴδη εἰσίοντα καὶ ἐξιόντα [eidē eisionta kai exionta] of *Timaeus,* 50.

43. See Chapter 1, above. And compare the following from a footnote to Section 2, Essay IX, of the *Friend:*

> Willingly would we designate what we have elsewhere called the mental initiative, by some term less obnoxious to the anti-Platonic reader, than this of *Idea* . . . did we not see, too clearly, that it is the meaning, not the word, which is the object of that aversion, which, fleeing from inward alarm, tries to shelter itself in outward contempt. [F I, 494.]

44. For example: "the necessity of contemplating the idea now as identical with reason, now as one with the will." (P 359.) Reason, as will, projects detachment and thus the existence of nature's and humanity's multeity. As reason, it (*a*) retains original attachment, (*b*) implements the recovery of lost attachment.

45. TM 2; 7; 21–22.

46. Shedd I, 465.

47. TM 2.

48. TM 24.

49. Shedd I, 433.

50. TM 7.

51. Compare *Speaker's Meaning,* by Owen Barfield (Middletown: Wesleyan University Press, 1967; London: Rudolf Steiner Press, 1971), Chapter 2.

52. Not altogether; there was a time, as Coleridge himself has elsewhere remarked in a footnote, when Newton toyed with the notion of an intervening ether.

---

* See however *The New Atlantis* of Francis Bacon, by Benjamin Farrington (Norfolk Lodge, Richmond Hill, Surrey. New Atlantis Foundation [Tenth Foundation Lecture], 1964). Professor Farrington's excellent book *The Philosophy of Francis Bacon* (Liverpool University Press, 1964) should also be consulted by everyone interested in the questions here raised.

53. "The utmost we ever venture to say is, that the falling of an apple *suggested* the law of gravitation to Sir I. Newton. Now a law and an idea are correlative terms, and differ only as object and subject, as being and truth." (F I, 467n.) See also note 58, below.

54. "A Power has no scientific sense, no philosophic genesis or derivation, where it is not coincident and commutable with a law; or introduced confessedly as the surrogate or substitute of a law not yet discovered,—and as a means, and part, of the process of the discovery . . ." [*Treatise on Logic* II, 39 (verso).]

Moreover power is always Will-power. Kant's paramount shortcoming was his failure to realise precisely this:

What should we think of a Physiologist who should deny the objective truth of the Circulation of the Blood, because it could not be shewn by the arteries alone without the veins? And yet the Kanteans argue not much unlike this, when in the Idea they separate the Reason from the Reason in the Will or the theoric from the practical Man. Anselm's and Descartes' error lay in not distinguishing the Idea in the Reason from the exposition of the Idea by the Reason.

On all this (and on gravity as the *vis centrifica*) compare, both as commentary and for its further implications, the marginalia to Tennemann on *Scotus Erigena,* reproduced in PL at pp. 434 and 438, from the second of which the above quotation is extracted.

55. F I, 500 and PL 145. See also Chapter 2, above.

56. TM 58.

57. *Treatise on Logic* II, 80; where natural science is dubbed, by contrast with logic, "the Poetic or Formal Science."

58. CL IV, 876. Idea is "anterior to all image," and not, as Kant, for instance, held, an abstraction from image (*Treatise on Logic* II, 24); it is abstractions that do *not* become ideas which fall under the despotism of the eye: ". . . abstractions descend into Images or total Impressions; but . . . an Idea never passes into an Abstraction, and therefore never becomes the equivalent of an Image . . . there is no interspace between Abstraction and Image for the Idea to occupy."

59. "The *term,* Idea, I had already defined, in the only way, in which the name of *any what,* that really or actually is, can be defined—viz., first, negatively, by contra-distinction—i.e. by determining what an Idea is *not*—2. positively, by some character common to all Ideas—ex gr. that in all we contemplate the Particular in the Universal, or the Universal in the Particular, the qualified (or determinate) in the Absolute, and the Absolute in the Qualified. This, however, is not *the* Idea which is *the* Form, in which the Absolute distinctly yet entirely and indivisibly is realised and revealed. This is that which cannot be *generalized,* on which the mind can exercise no modifying functions—that which can only be *contemplated*—that which is deeper than all intelligence,

inasmuch as it represents the element of the Will, and its essential underivability. Thirdly by reference to some Instance—as to the *Ideas* of Kepler, the Correlates of the Law of the Planetary Orbits contrasted with the conceptions of Ptolemy—who began with the phaenomena, the apparent Motions, as *data* —and then sought so to take them as that he might take them all together— i.e. *concipere, capere* haec *cum* illis—and the Conception or synopsis of a plurality of phaenomena so schematized as to shew the compatibility of their co-existence, is THEORY—a product of the Understanding in the absence or eclipse of IDEAS, or Contemplations of the Law, and hence necessarily conditioned by the Appearances, and changing with every new or newly discovered Phaenomenon, which Theory always follows never leads—while the Law being constitutive of the phaenomena and in order of Thought necessarily antecedent, the Idea as the correlative and mental Counterpart of the Law, is necessarily prophetic and constructive—*et Solem dicere falsum Audet,* and turns the contradiction of the Senses into proofs and confirmations of its Truths" [Snyder 136.]

60. F I, 177 note 1, and 459 note 2.
61. E.g. TM 58; PL 359–60.
62. E.g. *Treatise on Logic* I, 22–23.
63. P 358.
64. Compare marginal note on Thomas Taylor's *Proclus.* N.I (Notes) p. 456.
65. AR 163.
66. MS note (IS 196) (italics not in original).
67. F I, 156.
68. *Ib.:* "Whatever is conscious Self-Knowledge is Reason." Compare Chapters 4 and 5, above—and the following observations on (somewhat unexpectedly) the character of Don Quixote, who

had no knowledge of the sciences or scientific arts which give to the meanest portions of matter an intellectual interest, and which enable the mind to decypher in the world of the senses the invisible agency—that alone, of which the world's phenomena are the effects and manifestations,—and thus, as in a mirror, to contemplate its own reflex, its life in the powers, its imagination in the symbolic forms, its moral instincts in the final causes, and its reason in the laws of material nature. [*Miscellaneous Criticism,* ed. T. M. Raysor (London: Constable, 1936), pp. 100–101.]

69. TM 6.
70. F I, 470.
71. F I, 115.
72. F I, 106n.
73. *Treatise on Logic* 393 (Snyder 100–101). Some of the earlier letters are also relevant here, e.g. to Poole in March 1801 (CL II, 708): ". . . deep thinking is attainable only by a man of deep Feeling . . ."; to Wedgwood in January 1803 (CL II, 915); and to Southey in August 1803 (CL II, 960). See also IS 99 (Egerton 2801, f. 101).

74. "—a *constant Phaenomenon* becomes a LAW in the moment of its coincidence with an IDEA." (CL IV, 876.)

75. Shedd I, 451.

76. F I, 473-74.

77. CL IV, 809 and TL 568.

11. Coleridge and the Cosmology of Science

1. See Chapter 3, page 33, and Chapter 4, note 15.

2. TL 589.

3. See for instance the article by George R. Potter, *Coleridge and the Idea of Evolution* (PMLA. XL, 379-97), where he is congratulated on having *nearly* succeeded in anticipating the Darwinian theory. It could perhaps be argued that the post-Darwinian theory of mutations followed by adaptive radiation is a move away from Darwinism in the direction of the *Theory of Life.* But the concept of mutation has nothing in common with Coleridge's analysis of the origin of change in nature; it amounts to little more than the re-introduction of a small dose of "catastrophism" into the whole uniformitarian picture (see n. 7, below), which is left undisturbed by it. Moreover the theory of adaptive radiation presupposes an inorganic earth, very much as we have it today, on which the whole process could take place from the beginning. For Coleridge the earth has *become* inorganic to the extent that organisation has ceased; and the inanimate is always the formerly animate. The dead succeeds, not precedes, the living.

4. Note on Oersted, H. C. *Ansicht der chemischen Naturgesetze,* p. 42. BM (IS 192).

5. AR 304-5.

6. See IS 165 for a MS comment by Coleridge on Hutton's *An Investigation of the Principles of Knowledge.*

7. Letter dated 1829. See J. H. van den Berg, *The Changing Nature of Man,* translated from the Dutch by H. F. Croes (New York: Dell, 1964). To Coleridge, on the contrary, it was a self-evident absurdity to suppose "that a succession of different states should be the effect of the same agents in the same proportions of agency." (Unclassified MS in the possession of Victoria College, Toronto.)

The appearance of these rival options of uniformitarianism and catastrophism may be thought to offer an illustration of the relation between reason and "the moulds of the understanding." Substantial change, or change in time, being incomprehensible to the understanding, geological change appears there as two contradictories: *either* catastrophic *or* uniform—either a few sudden and violent rearrangements of *natura naturata* or an infinite number of very small ones.

8. See Chapter 3, note 5. Darwin took Lyell's *Principles of Geology* with him in his epoch-making voyage on the *Beagle*; and that unlimited extrapolation of present conditions, which uniformitarianism enables, is of course the indispensable scaffolding for his whole theory of evolution. Although, like geology, evolution is a historical discipline, it reacts in turn on practical sciences such as physiology, psychology and sociology. There is one almost invisibly deep hide-out for the entrenchment of error, to which Coleridge does not specifically refer in the pas-

sage quoted, though he touched on it in his two essays on Bacon (see Chapter 10, above, pp. 123–124). *Idola fori*—"idols of the market-place"—is the term Bacon himself coined to signify errors and limitations, originally intellectual but now inveterate in lexical meanings, which numerous important words have by imperceptible gradations acquired. And the effect of these is to blunt or ruin the very tools with which the mind has to set about correcting the errors or removing the limitations. In order to do that it must first smash the idols—and, alas, it has nothing but the idols themselves to smash them with.

Take as an example the limiting (and, as Coleridge held, erroneous) concept of *man* as a single biological species, and of any one man as a single member of that class. This is no longer a learned definition. It is *the* paramount lexical meaning; it is the word's 'reference'; and that in its turn determines the reference of countless other words associated with it. So that, whatever we may hear or say, or do, about man or men or mankind, or about a part of a man, such as his liver, his mind, his instincts or his behaviour, and however unhappily our opinions may differ, we are all happily agreed that it is *that,* or some part of that, *about* which we are differing.

9. For the ordinary person, to question an assumption so deeply entrenched in the general consciousness of his contemporaries is to be classed as a crank. For the scientist himself it is economically and socially dangerous. For a striking instance of this see *The Velikovsky Affair,* ed. Alfred de Grazia (New Hyde Park, N.Y.: University Books Inc., and London: Sidgwick and Jackson, 1966). Velikovsky's theories are not specially relevant here. They do not challenge the primary maxim, and it is doubtful whether he is even conscious of it. But, since his interpretation of a mass of astronomical, geological, archaeological and other evidence is 'catastrophic,' to admit that they are even worth investigating would involve conceding that the uniformitarian corollary might possibly be mistaken. (Albert Einstein had expressed the opinion that Velikovsky had nevertheless made out a *prima facie* case, which ought to be fully investigated. The book, fully documented, describes how various 'power structures' of the scientific establishment mobilised to suppress publicity and avert investigation.)

For comment on the "advancing frontiers of Knowledge" metaphor, and an interesting attempt to deal, as *epistemological* problems, with semantic fixation by textbook and the creeping establishment of speculative and mental limitation, see T. S. Kuhn, *The Structure of Scientific Revolutions* (Chicago: University of Chicago Press, 1962).

10. Egerton 2800, f. 155; and IS 185, where the remainder of the note may be read. In her own note the revered editor of *Inquiring Spirit* contrasts "the 'fancy' in this" with a brief and very practical note of Coleridge's on another matter altogether and advises us to set one against the other. Yet we should not forget that, on Coleridge's own premises, there is likely to be less there of fancy, as he defined it, than in the average textbook.

11. TL 592 and F I, 470 (IS 191). Compare TT 29.8.1827. And see Chapter 8, above, pp. 98–99.

12. As to Coleridge's relation to Goethe's voluminous scientific writings, we seem to know only that he was acquainted with the *Farbenlehre* (Theory of

Colour). I at any rate have not come across any reference to the *Botanical Writings,* and this is something of a mystery, having regard to his inquisitive appetite for, and wide reading in, contemporary German literature and his particular concern with science. Goethe's *Metamorphosenlehre* (Theory of Metamorphosis), which is their nucleus, was published in 1790. Not only is its method based on precisely what Coleridge demands, namely penetration from *natura naturata* into *natura naturans,* but its "archetypal plant" (*Urpflanze*) is the very embodiment of the idea of polarity as the basis of life. In some of the other writings Goethe's epistemology (so far as he develops it philosophically) is thoroughly Coleridgean. How the latter must have appreciated for instance, if he had had an opportunity of reading them, Goethe's brief note on "Experiment as Intermediary between Subject and Object" * or the longer account of his dispute with Schiller concerning the nature of "ideas" in the essay called "Fortunate Encounter," from which the following is taken:

> Batsch. with incredible enterprise, had set on foot a scientific society with fine collections and good apparatus. I normally attended its meetings and on one occasion found Schiller there. We happened to leave the hall together and entered into conversation. He appeared to have followed the lecture with interest, but he remarked with great understanding and insight, and in a way that gave me much pleasure, that such a fragmented approach to Nature could only put off any layman who might have been feeling inclined to tackle the subject.
>
> I replied that it might even alienate professionals also; and that there might well be another way of considering nature, not bit by separate bit, but as alive and actively working from the whole to the parts. Schiller asked to have this point elucidated, but without concealing his doubts and without admitting that the sort of thing I was talking about could originate from actual experience.
>
> We reached his house and the conversation tempted me in. I gave a spirited exposition of my theory of the metamorphosis of plants, endeavouring with the aid of a number of graphic sketches to make him see a symbolic plant. He listened and looked with great sympathy and incisive comprehension; but, when I had finished, he shook his head, saying, "That's not an experience, it is an idea". I was taken aback and somewhat put out, for the issue that was keeping us apart had been sharply underlined by his comment. The argument of his essay "On Grace and Dignity in Literature" recurred to my mind, and the old antipathy raised its head. Controlling myself however, I answered, 'I am very glad to hear that I have ideas without knowing it and even see them with my eyes.'
>
> Schiller, who had far greater tact and urbanity than I . . . replied in the style of an erudite Kantian. My stubborn realism led to a lively argument and a lengthy battle ensued, at the end of which an armistice was declared. Neither

---

* Goethe's *Naturwissenschaftliche Schriften* (*Goethes Werke,* Weimar, 1893), Vol. II, Part 2, p. 21: "Der Versuch als Vermittler von Object und Subject."

of us could claim the victory, yet each considered himself invincible. Remarks of his like the following made me very unhappy: 'How can there ever possibly be experience that is conformable with an idea? The very property that distinguishes an idea is that no experience can ever be congruous with it'. Yet if he took for an idea what I expressed as an experience, there must surely be some common ground between us somewhere to work upon.*

Conversely, how readily Goethe himself must have responded to such a dictum of Coleridge's as that: "The completing power which unites clearness with depth, the plenitude of the sense with the comprehensibility of the understanding, is the imagination, impregnated with which the understanding itself becomes intuitive, and a living power." † For Goethe's methodology concurs entirely with Coleridge's in rejecting any invented or fancied 'model' interposed between subject and object and relying instead on imagination to "complete," by realising, the identity of the idea with the law of nature. For both alike all genuine knowledge is at the same time self-knowledge.

See *Die Metamorphose der Pflanzen. Mit Anmerkungen und einem einleitenden Aufsatz von Rudolf Steiner: Die Entstehung der Metamorphosenlehre,* 2. Aufl. (Stuttgart: Verlag freies Geistesleben, 1966).

A good English translation of the *Metamorphosenlehre* (with illustrations) together with some of Goethe's related essays, by Bertha Mueller, appeared in 1952 under the imprint of the University of Hawaii. It contains particulars of previous English translations.

Such of Goethe's scientific writings as were then available were brilliantly edited for a general collection of German classics in the closing years of the last century by Rudolf Steiner, who subsequently also edited many of them (including all the botanical ones) for the definitive Weimar edition of the whole of Goethe's works. Steiner's original introductions and some of his notes and comments, contained in the first-named work (Kürschner, *National-Litteratur*), were assembled and published in 1926 in a single volume by Philosophisch-Anthroposophischer Verlag, Dornach, Switzerland (English translation: *Goethe the Scientist* [New York: Anthroposophic Press, Inc., 1950]).

The following may also be referred to: Rudolf Steiner, *Grundlinien einer Erkenntnisstheorie der Goetheschen Weltanschauung* (1886) (Verlag freies Geistesleben, 1960). English translation: *The Theory of Knowledge Implicit in Goethe's World-Conception* (London: Rudolf Steiner Press, 1940, and New York: Anthroposophic Press, Inc.). *Goethes Weltanschauung* (1895) (Dornach: Verlag der Rudolf Steiner—Nachlassverwaltung, 1963); English translation: *Goethe's Conception of the World* (Rudolf Steiner Press, 1928). Ernst Lehrs, *Man or Matter* (1951) (London: Faber & Faber, 1958). G. Adams and O. Whicher, *The Living Plant and the Science of Physical and Ethereal Spaces* (*A Study of the "Metamorphosis of Plants" in the Light of Modern Geometry and Morphology*) (Home Farm, Clent, Stourbridge: Goethean Science Foundation, 1949).

---

* *Ib.,* p. 13: "Glückliches Ereigniss."

† Shedd I, 461.

13. G. H. Schubert for instance; and see the list of French and English "activists" assembled by H. W. Piper in his essay, "Nature and the Supernatural in *The Ancient Mariner*" (Armidale, New South Wales: University of New England, 1955). Richard Owen and Louis Agassiz are one among those nearer to our own time, to whom the same applies.

14. BL I, 199.

15. *Coleridge* (London: Weidenfeld and Nicolson, 1968), p. 193.

16. It is not in the 1812 edition (that is, the original periodical in book form), but is included as part of Section 2, Essay VII, of the revised and augmented edition printed in 1818.

17. Compare Chapter 3, note 26. Coleridge not only attended Davy's lectures, but participated in some of his experiments. His friendship with Davy began before 1800. Familiar to and honoured by Coleridge in 1810 was the name of R. J. Boscovich,* later often acknowledged by Faraday as the first to advance against the "corpuscular" theory of material particles, the "point-atom" theory of intersecting forces. Faraday first met Davy in 1812 or 1813, travelled abroad with him between 1813 and 1815 and became his laboratory assistant at the Royal Institution in 1815. For a fuller account of Coleridge's influence, through Davy, on Faraday and an estimate of its significance in the history of science, see L. Pearce Williams, *Michael Faraday* (London: Chapman and Hall, 1965), pp. 62–71.

Actually the affinity between the two minds (Coleridge's and Faraday's) was closer than Williams's imperfect understanding of Coleridge allows him to assume; for later in the book he lets fall the surprising observation that Faraday "did not, like Coleridge, draw a sharp line of demarcation between mind and matter." Nevertheless, when after Coleridge's death his disciple J. H. Green endeavoured to interest Faraday in Coleridge's philosophy, he was unresponsive. Faraday preferred to keep his religion and his science quite separate. See Bence Jones, *Life and Letters of Michael Faraday* (Longmans, Green, 1870).

Yet the following, from Faraday's account, in a letter to a friend, of a discourse entitled *A Speculation touching Electric Conduction and the Nature of Matter,* given by himself at the opening of the weekly evening-meetings of the Royal Institution in January 1844, could almost have been written by Coleridge:

A mind just entering on the subject may consider it difficult to think of the powers of matter independent of a separate something to be called *the matter,* but it is certainly far more difficult, and indeed impossible, to think of or imagine that *matter* independent of the powers. Now the powers we know and recognize in every phenomenon of the creation, the abstract matter in none; why then assume the existence of that of which we are ignorant, which we cannot conceive, and for which there is no philosophical necessity? . . .

The view now stated of the constitution of matter would seem to involve necessarily the conclusion that matter fills all space, or, at least, all space to which gravitation extends (including the sun and its system); for gravitation

---

* F II, 11 and note 1. And see Supplementary Note, p. 248, below.

is a property of matter dependent on a certain force, and it is this force which constitutes the matter. In that view matter is not merely mutually penetrable, but each atom extends, so to say, throughout the whole of the solar system, yet always retaining its own centre of force.*

18. Williams includes in his book some interesting extracts from Faraday's correspondence with Whewell, to whose Greek scholarship he appealed for help with the new terminology he was beginning to need. Some of the terminology of electronics—e.g. *ion, anode, cathode,* etc.—was born from this co-operation (Faraday had first suggested *east-ode* and *west-ode*).

19. Polarity, for Coleridge, is the "most general form" under which the tendency to individuation acts. (TL 578.)

20. A possibility Coleridge himself clearly foresaw. See the long footnote in the *Theory of Life,* which concludes with the *envoi:* "This explanation, which in appearance only is a digression, was indispensably requisite to prevent the idea of polarity, which has been given as the universal law of Life, from being misunderstood as a mere refinement on those mechanical systems of physiology, which it has been my main object to explode." (TL 580–81.)

21. AR 48 (IS 103). See also (on Space, Time and Motion) AR 56–57.

22. According to Faraday "gravitation is a property of matter dependent on a certain force, *and it is this force which constitutes the matter.*" (See note 17, above.) According to Coleridge: "gravitation combines and includes the powers of attraction and repulsion, which are the constituents of matter, as distinct from body" (Shedd I, 466.). By contrast with gravitation, it is the bi-polar forces which constitute *bodies,* both inorganic and organic—and all qualities.

One of the things that puzzled and distressed Faraday was the non-polar nature of the force of gravity. He tried hard, but failed, to fit it into his novel concept of "lines of force" (non-material but physical), the eventual reluctant acceptance of which by his contemporaries ended the birth-pangs of modern physics.

For Coleridge (who held that "after the Things are made, the same Powers re-appear *in* the Things"): "—the Ideal Power of Gravity re-appears in the Real Power of Magnetism." (Egerton 2801, f. 144 [verso].)

23. Compare the following, from *Aids to Reflection:*

I am persuaded . . . that the dogmatism of the Corpuscular School, though it still exerts an influence on men's notions and phrases, has received a mortal blow from the increasingly dynamic spirit of the physical sciences now highest in public estimation. And it may safely be predicted that the results will extend beyond the intention of those, who are gradually effecting this revolution. It is not chemistry alone that will be indebted to the genius of Davy, Oersted, and their compeers . . . [AR 301.]

24. F I, 521. The obvious objection to associating science with delusion is, of

* *Experimental Researches in Electricity* (London: 1844), II, 291, 293.

course, the fact that, anyway, it works. It stamps out smallpox, lights and warms our houses, distributes the motor car and even carries our bodies, incredibly, to the moon and back. It cannot therefore be "untrue." But, is this objection necessarily valid, even for a pragmatist? Today there are some, even among those whose definition of truth is solely pragmatic, who are beginning to doubt whether technological efficiency is an altogether conclusive criterion. The question is whether it is *necessarily* absurd to classify as fiction and fancy respectively the maxims adopted for interpreting nature and the notions, culture and apparatus erected on them—notions and apparatus which, while they undoubtedly enable man to lighten his material burdens, at the same time enable and encourage him to disfigure, pollute and perhaps destroy his planet. Add that, in the cool perspective of history, interpretation of sequence as causality was the mother not only of technology, but also of superstition.

25. Egerton 2801, ff. 143 (verso) and 144. (The sign between "Light" and "Gravity" is odd and irregular. It is somewhat, but not much, like "&," and it is just possible that Coleridge intended to write ")(("—his symbol for the relation of polarity.)

26. As to that, Coleridge has left us his own opinion uttered less than a month before his death:

You may not understand my system, or any given part of it,—or by a determined act of wilfulness you may, even though perceiving a ray of light, reject it in anger and disgust: but this I will say, that if you once master it, or any part of it, you cannot hesitate to acknowledge it as the truth. You cannot be sceptical about it. [TT 28.6.1834.]

It is true there is one ground for withholding acknowledgment which his confident defiance overlooked. Compare Chapter 5, note 25, above.

27. For instance, by some of Heisenberg's reflections on quantum theory and the principle of complementarity:

The demand to describe what happens in the quantum-theoretical process between two successive observations is a contradiction *in adjecto,* since the word "describe" refers to the use of classical concepts, while these concepts cannot be applied in the space between observations; they can only be applied at the points of observation.

The fact that natural science does not simply describe and explain nature, but is a part of the interplay between nature and ourselves . . . makes the sharp separation between the world and the I impossible.

. . . methods and object can no longer be separated.

If one follows the great difficulty which even eminent scientists like Einstein had in understanding and accepting the Copenhagen interpretation of quantum theory, one can trace the roots of this difficulty to the Cartesian partition. This partition has penetrated deeply into the human mind during the three centuries following Descartes and it will take a long time for it to be re-placed by a really different attitude toward the problem of reality.

For the above and further citations see John Lukacs, *Historical Consciousness* (New York: Harper & Row, 1968). In *Causality and Chance in Modern Physics* (see Chapter 2, page 22, and n. 1) it is the Cartesian *co-ordinates* that are brought in issue by the author, David Bohm.

28. F I, 490.

29. If the scientific "entrenchment" of uniformitarianism is made evident by the phenomena of closed minds (n. 9, above), it is rather among the open minds that we find evidence of the even deeper entrenchment of Cartesianism—and of the bastard realism begotten on it by the followers of Kant. It is the adventurous minds, willing and anxious to re-open the whole issue of the validity of science, that are here most revealing. It is in *philosophies* of science that the primary maxim will be found to be entrenched *a priori*.

Sir Karl Popper, for instance, in *The Logic of Scientific Discovery,** concedes that truth must be subjective, in order to be absolute. *And he assumes* that what is subjective cannot also be objective. We have therefore to choose between "this pair of opposites, *subjective-absolute* and *objective-relative*," and this is "one of the most profound epistemological truths which can be gathered from the study of nature." The "truths" of science are therefore relative only, and

> The empirical basis of objective science has thus nothing 'absolute' about it. Science does not rest upon rock-bottom. The bold structure of its theories rises, as it were, above a swamp. It is like a building erected on piles. The piles are driven down from above into the swamp, but not down to any natu-ral or "given" base; and when we cease our attempts to drive our piles into a deeper layer, it is not because we have reached firm ground. We simply stop when we are satisfied that they are firm enough to carry the structure, at least for the time being.

"Objective," in fact, means nothing more than "intersubjectively testable."

Michael Polanyi's "personal knowledge" on the other hand is existential rather than relativist. He maintains that

> the actual foundations of our scientific beliefs cannot be asserted at all. When we accept a certain set of presuppositions and use them as our interpretative framework, we may be said to dwell in them as we do in our own body. Their uncritical acceptance for the time being consists in a process of assimila-tion by which we identify ourselves with them.†

To which Coleridge would, I think, have replied that the proposition that we "dwell" in our own body is itself a presupposition, which need not be accepted uncritically and can in fact be demonstrably refuted. For Polanyi however it is so

---

* London: Hutchinson, 1959, pp. 111, and 111n (citing H. Weyl).

† *Personal Knowledge* (London: Routledge, 1958), p. 60.

deeply entrenched that he treats it as self-evident and seeks therefore, to arrive at an epistemology of the understanding alone.

30. Compare Chapter 9, above, note 38.

31. See note 12, above.

Supplementary Note (see n. 17, above):

More significant in the general context of this chapter is Coleridge's incidental reference to Boscovich in a note on the flyleaf of Kant's "Metaphysical Foundations of Natural Science." * This relatively brief treatise is more thickly annotated than any other volume I have come across, and the marginalia make it obvious that it was ardently studied and pondered by Coleridge—probably at about the time when he was studying another † of Kant's *Vermischte Schriften*, which he was to describe later (AR 305n) as "the first product of the dynamic philosophy in the physical sciences, from the time, at least, of Giordano Bruno, whom the idolaters burned for an Atheist, at Rome, in the year 1600." Compare however Appendix, below.

12. Man and God

1. Thus, he would certainly have diagnosed the so-called "God is Dead" movement, which was much in vogue at about the time the writing of this book was commenced, as yet another futile attempt to strait-waistcoat the truths of reason within "the moulds of the understanding": Either God is in man, or he is not. If he is, then God (= *other* than man) is "dead."

Prophetically he had concluded, in a Notebook entry made as early as 1805:‡ "No Trinity, no God." Later, in his *Notes on Waterland* (Shedd V, 413), he expatiated: "The whole delusion of the Anti-Trinitarians arises out of this, that they apply the property of imaginable matter—in which A. is, that is, can only be imagined, by exclusion of B. as the universal predicate of all substantial being." The "despotism of the eye" has much to answer for!

2. P 362.

3. "The Idea of God *involves* that of a Tri-unity." (CL II, 1196. October, 1806, to Clarkson. Original not italicized.) It is characteristic of polar causality, as distinct from mechanical causality, that the cause remains present in the effect and is, from one point of view, identical with it. There is nothing to distinguish the negative from the positive pole—except the position. Thus, in the case of the Absolute, or First, Cause: "it can only be the *Relation* which distinguishes the Product or Consequent from the Producent or Antecedent . . . which constitutes the Alterity; as in a Son who should be in all respects the same as the Father,

---

* *Metaphysische Anfangsgründe der Naturwissenschaft* (BM.). The note on the first flyleaf is headed with the date 1819.

† *Gedanken von der wahren Schätzung der lebendigen Kräfte* ("Reflections on the correct Evaluation of living Forces").

‡ N 2448. Compare note 45, below.

except that he is the Son and not the Father." (Tennemann, Vol. VIII [2]. Note on 1st and 2nd flyleaf. Compare TT 23.6.34.)

4. Compare Shedd V, 109–10 (*Notes on Donne*).

5. Shedd V, 407 (*Notes on Waterland*). (H. N. Coleridge in his *Notes on the Confessions of an Inquiring Spirit* [CIS 239] quotes "substantive" for "substrative.")

For the reasons stated in the Introduction I am not concerned to combat the absurd but persistent tradition that Coleridge's Trinitarianism was a kind of escapist "lapse" into religious orthodoxy towards the end of his life. Were it otherwise, there would be enough documentary ammunition and to spare, with which to confirm Shawcross's considered opinion: "Nothing, I believe, is more remarkable with regard to Coleridge than the comparatively early maturity of his ideas." (BL I, v.) He had been a trinitarian, though not always a Christian one, from the time when he "conjured over the *Aurora* at school."

On *"Idea Idearum"* compare Chapter 11, above, p. 140.

6. Shedd V, 402 (*Notes on Sherlock*).

7. CIS 137 (*Formula of the Trinity*). God's projection of himself as other is the foundation of all natural "distinctities" and the source of the human reason's ability to distinguish without dividing.

8. P 362.

9. That is to say, the term *separative projection* attempts to re-state the technical meaning of the word *proceeding*—somewhat as Aquinas did in the opening words of his Hymn: *Verbum supernum prodiens Nec Patris linquens dexteram* (Supernal Word proceeding, yet never leaving the right hand of the Father), "dextera" being the well-recognised verbal image for "power." To distinguish, further, between the Word and the Spirit is to distinguish between the *Act* of begetting and the Product, in a realm where we have no *naturans*)(*naturata* contrast to help the imagination:

> . . . to will causatively with foreknowledge is to *create,* in respect of all finite products. An absolute and co-eternal Product (improperly so called) is either an Offspring, and the productive Act a *Begetting,* or a Procession. The *Word* begotten, the Spirit proceeding. [Note on flyleaf of John Scotus Erigena's *De Divisione Naturae.* PL 434. (See also n. 17, below.)]

10. TT 15.10.33. Compare F I, 316n.

11. Shedd I, 463n.

12. Note on pp. 148 and 149 of *Aids to Reflection,* 1825 (copy presented to John Coleridge). BM. Compare p. 145, above.

Thus, the spirit alone, and not the soul, is wholly "supernatural." (AR 46n.) Soul abides in the polarity: man)(nature. It is "psychosomatic." (For Coleridge's coinage of this term see IS 52 [p. 67]; and compare F I, 467n.)

13. MS Commonplace book. See the whole passage quoted by Muirhead (pp. 122–24).

14. Vol. I, 93 (BM). The note is in pencil, and I am not sure if I have correctly deciphered the two words *ignorant* and *Abyss.* As regards the accompanying diagram, there is a marginal note to Scotus Erigena (*Scholia on Gregory*), where

Coleridge denotes "☉" as his 'idiosymbol' for "Identity, or Co-inherence of two in one previously to the manifestation of the One as two." It is also of course the astrological symbol for the sun as planet. Compare also N 2784.

15. See TT 18.3.27. And compare the following somewhat clearer presentation in the *Treatise on Logic* (I, f. 27):

> All words express either being or action or the predominance of one over the other. In philosophical grammar they are either substantives or verbs, or as adnouns [adjectives] and adverbs express the modification of the one by the other. But the verb substantive (am, sum, εἰμί) expresses the identity or coinherence of Being and Act. All other words therefore may be considered as tending from this point, or more truly from the mid-point of the Line, the *punctum indifferentiae* representing the *punctum identitatis,* even as the whole Line represents the same point as produced or polarised.

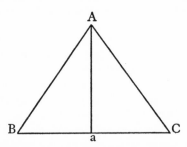

In this simple diagram A = the point of identity is supposed to generate by perpetual eradiation the line B.C., the Pole B representing Being in its greatest predominance, the pole C action in like manner. While the point a, expressing the indifference of Being and Action, of substantive and verb, is the more especial Representative or Analogon of the Point A, *as* a point. A, the point of identity, is Verb and Substantive in one and as one. a, the point of indifference, is *either* verb *or* substantive, or even both at the same time, but *not* in the same relation. Such in Grammar is the Infinitive . . .

16. TT 6.1.23.

17. On the proper translation of ἐγένετο (egeneto) in John 1.2. ("It is not *made,* but *became*") see e.g. Shedd V, 414 (*Notes on Waterland*). On the difference between "generation" and "fabrication" see N 2444. On the concept of "creation out of nothing" see the note on Scotus Erigena referred to in note 9, above, from which I take the following:

> this difficulty . . . arises wholly out of that Slavery of the Mind to the Eye and the visual Imagination or Fancy under the influence of which the Reasoner must have a *picture* and mistakes surface for substance. Such men, and their name is *Legion*—consequently *demand* a *Matter* as a *Datum.* As soon as this gross Prejudice is cured by the appropriate discipline, and the Mind is familiarized to the contemplation of Matter as a *product* in time, the resulting Phaenomenon of the equilibrium of the two antagonist Forces, Attraction and

Repulsion, *that* the Negative and this the Positive Pole of **I** gravity (or the Power of Depth) the difficulty disappears—and the Idea of *Creation* alone remains.

On the *proper* concept of "substance"—i.e. after liberation from the "gross Prejudice"—see the ensuing note.

18. Although creation is not an "emanation," the concept of "creation out of nothing" does *not*, for Coleridge, signify that the "being," or "substance," of man is other than the being of God:

> It is doubtful whether to Bruno or to Jakob Behmen belongs the honour of daring to announce the *substantial* meaning of the (*verbally* by all Christians) acknowledged Truth, that God hath the *Ground* of his own Existence in himself and that all things were created out of the *Ground*.

But the words *being* and *substance* are themselves "a mere mode of fixing our thought, a sort of mental Word by and through which we represent to ourselves Power or Act generally." In God being and act are one: Coleridge himself finds it impossible "to conceive or imagine action as a mode of passivity, no act having been presupposed." (Notes on Jacobi's *Über die Lehre des Spinoza,* pp. 284 and 1067 [BM].) On the difference between emanation and creation consult also P 354.

19. AR 46n and 48 (IS 103).

20. Marginal note on Kant's *Religion innerhalb der Grenzen der blossen Vernunft.* H. Nidecker, *Revue de Littérature Comparée* (1927), VII, 146. And Muirhead 250.

The original note reads: "Χριστος = κοσμος ἐπιστημάτικος ᾿Ανθρώπων [Christos = kosmos epistematikos anthrōpōn], sensorium quasi commune? Idea totalis cogitationum omnium modificatrix? Item—whether numerical Difference may not be an exclusive property of Phaenomena—and distinctness belong only to Noumena?—so that ὁ Χριστοειδῆς Χριστος γ[ιγ]νεται [ho Christoeidēs Christos gignetai]."

Muirhead comments that Coleridge "veils these speculations in Greek and Latin terms." The Notebooks make it clear that he did resort to the dead languages, among other devices, for "veiling" purposes even in notes intended for his own eyes alone. Delicacy, or awe, may well have been at the back of it. On the other hand his habit of dropping into Latin or Greek, for increased clarity, vividness or brevity, is persistent throughout his prose; and there is a note in his copy of Southey's *Life of Wesley,* which suggests that the relation of identity between the Christ and heart-filled minds, so far from being a fearfully esoteric notion, must be the normal one for thoughtful men, though not for "the generality of Christians":

> . . . if that popular and common-sense view of men as individuals *other* than The Son of Man be meant—which view alone the generality of Christians can understand—or if any view but that of the transcendent union, in which we have our being personality, and freedom in the being, person and will of God —then it is clear that the term *merit* is used in two diverse senses as applied

to Christ and applied to man. [*Life of Wesley* (Longmans, 1864, in which Coleridge's notes are printed), II, 142; and compare Shedd V, 68 (*Notes on Field on the Church*).]

21. The long letter to Tulk (CL IV, 767), in which these words occur, should be read for Coleridge's philosophy as a whole and its relation to science. It is near the end of it that he observes:

> It is peculiar to the Philosophy, of which I have given this sketch as far as its introductory Science is concerned, to consider matter as a Product—coagulum Spiritus, the pause, by interpenetration, of opposite energies—and that while I hold no matter as *real* otherwise than as the copula of those energies, consequently no matter without Spirit, I teach on the other hand a real existence of a spiritual World without a material.

22. For a treatment of the issue of pantheism, as it appeared during the first fifty years after Coleridge's death, see Shedd's Introduction to the *Complete Works*. For an up-to-date and historical treatment of it see Professor Thomas McFarland's monumentally erudite *Coleridge and the Pantheist Tradition* (Oxford: Clarendon Press, 1969). Both are defences of Coleridge against the charge of pantheism. Neither of them however concerns itself more than superficially with polarity.

In addition to the specifically theological approach to the all-important distinction between pantheism (which Coleridge sometimes equated with atheism) and theism, there is what should probably be called the Pythagorean approach. I do not seek to discourage anyone from pursuing the distinction between the triad and "the adorable tetractys, or tetrad," and the further distinction between that and the pentad, which the eschatology of redemption would seem to import. See, for instance, PL 109; TT 24.4.32 and AR 127n. But I doubt if either the theological or the Pythagorean way will be well discerned in the twentieth century without taking some help from that more forward-looking attire of Coleridge's thought, in which it met and conversed with natural science.

The passage from the closing paragraphs of the *Theory of Life* ("Porphyrogeniti Sumus . . .") which was quoted in Chapter 5, above, continues as follows:

> Nor does the form of polarity, which has accompanied the law of individuation up its whole ascent, desert it here. As the height, so the depth. The intensities must be at once opposite and equal. As the liberty, so must be the reverence for law. As the independence, so must be the service and the submission to the Supreme Will! As the ideal genius and the originality, in the same proportion must be the resignation to the real world, the sympathy and the intercommunion with Nature. In the conciliating mid-point, or equator, does the Man live, and only by its equal presence in both its poles can that life be manifested.

Whereas the arch-pantheist "Spinoza's is a World with one Pole only, and consequently no Equator . . ." (CL IV, 548n.)

Polarities may be raised on polarities. Not only the *Theory of Life* itself, but Coleridge's whole theory of life is founded on a perception that the "productive Unity" of a given polarity (the one Power, of which its two forces are the "separative projection") may itself be a prior polarity functioning in another relation or another dimension. Thus, the (from man's point of view) "ultimate" polarity is not that between God and nature, but that between God the Father (or reason, in its aspect of will) on the one hand and the whole polarity of man ⩞ Logos on the other. Man and nature together remain, through the Son, "in the bosom of the Father," who produced them both, the latter directly, the former, indirectly. Compare the observations on the meaning of ὁ ὢν εἰς τὸν κόλπον τοῦ πατρός [ho ōn eis ton kolpon tou patros] in John 1.18, in the *Notes on Waterland* (Shedd V, 412) and elsewhere.

23. F I, 490.

24. F I, 516, and BL Chapter XIII. At some later date Coleridge deleted, in one copy of the *Biographia Literaria,* the ensuing sentence "and as the repetition in the finite mind of the eternal act of creation in the infinite I AM." It has been assumed that he was afraid of pantheism. Professor McFarland, for instance, holds that he had come to dislike the suggestion of the eternal act of creation being itself a kind of "imagination." (*Coleridge and the Pantheist Tradition,* p. 331.) Personally I suspect that it was the word *repetition* in the *Biographia* definition with which he was dissatisfied—either as inadequately expressing this "priestly" function, or as too much suggesting the mind of *l'homme particulier,* or on both grounds. Compare TT 28.6.34.

25. As understanding, it is "relatively subjective to the objective." As pure reason, it is also "relatively objective to the subjective." And one aspect of this objectivity is conscience. Compare CIS 138 (*Formula of the Trinity*).

26. Shedd V, 91 (*Notes on Donne*).

27. CIS 103 (*Essay on Faith*).

28. Shedd V, 91 (*Notes on Donne*); and compare 107:

faith is the *apotheosis* of the reason in man, the complement of reason, the will in the form of the reason.

We (that is the human race) *live by faith.* Whatever we do or know that in kind is different from the brute creation, has its origin in a determination of the reason to have faith and trust in itself. This, its first act of faith, is scarcely less than identical with its own being. [Shedd I 430.]

29. Compare Chapter 5, p. 65 and n. 18, p. 212, above.

30. Shedd I, 425.

31. See the seven *Letters on the Inspiration of the Scriptures,* CIS 3–102; and compare F I, 516.

32. Shedd I, 427. A prophetic comment surely on the brand-new 'science' of *Futurology!*

33. Shedd I, 450. See also the concluding apostrophe (p. 451), in which he exemplifies, from the history of science, the 'physical ideas' to which he has been referring.

34. Shedd I, 429.
35. Shedd I, 437. See also AR 191–93n (Aphorism X on *Original Sin*).
36. *Ib.*
37. BL II, 230 (*On the Principles of Genial Criticism*).
38. F I, 497–98. Compare Chapter 5, above, pp. 60–61.

39. "Christ, the Logos, *Deitas objectiva, centred Humanity* (always pre-existing in the Pleroma) in his *Life,* and so became the *Light* = Reason, of Mankind. This eternal (i.e. timeless) act he *manifested* in time—σάρξ ἐγένετο [was made flesh: John 1.14]—and dwelt among men, an individual Man, in order that he might dwell in all his Elect, as the Root of the divine Humanity in time" [F I, 316n].

And compare *ib.* 112 and CS 370.

40. ". . . relatively taken and inadequately, the germinal powers of every seed might be generalized under the relation of Identity." (AR 127n, at p. 129.)

41. To be distinguished of course from the "actual" sin attributed in the Book of Genesis to Adam. For Coleridge on original sin, see in particular AR 191–240. References elsewhere are very numerous. Especially relevant here perhaps is the following from the *Notes on Donne* (Shedd V, 105):

What is the consequence of the apostasy? That no philosophy is possible of man and nature but by assuming at once a zenith and a nadir, God and *Hades;* and an ascension from the one through and with a condescension from the other; that is, redemption by prevenient and then auxiliary grace.

Nature and the human soul both depend upon "the admission of a nature into a spiritual essence by its own act." (AR 201.) The fact that that admission presupposes an apostasy, and is therefore a "corruption"—even though without it there could have been no human souls and no nature at all—is the mystery of evil.

42. AR 211, with especial reference to the myths of Prometheus and of Io. See however the whole idea worked out in much greater detail in *The Prometheus of Aeschylus.*

43. Shedd V, 546 (*Notes on Asgill's Treatises*).

44. CIS 109 (*Essay on Faith*).

45. "All religion is revealed:—*revealed* religion, is, in my judgment, a mere pleonasm." (TT 31.3.32.) Compare CIS 98.

Christianity has . . . its historical evidences, and these as strong as is compatible with the nature of history, and with the aims and objects of a religious dispensation.

Nevertheless:

The truth revealed through Christ has its evidence in itself, and the proof of its divine authority in its fitness to our nature and needs;—the clearness and cogency of this proof being proportionate to the degree of self-knowledge in each individual hearer. [CIS 63 (*Letter IV. On the Inspiration of the Scriptures*).]

It is possible therefore to have faith without belief and, judging by the *Notebooks* (N 2448, for instance), this was Coleridge's position in 1805. The same process looks very different according to whether it is seen from outside or from within. To the acute but shallow mind of Hazlitt, Coleridge's Anglican theology looked like a pusillanimous lapse or surrender. But it is clear from the Notebooks (N 2444–48 in particular) that, for Coleridge himself, what was going on beneath all the misery he endured in Malta in 1804 and 1805, looked like what he was afterwards to describe as: "a gradual opening out of the intellect to more and more clear perceptions of the strict coincidence of the doctrines of Christianity, with the truths evolved by the mind, from reflections on its own nature." (CIS 187 [*Evidences of Christianity*].)

For the converse predicament, of belief without faith, see for instance, Shedd V, 370 (*Notes on Leighton*).

46. Compare page 154, above. Coleridge assumed a possible experience of time itself as organic and not merely linear. Such an experience is clearly relevant to the possibility of prophecy. While I am not competent to pronounce on the ancient Hebrew language, and least of all on its verbs, it is a fact that some Hebrew grammars put it that, in that language, the *future* tense was used for history and the *past* for prophecy. If this be so, it would seem to suggest that a decidedly organic experience of time functioned at a deep level of the nation's consciousness, or of its unconscious—rendering it a peculiarly apt source or vehicle for prophetic expression.

47. Compare Shedd I, 425.

48. "What then can we think of a theological theory, which . . . makes its whole *religion* consist in the belief of miracles! As well might the poor African prepare for himself a fetisch by plucking out the eyes from the eagle or the lynx, and enshrining the same, worship in them the power of vision. As the tenet of professed Christians . . . it is even more absurd, and the pretext for such a religion more inconsistent than the religion itself. For they profess to derive from it their whole faith in that futurity, which if they had not previously believed on the evidence of their own consciences, of Moses and the Prophets, they are assured by the great Founder and Object of Christianity, that neither will they believe it, in any spiritual and profitable sense, though a man should rise from the dead." [F I, 432 (cf. Luke 16.31).]

Observe both the wording and the order of the last sentence: first, the *evidence* of their own consciences ("fidelity to our own being"), then Moses and the Prophets in that light, and finally the miracle in the light of both. And compare CIS 159–61 (*Definition of Miracle*); and Chapter 7, note 41, above.

49. Shedd V, 83–84 (*Notes on Donne*). And compare 365 (*Notes on Leighton*) on the meaning of "the blood of Christ."

50. Shedd V, 260 (*Notes on the Pilgrim's Progress*).

13. Man in History and in Society

1. TL 573.
2. TL 577.
3. Shedd I, 463.
4. TT 12.9.1831. The remark was made at table. As to the bold claim in the first sentence, Hegel's *Phenomenologie des Geistes* (1807) and his *Encyclopedie der Philosophischen Wissenschaften* (1817) do not appear to have been known to Coleridge; otherwise the second in particular (now partly available in translation by A. V. Miller, as *Hegel's Philosophy of Nature* [Oxford: Clarendon Press, 1970]) might well have caused him to modify it.
5. See *The Idea of History* (Oxford: Oxford University Press [paperback], 1961).
6. TT 12.3.1827.
7. Shedd I, 470. Compare the characterisation of Shakespeare as "a nature humanized, a genial understanding directing self-consciously a power and an implicit wisdom deeper than consciousness." (Raysor I, 224.) And, also from the *Lectures on Shakespeare*: "Man, in a secondary sense, may be looked on in part as his own creator, for by the improvement of the faculties bestowed upon him by God, he not only enlarges them, but may be said to bring new ones into existence. The Almighty has thus condescended to communicate to man, in a high state of moral cultivation, a portion of his own great attributes." (Raysor II, 36.)
8. CL II, 1196.
9. *Lectures* quoted BL II, 269: "Shakespeare in composing had no I, but the I representative." Compare the observations on "the supposed irritability of men of genius" in Chapter II of the *Biographia Literaria*, and on selfishness and genius in TT 23.7.1827.
10. CL II, 1197.
11. CL II, 1198.
12. CL II, 1196.

13. "And here the peculiar, the philosophic, genius of Greece began its foetal throb. Here it individualized itself in contra-distinction from the Hebrew archology, on the one side, and from the Phoenician, on the other. The Phoenician confounded the indistinguishable with the absolute, the *Alpha* and *Omega,* the ineffable *causa sui.* It confounded, I say, the multeity below intellect, that is, unintelligible from defect of the subject with the absolute identity above all intellect, that is, transcending comprehension by the plenitude of its excellence." [P 353.]

14. TT 13.7.1832.
15. From the *Prospectus* (PL 67).
16. MS note on Gillman's copy of the *Statesman's Manual* (IS 169).
17. F I, 505.
18. TT 9.7.1832. It is interesting to compare with this observation on the language of Homer some of those made by Bruno Snell in *The Discovery of the*

Mind (Cambridge: Harvard University Press, 1953; New York: Harper Torch-
book, 1960).

19. This is what Collingwood apparently failed to realise. It is remarkable
that, in the course of justifying his doctrine that the historian "re-enacts" the
thought of the past, he laid his finger so firmly on "the queen bee in the hive
of error" (the assumption that the *same* thought in two minds is still, numerically,
two thoughts)—and failed to realise that the lady had taken with her, on her
flight into the superindividual, the material for his own impassable barrier between natural and historical events; the assumption, namely, that the act of
thought is confined to a spatially detached human organism. Compare Chapter 5,
above.

20. The part played by language in detaching man from nature has been
considered in great detail by Ernst Cassirer in Vol. I ("Language") of his *Philosophy of Symbolic Forms*. (New Haven: Yale University Press, 1953.)

21. CIS 115–16. Theories of the origin of human society, via caveman, from
the animal herd, were already beginning to appear. The view implicit here is incompatible with them, and Coleridge accordingly rejected them:

> I attach neither belief nor respect to the Theory, which supposes the human
> Race to have been gradually perfecting itself from the darkest Savagery, or,
> still more—boldly tracing us back to the bestial as to our Larva, contemplates
> the Man as the last metamorphosis, the gay *Image*, of some lively species of
> Ape or Baboon. [Egerton 2801, ff. 15–17.]

22. CIS 107–8. The *Essay on Faith* is extant in more than one version. I do
not know how far these are due to Coleridge's own recensions and how far to
liberties taken by others—H. N. Coleridge, for instance, in editing CIS. I have
used both CIS and the MS version in Egerton 2801, f. 217 etc., the differences being
mainly of punctuation and the use of capitals. See also Muirhead 108 and 268 for
a summary of the same argument in the as yet unpublished *Opus Maximum*. And
compare the *Notes on Donne* (Shedd V, at pp. 91, 106 and 107), and CL II,
1197. The *Essay* itself has recently been reprinted in *Religious Thought in the
Nineteenth Century*, ed. B. M. G. Reardon (Cambridge University Press, 1956).
Professor McFarland has wisely compared this part of it with Martin Buber's *I
and Thou*, adding the judicious comment:

> We note that the I-Thou of Coleridge differs, in its initial emphasis, from the
> I-Thou of Buber, by being a deduction from the nature of consciousness rather
> than, as in Buber, an axiom of experience. The step with which Buber begins:
> one human confronting another as an I to a Thou, is for Coleridge a secondary
> realization of a polarity that has arisen in the individual consciousness itself.
> [*Coleridge and the Pantheist Tradition*, pp. 236–39.]

23. Compare CS 129n.

24. *Essay on Faith* (CIS 109):

—the equation of Thou with I, by means of a free act, negativing the sameness
in order to establish the equality, is the true definition of conscience. But as

without a Thou there can be no You, so without a You no They, These or Those; and as all these conjointly form the materials and the subjects of consciousness, and the conditions of experience, it is evident that the conscience is the root of all consciousness,—*a fortiori*, the pre-condition of all experience,—and that the conscience cannot have been in its first revelation derived from experience.

25. "Nature is a line in constant and continuous evolution. Its beginning is lost in the supernatural: and for our understanding therefore it must appear as a continuous line without beginning or end. But where there is no discontinuity there can be no origination, and every appearance of origination in nature is but a shadow of our own casting. It is a reflection from our own will or spirit. Herein, indeed, the will consists. This is the essential character by which Will is opposed to Nature, as spirit, and raised above nature as self-determining spirit—this namely, that it is a power of originating an act or state." [AR 196n.]

26. Coleridge speaks both of "the will of reason" and of "reason in the form of will." (Egerton 2801, f. 77) Compare also, in P 359 (on the relation between idea and law), "—the necessity of contemplating the idea now as identical with the reason, and now as one with the will, and now as both in one, in which last case I shall, for convenience sake, employ the term *Nous* the rational will, the practical reason."

27. PL 111-12. For the ensuing polarity between Greece and Rome, with the Hebrew now as "the fixed mid point of the living line," see F I, 505-6; and compare Chapter 12, note 15, above.

28. Notebook Entry, 1810, quoted in PL at page 42-3.

29. PL 112.

30. CS 123ff.

31. F I, 118-19; with which compare the sentence he selects (F I, 123) from Machiavelli: "There are brains of three races. The one understands of itself; the second understands as much as is shewn it by others; the third neither understands of itself nor what is shewn it by others."

32. F I, 326ff. His other reason for re-printing the 1795 Address was, that it had recently been referred to (by Hazlitt) "in an infamous Libel in proof of the Author's former Jacobinism."

33. F I, 508.

34. Compare CS 173: "—as no bridge ever did or can possess the demonstrable perfections of the mathematical arch, so can no existing State adequately correspond to the idea of a State"—and the ensuing observations. And consult *Coleridge and the Idea of the Modern State,* by David P. Calleo (New Haven: Yale University Press, 1966).

35. CS 48.

36. "The Clerisy of the nation, or national Church, in its primary acceptation and original intention, comprehended the learned of all denominations, the sages and professors of the law and jurisprudence, of medicine and physiology,

of music, of military and civil architecture, of the physical sciences . . . in short, all the so-called liberal arts and sciences, the possession and application of which constitute the civilization of a country, as well as the theological." [CS 49.]

37. F I, 507.
38. CS 101.
39. CS 80.
40. Coleridge tends to "desynonymize" the two terms, using *state* in the exclusive, and *nation* (or occasionally *commonwealth*) in the inclusive, sense; and at one point he does so explicitly: "—we must, in addition to a grounded knowledge of the State, have the right idea of the Church. These are two poles of the same magnet; the magnet itself, which is constituted by them, is the constitution of the nation." (CS 34.) But, since the purely "secular" state in itself is nevertheless a dynamic institution, the distinction is not in all contexts rigidly maintained.
41. F I, 192.
42. CS 15.
43. F I, 193–94.
44. CS 102–3.
45. CS 15 and 417n; and elsewhere.
46. A considerable part of Sir Karl Popper's *The Open Society and Its Enemies* is devoted to his brilliant onslaught on Plato. For some much deeper reflections on the problem of historical causality see John Lukacs, *Historical Consciousness or the Remembered Past* (New York: Harper & Row, 1968), Chapter 4.
47. Marginal note in Lessing's *Philosophische Aufsätze, Sammtliche Schriften,* VII, 245 (BM).
48. It is a token of Coleridge's fundamental wisdom that he saw, or foresaw, what the German idealists failed to see—the spiritual danger inherent in the abstract concept of an "ethical" state, and the vital distinction between *that* and the state itself as moral idea. Against that danger the bare *theory* (which they also held) that the self-realisation of the individual is the concern of the state, affords no protection. Unembodied, as idea and correlative law, in the constitution itself, the theory must lose all substance and will merely accompany, as lip-service, the actuality of Hegel turning into Marx and *Historismus* ending in totalitarianism. Compare *Bentham, Coleridge and the Science of History* (especially the excellent chapter on "Coleridge's Historical Thought") by Robert Preyer (Bochum-Langendreer: Verlag Heinrich Pöppinghaus OHG., 1958).
49. That is, the landed proprietors, and the commercial and industrial interest. Rather surprisingly, in view of his penetration, Dr. Preyer (see previous note) takes Coleridge to task for this, affirming (p. 24) that "there has never been a stationary party of permanence in England: what the historian observes is the conflict among groups who want to move in different ways" and, more generally, that "Coleridge's notion of the composition of the Permanent and Progressive interest is grossly unhistorical." In reply to the first objection I should insist that Coleridge did not mean by "the Permanent interest" any consciously formulated 'conservative' platform, but rather an idea working largely in the unconscious; and in

reply to the second, that it is simply not true. No-one who has any acquaintance with the English law of property and its history can feel any doubt of a very deeply rooted link, both practical and psychological, between (*a*) property in land and "retained attachment" to the soil and with that to tradition and the past, and (*b*) personal property and "detachment" both from the soil and from tradition. Compare Owen Barfield, "Poetic Diction and Legal Fiction," in *The Importance of Language,* ed. Max Black (Englewood Cliffs, N.J.: Prentice-Hall, 1962).

50. *The Idea of Coleridge's Criticism,* p. 25.

51. CS 181. With which however contrast (Letter to Joseph Cottle, April, 1814):

> Mind, therefore, may be regarded as a distinct genus, in the scale ascending above brutes, and including the whole of intellectual existences; advancing from *thought* (that mysterious thing!), in its lowest form, through all the gradations of sentient and rational beings, till it arrives at a Bacon, a Newton, and then, when unincumbered by matter, extending its illimitable sway through Seraph and Archangel, till we are lost in the GREAT INFINITE! [CL III, 483.]

52. *Notes on Henry More.* Shedd V, 117.

53. From a Note on Kant's objections to Anselm's ontological proof. Tennemann Vol. VIII (1st Part): end flyleaves and backboard. (Compare PL 437.)

54. *Die Rätsel der Philosophie,* 8th ed. (Dornach: Rudolf Steiner Nachlass-verwaltung, 1968).

55. Note on the *De Divisione Naturae* of John Scotus Erigena. *Liber Quintus,* 285 (PL 435).

Appendix. Polar Logic

1. For a collection of references to Bruno in Coleridge's works see the article "Coleridge on Giordano Bruno" by A. D. Snyder, MLN. XLII (1927). For the probable extent of his reading see the various references indexed under "Bruno" in N I and II.

2. For the marginal note in full see pp. 182–183, below.

3. N II, 2264 and 2254n.

4. Tennemann Vol. IX, end flyleaf 2. Compare PL 450–51. For a full and fascinating account of Bruno's "attempts in Mnemonic" see *The Art of Memory,* by Frances A. Yates (London: Routledge, 1966). Dr. Yates has shown that these do indeed "throw a light on his whole philosophy." But, as far as I know, no-one except Coleridge has suggested that the same can be said of his attempts in Logic.

5. *Raymundi Lullii opera ea quae ad inventam ab ipso artem universalem etc. Pertinent* (Zetzner, 1617). First printed in 1598, reprinted 1609, 1617 and 1651. The British Museum has four copies in all, but only one of the first and only previous edition (1589) of the *De Progressu,* which was not reproduced again until after Coleridge's death. See Salvestrini's Bibliography (*Bibliotheca Bibliographica Italica,* Vol. 12, 1958).

6. The marginal note in Tennemann, to which we have already referred, continues: "O for a real life of Bruno, and analysis of his Writings!" In the "Critical History of Philosophy by several hands," which Coleridge goes on to desiderate: "the one article of Giordano Bruno would occupy the same man who had before taken R. Lully."

7. Egerton 2801, f. 126. (This and the surrounding folios appear to constitute the "article on 'the polar logic'" alluded to in IS 306n.). For the conclusion of the opening paragraph of the letter see note 29, below.

8. *Treatise on Logic* II, 401–2 (Snyder 126).

9. Coleridge's disciple J. H. Green interprets "polar logic" in this portmanteau sense. See *Spiritual Philosophy* (Part II, Chapter IV, entitled: "Dialectic, or the Polar Logic, and its Office in the Conversion of Conceptions into Ideas"). Thus:

It may be assumed that the Polar Logic which we adopt from Coleridge's statement (Common Place Book No. 3) is an adequate description of the Relations, or elementary factors, required in the Polar Logic in order to the Conciliation of Opposites and, in perpetuating their distinction, to secure their unity; viz:—

	Identity	
Thesis	Indifference	Antithesis
	Synthesis	

And later

Reason implies the *Polar Form,* for the indispensable purpose of securing what is essential to its nature, namely, *Unity* and *Distinction*; and this will have been accomplished when a *genetic One* distinguishes itself into the correspondent factors, *Integral* and *Differential,* and produces a *Totality* in which the Distinctions are preserved whilst the Unity is ever secured . . . the identity of Will and Reason; this identity manifesting itself in its dynamic co-factors or correlatives, as Thesis and Antithesis; Reason in the form of Will, or Distinction in Unity; and correspondently thereto, Will in the form of Reason, or Unity in Distinction . . . whilst in the Synthesis or Totality, we contemplate the living perpetuity of Unity in Distinction, and of Distinction in Unity. [245 and 272.]

I have not succeeded in identifying "Common Place Book No. 3."

Coleridge's occasional attribution of a "logic of trichotomy" to Kant and his repeated emphasis on its appearance in Baxter might stand an Appendix to themselves. As to Kant, the *word* "trichotomy" occurs in a brief Introduction to later editions of the *Critique of Pure Reason,* and I am induced, with some trepidation, to suggest that Coleridge was over-excited by it. In a marginal note on an early work of Kant's on *Optimism* he even goes so far as to say that Kant "owed his after greatness" to having "exchanged" the Logic of Dichotomy for the Logic of Trichotomy.* By the time he wrote the passage quoted above from the *Treatise*

---

* *Revue de Littérature Comparée* (1927), VII, 526.

on Logic (p. 182, above) however he had modified this view considerably; for the passage continues:

> Baxter saw far more deeply into the grounds, nature and necessity of this division as a Norma Philosophiae and the evils and inconveniences of the ordinary Dichotomy when carried from its proper province, that of common Logic, into Philosophy and Divinity, than Kant did more than a century after. The sacred fire however remained hid under the bushel of our good countryman's ample folios.

On the world of difference between Kant's trichotomy and Coleridge's see Muirhead 85n; and compare H. J. Paton, *Kant's Metaphysics of Experience* (London: Allen & Unwin, 1936) I, 305–6.

As to Baxter, the relevant volumes appear to be: *Catholick Theologie, Reasons of the Christian Religion,* and (his only Latin work) *Methodus Theologiae Christianae.* Coleridge read and slightly annotated *Catholick Theologie*; but it is doubtful if he ever read the *Methodus Theologiae* (see MS quoted in Snyder at p. 128). Baxter's trichotomy is rather assumed by him throughout than argued for; but see, e.g. *Reasons of the Christian Religion,* "In Defence of the Soul's Immortality," Objection VIII (". . . He that feeleth not that his understanding doth *agere* as well as *pati* (when he is studying, reading or writing) is a stranger to himself . . .") and *Methodus Theologiae, Praefatio* p. 6. Baxter's trichotomy was in no sense a discovery of his own. It is clear, not only from the content of the volumes referred to, but from their very numerous marginal references, that he stood in the main tradition of Augustinian—or Augustinian and Hermetic—trinitarianism, of which more is shortly to be said. Thus, the authorities he refers to include not only Augustine (*De Trinitate*) but also Ramon Lull and Ficino.

10. For a careful and sympathetic epitome of the Art of Ramon Lull, see the article by Frances A. Yates in the *Journal of the Warburg and Courtauld's Institute,* Vol. 17, No. 1/2 (1954). Dr. Yates draws attention to the fact that a great deal of Lull's voluminous writings is still unpublished and remarks thereon: "A vast and virtually unknown country lies waiting here for exploration." For Lull's definition of *contrarietas* see Chapter 7, above, p. 89, and n. 43, p. 221.

11. Compare BL I, 94.

12. Compare the two letters to J. H. B. Williams and J. H. Green in December 1817. CL IV, 789 and 791.

13. It was for the same reason that he valued the German *Naturphilosophen.* Compare Chapter 10, above, and CL IV, 793.

14. F I, 94.

15. Egerton 2801, f. 15. The passage is quoted in *Coleridge on Giordano Bruno* (see n. 1, above), p. 431. And see, further, No XI of the *Philosophical Lectures,* where the doctrine attributed to Bruno is practically a summary of Coleridge's own system. PL 323 and 326.

16. The earliest instance of *polarity* in English given in the O.E.D. is from Sir Thomas Browne in 1646. For reasons given in the ensuing note its Latin or Italian equivalent is unlikely to have appeared much, if at all, earlier. Alessio's *Etymological Dictionary* assigns 1749 as its date in the Italian language.

17. The terms *pole* and *polar* were originally used only of the celestial poles and, by extension, of any geometrical sphere. Their application to the terrestrial poles appears to have coincided approximately with the advent of Copernicanism, the sense being wholly or predominantly geographical. Subsequent connotation of a force, or forces, that could be thought of as polar, can hardly have preceded the discovery, or the confirmation and publicizing, of terrestrial magnetism; and Gilbert's *De Magnete* was published in 1600, the year of Bruno's death. It is thus inherently improbable that Bruno should ever have spoken, or even thought, of a universal law of polarity as Coleridge conceived of it.

Nevertheless, in view of his very definite statement, I took the precaution of consulting Dr. Frances Yates, author of *Giordano Bruno and the Hermetic Tradition,* and of the *Art of Memory,* to which I have already referred, and which is very largely concerned with Bruno's writings. Dr. Yates was good enough to inform me that she remembers no passage in which Bruno uses the word *polarity*. She also took the trouble to draw my attention to a passage from the *Cena de le Ceneri,* in which he refers to three movements of the Earth: round its own centre (light and darkness, day and night); round the sun (the four seasons); and a third movement "towards the so-called poles and opposite hemispheric points." This last movement is "for the renewal of the epochs (*secoli*) and the changing of earth's countenance, so that, where there was sea, there may be dry land, where there was heat, there may be cold, where there was tropic, there may be equinox and, lastly, that there may be mutation (*vicissitudine*) of all things, alike in this and the other stars rightly called 'worlds' by the genuine ancient philosophers." She added: "I may be wrong but I fancy that Bruno would always think of the actual poles as here."

Bruno is clearly thinking primarily of the geographical poles. Nevertheless it is interesting that he evidently conceives of a motion "towards" the poles, which seems to imply motion in two opposite directions, and that he associates this with the continuous change of matter. Could this have particularly struck Coleridge and lingered somewhat confusedly in his memory?

The *Cena de le Ceneri* is on his Bruno reading-list, jotted down while he was in Malta (N II, 2264). He may very well therefore have read it while he was learning Italian or at least while that language was still fresh to him. We know his delight in the subtle turns of linguistic usage. I add, not as a too ingenious theory but as an idle speculation, the possibility that his attention was caught by the Italian idiom, "i chiamati poli" (Latin *clamare,* with which he had been familiar from boyhood, meaning always "to call out loud" and never "to call," in the sense of naming), and held suspended a little longer than would otherwise have been the case on the "so-called poles"—"so-called" perhaps because in Bruno's time the semantic transference from celestial to terrestrial poles was still in ambivalent progress. A purely terrestrial law, or a "universal" one?

18. On Lull and Cusa, see E. Colomer, *Nikolaus von Kues und Raimund Llull* (Berlin: 1961). On Cusa and Bruno, see H. Védrine, *La Conception de la Nature chez Giordano Bruno* (Paris: 1967).

19. The modern development foreshadowed by Cusa is surely, not the Physics of polarity, but the "centro-peripheric" Projective Geometry developed in the

nineteenth century. I am not able to say whether this geometry of finity and infinity was in fact indebted to him. On its relation to biological polarity, and particularly to Goethe's *Metamorphosenlehre,* see *The Living Plant and Ethereal Spaces (A Study of "the Metamorphosis of Plants" in the light of Modern Geometry and Morphology)* (Chapter 11, n. 12, above).

20. Compare H. Védrine, *op. cit.,* p. 170.

21. "Twinned nature, which both is made and makes, which both creates and is created." Quoted by Coleridge from Scotus Erigena's *De Divisione Naturae.* (F I, 146.) Coleridge comments on page 41 of Boehme's *Aurora:* "By Quality Behmen intends that act of each elementary Power, by which it energizes in its particular kind. But in the Deity is an absolute synthesis of opposites. Plato in Parmenide and Giordano Bruno passim have spoken many things well on this aweful Mystery— the latter more clearly." (Compare BL I, 103.) It is the absolute synthesis in the Deity, and not the act of each elementary Power, on which Bruno is said to have spoken more clearly.

22. Actually, the importance in Bruno of coincidence of opposites in *any* sense is disputed. E. Troilo, in *La Filosofia di Giordano Bruno* (1907), denies it any fundamental importance; it is "not more than an episode in his philosophical system." H. Védrine on the other hand (*op. cit.,* p. 168) considers that his philosophy would be incomprehensible without it: "elle seule, en effet, permet d'attribuer un statut au fini et de montrer de quelle manière il peut se médiatiser dans l'infini." This seems the better opinion.

23. TT 30.4.1830.

24. AP 73.

25. Compare the chapters on Bruno in Yates, *Art of Memory,* and particularly pp. 230, 256–57 and 299.

26. F. Tocco, in *Le opere latine di Giordano Bruno* (Florence: 1889), gives it a single page, in which he dismisses it as "un magro compendio della topica Aristotelica." Coleridge evidently thought otherwise.

27. See, for instance, his *De Triplici Minimo et Mensura.*

28. See Chapter 6, note 9.

29. The letter on Polar Logic, quoted on pp. 181–182, above ("A could not be affirmed to be A. but by the perception that it is not B . . ."), continues as follows:

> Well then, we know A by B: and B. by A. We know that between A and B. there is first a something peculiar to each, *that,* namely, by which A is A and *not* B, and B is B and *not* A. and secondly, a something common to them, a one in both; namely that which is expressed by the copula, *is;* and thirdly, that the latter, = Being, is in order of thought presupposed in the former. What is last in Reflection, is first in the *genesis,* or order of causation . . .

With which compare:

> . . . Dichotomy, or the primary Division of the ground into Contraries, is the necessary form of reasoning, as long as and wherever the intelligential faculty of Man weens to possess within itself the centre of its own System; and vice

versa, the adoption of Dichotomy under the supposition of its being the legitimate and only form of distributive Logic, naturally excites, and seems to sanction this delusive conceit of Self-sufficiency in minds disposed to follow the clue of argument at all hazards, and whithersoever it threatens to lead them, if only they remain assured that the thread continues entire . . . [MS forming part of the "Opus Maximum." Snyder 128–29.]

30. "There is, thirdly, the middle of extremes, into which things that would otherwise be separates come together. Whence action is understood to be the middle between agent and patient . . ." (*Raymundi Lullii Opera ea* . . . , p. 702.) Lull defines "medium" as *subiectum, in quo finis influit principio, et principium refluit fini*—"wherein the end flows into the beginning and the beginning flows back into the end." (*Ars Brevis,* cap. VI.)

31. *Treatise on Logic* II, 62. The point is, that meaningful predication (as, for instance, between species and genus) already implies a metaphysics of "descent" and "ascent."

32. Compare:

(1) Note on Baxter's *Catholick Theologie* (p. 9): "For in reason, tho' not in the sensuous Fancy, *Negations* are as true causes as positives . . ." (Baxter had affirmed that "possibility" and "futurity" are not attributes etc. but only "Conceptions in the mind of Creatures concerning that which is not").

(2) Negative Quantities = opposed forces. Logical by Contradiction ends in absolute nothing, nihil *negativum*, quod est etiam irrepresentabile—a ball in motion & at the same time not in motion, motion in each sentence having been used in the same sense, is a contradiction in terms. In Nature it is *not,* or rather say, it isn't, so as not to give a moments reality by the use of per se, *is*—but there are oppositions without contradiction, & real— nihil privativum cogitabile—two tendencies to motion in the same body, one to the N. other to S., being equipollent, the Body remains *in rest.*— the second assumed Tendency is a real negative Quantity—better therefore called a *privative* Quantity. $-4-5 = -9$ is mere pedantry—there is no real *sub*traction; it is true addition. $-$ and $+$ have no meanings but as symbols of opposition. [N 2502.]

(3) . . . The Reasoning on this page might be cited as an apt example of the inconveniece of the Dichotomic Logic . . . Two terms in manifest correspondence to each other are yet opposed as contraries, without any middle term; the consequence of which is that one of the 2 becomes a mere negation of the other, *ex. gr.* Real $-$ Unreal $= 0$ . . .

Compare *the Logic of* dichotomy with that of Trichotomy, or what is the same, the Pythagorean Tetractys. In this we seek first for the Unity, as the only source of Reality, and then for the two opposite yet correspondent forms, by which it manifests itself. For it is an axiom of universal application, that "Manifestatio non datur, nisi per alterum" . . . Thus the finite and infinite are the 2 necessary forms of Being manifested, which can never be divided—the instances in which either is assumed singly, will be found mere abstractions, or else mere forms of subjective imagination, such as are Atom, or Infinite Space. And what is Space? A something with the attributes of Nothing. But in *real* Science we must say—

1. Being
or identity of Finite and Infinite
2. The Finite in the Infinite)(the Infinite in the Finite
[Marginal Note on Swedenborg's *De Infinito et Causa Finali*—from a transcript in the possession of Victoria College, Toronto.]

33. "Year after year, day after day, I see more clearly and feel more livelily the importance of Trichotomy in all *real* definition." (Note on flyleaf of Baxter's *Catholick Theologie*.)

Rather than offer to translate the particular passage quoted from the *De Progressu,* I give my own tentative impression of what Bruno seeks, among much else, to find in his "field of Definition." The two titles of the whole treatise contain the words *venatoria* and *venatio:* a "hunt" or "chase"; and the chase seems now and then to be something like a chase after an absolutely univocal term— by the process of gradually peeling and paring away such parts of its meaning as would also be covered by some other term, and then seeing what is left. You take away from a word like *bravery,* first, on one side, what is also connoted by a word like *rashness;* then, on the other, what is also connoted by a word like *stoicism* or *endurance.* But the core you have left still requires peeling, if it is to be left absolutely univocal—it is still of the same, essentially peelable, nature. The implication seems to be that, when all the peeling has been done that ever could be done, what is left will still be—not a point, but two arrows pointing inward from, or a single two-headed arrow pointing outward towards, the two opposite directions from which you have been reducing in order to arrive at what is left. We could perhaps express it that any ultimate unit of meaning there may be is not "atomic" but nuclear. A logic of qualities, which is not to end in destroying what it sets out to analyse, must therefore itself be nuclear.

I am not affirming with confidence that this is exactly what is to be found in these sections of Bruno's *De Progressu.* It is certainly not *all* that is there. But I do believe with some confidence that it is not far from what Coleridge himself divined in them. J. L. McIntyre (*Giordano Bruno.* London, Macmillan, 1903, at p. 178) quotes as follows from the *De la Causa Principio et Uno* (Lagarde, 288–89):

He who would know the greatest secrets of nature, let him regard and contemplate the minima and maxima of contraries and opposites. *Profound magic it is to know how to extract the contrary after having found the point of union.*

Aristotle, said Bruno, was striving towards, but did not attain it:
. . . remaining with his foot in the *genus* of opposition, he was so fettered

that he could not descend to the *species* of contrariety . . . but wandered at every step, as when he said that contraries could not exist in the same subject.

34. I suggest that this, and nothing less, is the mental discipline required to bring about what Coleridge elsewhere called "communication by the symbolic use of the understanding" (Chapter 3, n. 29, above). We are to be logical without the logic-bred illusion that we are therefore being "literal." We have to learn to think, not less but *more* logically, without ever forgetting that the terms we are logically combining are not labels, but that each of them in itself is a symbol that flouts, by transcending, the requirements of logic; for only so shall we come not merely to accost, but to *discern* the related energies whence causality originates.

Index

Abernethy, John (1764–1831): 206 n. 8

Abraham: 156

Abrams, M. H., *The Mirror and the Lamp*: 59, 60, 125, 210 nn. 1–4, 215 n. 12, 229 n. 38

Abstraction(s): 24, 31, 41–42, 99 ff., 153; and language, 20–21; and definition, 46; and causality, 220 n. 41; and hypothesis, 126, 234 n. 33; enabled by reason, 109; and "occult qualities," 199 n. 13; power of—atrophied by persistent fancy, 21, 100–101, 223 n. 37, 238 n. 58

Accuracy: 101, 111

Act: chapter I *passim*, 164, 221 n. 2, 250 n. 15, 251 n. 18; and Product, chapter I *passim*, 24, 25, 33, 249 n. 9; of consciousness, 59, 76, 155, 164; *and see* Imagination

Action and Passion: 57, 78, 86, 97, 193, 198–199 n. 9, 213 n. 24, 216 n. 3; *and see* Fancy (active and passive)

Actual and Potential: 57, 77, 85, 124, 125, 153, 161, 162, 170–172, 229 n. 38

Adam: 230 n. 45, 254 n. 41

Adams, G. (1894–1963) and O. Whicher, *The Living Plant and the Science of Physical and Ethereal Spaces*: 241 n. 12

Addison, Joseph (1672–1719): 78

Aeschylus: 114, 115, 121, 122, 130, 145, 233 n. 20, 254 n. 42

Agassiz, Louis (1807–1873): 244 n. 13

"Agere et Pati": *see* Action and Passion

Akenside, Mark (1721–1770): 78

Alazonomastix Philalethes (pseud.): 229 n. 36

Alessio, *Etymological Dictionary*: 262 n. 16

Ammonius Saccas (3 cen. A.D.): 214 n. 8

Animism: 25, 188

Anselm, St (c. 1033–1109): 238 n. 54, 260 n. 53

Apostasy: 155, 254 n. 41; *and see* Original Sin

Appleyard, J. A., *Coleridge's Philosophy of Literature*: 4, 5, 7, 74, 196 n. 16, 197 n. 18, 200 n. 4, 213 n. 25, 215 n. 12, 216 n. 14, 233 n. 11

Aquinas, St Thomas (1225?–1274): 249 n. 9

Archimedes (c. 287–212 B.C.): 28, 130